True Loves

True Loves

FINDING THE SOUL IN LOVE RELATIONSHIPS

Alex T. Quenk & Naomi L. Quenk

Davies-Black Publishing
Palo Alto, California

Published by Davies-Black Publishing, an imprint of Consulting Psychologists Press, Inc., 3803 East Bayshore Road, Palo Alto, CA 94303; 800-624-1765.

Special discounts on bulk quantities of Davies-Black books are available to corporations, professional associations, and other organizations. For details, contact the Director of Book Sales at Davies-Black Publishing, an imprint of Consulting Psychologists Press, Inc., 3803 East Bayshore Road, Palo Alto, CA 94303; 415-969-8901; Fax 415-988-0673.

Cover art: Jim Dine, *The Southern Cross #3*, 1995. Acrylic and oilstick on canvas, $48^{1}/_{4}$ x $36^{1}/_{4}$ in. (122.6 x 92.1 cm).

Cover photograph: Ellen Page Wilson. Photograph courtesy PaceWildenstein.

01 00 99 98 97   10 9 8 7 6 5 4 3 2
Printed in the United States of America

Library of Congress Cataloging-in-Publication Data
True loves : finding the soul in love relationships / Alex T. Quenk and Naomi
   L. Quenk.
       p. cm.
   Includes bibliographical references and index.
   ISBN 0-89106-107-X
   1. Love. 2. Couples. 3. Interpersonal relations. I. Quenk, Naomi L.
   II. Title
HQ801.Q45 1997
306.7—dc21   97-15324
                                                CIP

FIRST EDITION
First printing 1997

For our children
Karin, Kaleb, and Rachel

Contents

PART 3   ENDURING LOVE RELATIONSHIPS

Preface

During the many years we have worked with couples who were having difficulties in their relationships, we have come to understand that there is no single true, valid, or mature love relationship. We have observed a number of very different loving, fulfilling, and meaningful relationships among the couples we have seen, regardless of the issues that brought them to us. To our surprise, these satisfying relationships have not necessarily met the standards of our dominant societal and professional notions of what constitutes a "mature and meaningful" relationship. Couples who by such standards might be judged as immature, unhappy, unloving, or in distress have actually been quite happy with each other, loved each other, and found their relationships fulfilling. Similarly, couples who appeared to meet societal and professional notions of a "good relationship" have been quite dissatisfied, felt unfulfilled, and had serious doubts about their love for each other. We have found these observations to be true not only for married and heterosexual couples, but for unmarried and gay and lesbian couples as well.

Gradually it became clear to us that there is not one standard by which relationships should be judged, but many standards. We began to look *within the relationships themselves* for appropriate standards, rather than relying on external societal, cultural, or professional criteria. By listening openly and carefully to what people said about their desires, expectations, needs, and values in love relationships, we came to perceive four clear and coherent patterns that appear as *archetypes of relationships.* We have identified these archetypes as four distinct *Soul Images* that in combination form the *true loves* we describe in this book.

In preparing to present our approach, we reviewed the numerous attempts that others have made to explain, analyze, promote, improve, and understand intimate relationships. We found that these systems range from simplistic schemes based on gender stereotypes to philosophical studies on the nature of love, and from unsophisticated magazine surveys to careful research examining the relationship of personality, social, and background characteristics to marital success or satisfaction. Regardless of the focus and level of complexity of these attempts, however, it was evident to us that most of them contained either explicit or implicit biases about love and relationships. Often such biases seemed to correspond to the prevalent views of our culture about what characterizes a good and mature love relationship—for example, equality, mutual respect, self-sufficiency, responsibility, caring, and commitment. In other instances, the prevalent cultural bias seemed to be rejected in favor of an alternative perspective, such as satisfying the needs of each partner for unconditional love and acceptance. In our view, the best of these perspectives describe *part* of the picture, but none honors the full range of possible relationships that in our experience can be equally mature and satisfying. When people evaluate relationships using either society's or some other single standard of appropriateness and maturity, valid differences among relationships go unrecognized and are misunderstood.

Our thoroughly different approach to love relationships provides a solid foundation for appreciating and capitalizing on the reality of differences in individuals and couples. By applying any single standard to relationships, the true meaning and importance of people's attitudes and behaviors is likely to be missed, leading to erroneous and damaging conclusions. Biased and potentially detrimental beliefs about "good" and "bad" relationships can influence the couple themselves, the people who know and care about them, and the counselors and therapists to whom they might turn for help. A perspective that is sensitive to different standards for assessing relationships allows us to fully appreciate and understand relationships that either are different from our own or deviate from what we have come to define as mature or appropriate.

For example, we have all had the experience of meeting a couple at a dinner party and wondering why they are together and why their relationship has lasted. They seemed to have very little in common, or they frequently insulted each other. One may have appeared to be extremely quiet and the other quite boisterous, or perhaps both complained about each other to the other guests. Maybe there was nothing obviously amiss in their relationship, but they "just didn't seem to go together."

How do we come to such conclusions? In general, we tend to judge other people's relationships from the perspective of our own implicit standards. We are likely to assume that our standard is a proper one and that if a relationship diverges markedly from our criteria, then it is not a "good" relationship.

In our approach, however, in order to understand and judge love relationships, we first must understand the differences among them and how these differences affect the individuals involved. These differences are embodied in the four archetypal "Soul

Images" we have identified. Only by understanding these images and how they emerge when two people live out their love relationship can we be in a position to form a fair opinion about whether a particular relationship is "good" for the couple involved.

True Loves provides the basis for identifying different but equally satisfying types of love relationships. It demonstrates through numerous illustrative everyday examples that there are many different kinds of "mature" and fulfilling relationships, and explains how and why they are all expressions of "true love." We have found that the insight and practical knowledge couples acquire through an understanding of our approach greatly enhance their appreciation and acceptance of each other and provide an effective vehicle for resolving conflict and sustaining the true love in their relationships.

Acknowledgments

We are grateful to friends and colleagues who critiqued early versions of this book and offered illustrative examples from their own and others' experiences. Thank you to Peggy Adams, Larry Alexander, Nancy Barger, David Coleman, John DiTiberio, Liza Eilers, Lorrie Fenton, Catherine Fitzgerald, Christen Galloway, Betsy Kendall, Linda Kirby, Chris Koloskous, Jan Mitchell, Wayne Mitchell, Laurie Prehn, Tom Prehn, Roberta Rice, Eric Rounds, Kim Spencer, Kim Viano, and Thomas Viano.

We also appreciate the many psychotherapy clients with whom we have worked over the years. Clients, both individuals and couples, enhanced the foundation for the ideas presented in this book. Their experiences provided the basis for many of the composite examples and anecdotes used throughout the book.

Lee Langhammer Law, Division Director of Davies-Black Publishing, enthusiastically supported the development and progress of this book. The care and attention of Laura Simonds,

Director of Sales and Marketing, and Jill Anderson-Wilson, Managing Editor, helped bring the work to successful completion. Brian Jones edited the manuscript with meticulous care and made helpful suggestions that improved its clarity and meaning.

I | *The Soul Images of Love*

There is only one happiness in life, to love and be loved.

George Sand, *Letter to Lina Calamatta*

If "to love and be loved" is indeed the one happiness in life, does that mean that there is only one way of loving and being loved? The obvious and true answer is that there are many ways of loving and being loved. Just as people are different, their expressions of love are different, and love's meanings are different. Furthermore, these differences have some remarkable effects on what happens in love relationships, including their satisfactions and joys as well as their misunderstandings, disagreements, and quarrels.

This book is about how and why these differences occur. Here are some examples:

> A wife gets terribly hurt and angry when her husband visits his brother without telling her. Her husband tells her that she is "crowding him."

1

A husband encourages his wife to take a job in a city four hundred miles away. *Both* believe this will enhance their love for each other.

A couple agree to take separate vacations one year. In contrast, another husband becomes quite upset when his wife goes on a business trip.

A husband and wife are surprised and amused when they discover that their friends suspect that both of them are having affairs with colleagues at work.

These brief examples reveal different perspectives on love and loving relationships. Yet all of the couples described love each other and believe that their marriages are happy. Implicit in the descriptions of these couples are aspects of four of the ten love relationships we discuss in this book. They are all "true loves"— genuine, authentic, satisfying, fulfilling ways of living love relationships. Each, however, has a distinct character that is expressed through its joys and sorrows, its sources of contentment, and its tensions and stresses.

In spite of the general agreement that there are different ways of experiencing and expressing love, relationships are often judged from a single vantage point. Sometimes the perspective used is the judger's own point of view—that person's beliefs about what is appropriate for his or her own love relationship. Other times a person's perceptions of society's view of what constitutes a "good" relationship becomes the standard.

In this book we will present a straightforward and accessible way of distinguishing the ten different types of love relationships and thereby enable you to understand and appraise their distinct features from within their unique perspective. You will then be able to more fully appreciate and assess your own love relationship as well as those of others. Our goal is to broaden your perspective about love relationships and the variety and nature of true love.

Different Ways of Loving

Why are there ten relationships and not seven, twelve, or fifteen? What accounts for the characteristics that appear in one kind of relationship and not in another? The answers to these questions lie in the way we arrive at the ten true loves. It is based on a unifying and comprehensive way of understanding and describing human nature—C. G. Jung's notion of *archetypes*.

What Are Archetypes?

Not a day goes by without our thinking and talking about archetypes. Perhaps you're not familiar with the word, or if you have heard it, maybe you think it has something to do with mysterious, esoteric things like Greek gods and ancient rituals. Actually, there is nothing mysterious or complicated about archetypes. You see them in operation every time you read a newspaper announcement of a birth, wedding, anniversary celebration, obituary, or religious festival. These everyday events are just a few of the many areas of living that reflect archetypes—inborn, natural patterns of responding to typical human situations and experiences. It is through these natural patterns that we know ourselves as individuals and experience our connection to each other and the world.

Archetypal patterns influence our interpretation of our own and others' behavior. They account for many of the differences within and between people and cultures. For example, all religions attempt to answer the same basic questions about the meaning and purpose of life. These questions include the following:

- Why am I here?
- What I am I supposed to do while I'm here?
- Why do I suffer?
- What happens to me when I die?

The differences among the many religions result from the different answers that each one gives to these basic questions. From an archetypal point of view, these basic questions embody archetypal patterns. The answers to the questions present different expressions of the same archetypal patterns. We can think of archetypes, therefore, as the questions all of us implicitly ask ourselves about what is meaningful and important in our lives. How we answer these questions and express those answers depends on which archetype is central to our nature. The expressions of different central archetypes account for many of the differences among us. And so it is with love: The questions we ask ourselves about the meaning of love and how it will be experienced and lived out in our lives are also embodiments of universal archetypal patterns that are essential to us as human beings.

An archetypal approach assumes that each of us is born with an inclination to live out "the natural life cycle of our species—being mothered, exploring the environment, playing in the peer group, [going through] adolescence, being initiated, establishing a place in the social hierarchy, courting, marrying, childrearing, hunting, gathering, fighting, participating in religious rituals, assuming the social responsibilities of advanced maturity, and *preparation for death*" (Stevens 1982, p. 40). People living in all cultures and historical periods reveal a remarkable similarity in the way they deal with these areas of life, though cultural, historical, and individual factors color the particular expression of any archetype.

Perhaps most striking is that particular social structures like marriage, warfare, and religion exist at all, since there is no logical necessity for them. It is as if all human beings are born "programmed" to experience and express major life circumstances and events in relatively specific ways. Jung was struck by these seemingly unexplainable similarities across cultures. He also observed that the same themes appear in a wide variety of myths, legends, stories, and symbols from different cultures and time periods. This uniformity of themes across cultures and historical eras led him to propose archetypes as universal "systems of readiness for action" (1970, p. 31). Archetypes give form and structure to our instincts, perceptions, and understanding. They are like blueprints or plans that we make real, rather than specific contents, images, ideas, or memories. Jung and other observers have written a great deal about archetypes and the manner in which they influence many aspects of our lives. The following discussion highlights the features of archetypes that are particularly relevant for this book.[1]

Archetypes Work in the Background to Guide Our General Behavior We don't usually think about archetypes when we go about our daily lives. Their influence is so much a part of our being human that our particular expressions of them seem natural and inevitable. For example, we take it for granted that some custom or ritual accompanies the birth of a child, whether it be baptism, circumcision, or even giving out cigars. Or, we accept without much thought that the majority of human beings live in families and social groups, and that one or another political system is always in place.

Each of Us Has Many Archetypes or Patterns of Behavior Available to Us In lower animals, archetypes take the form of instincts that are specific to the life cycle and environmental conditions the animal will face. Every individual animal of a species behaves in the same way in response to an instinctual pattern. In contrast, human archetypes are more complicated patterns with less precise details. For example, all baby geese exhibit the instinctual behavior known as imprinting—following the first moving object they see after birth (usually their mothers), and all bears hibernate in response to increasing cold temperatures. Human babies' responses to mothering are more varied and individual, as are the potential ways humans ensure their safety and security in response to environmental changes.

Not All of the Available Patterns of Behavior Are Used by Any Particular Individual   The complexity of human beings is such that archetypal patterns are too numerous for any one person to use during a lifetime. Many patterns lie dormant in an individual or are irrelevant in the particular historical or social context in which a person lives. For example, forty years ago the prevailing archetype of a man in our society included the expectation that he would grow up and be the sole financial and social support of his wife and children. The accepted female archetype was that of a wife and mother who relied on her husband and had limited responsibilities outside the home. Today, there is a wider variety of gender archetypes available to men and women.

Each of Us Is Capable of Reflecting On and Understanding Archetypes Through Images, Symbols, and Stories   Once you know what archetypes are and how you might recognize them in operation, you can think about them and be more aware of their influence in everyday affairs. However, as we pointed out earlier, you already knew about archetypes as peculiarly human patterns that enable us to know, understand, and interpret our own and others' behavior.

When we are not consciously aware of archetypes, the most common way we experience them is through enduring stories or the symbols and images of poetry and art. Pinkola Estes succinctly describes the archetypal aspect of stories when she says, "In dealing with stories, we are handling archetypal energy, which we would metaphorically describe as being like electricity. This electrical power can animate and enlighten" (1992, p. 509). This energy is evident in the classic theme of Dr. Jekyll and Mr. Hyde, which explores the archetypal coexistence of good and evil, and in the many reenactments on film of the Frankenstein story, which reflects similar archetypal themes. The archetypal Wanderer appears in works from the *Iliad* and the *Odyssey* of Homer to *Travels with Charley* by John Steinbeck (1962). These and many other universal themes tend to evoke in us immediate recognition and a sense of larger meaning. They seem both familiar and strange, common yet unique.

We Cannot Consciously Choose an Archetype Which archetypes become prominent in our lives is determined by the interplay of the important themes that characterize the culture in which we live, our social identity, and our particular life experiences and circumstances. Compare, for example, a musically talented man raised in a family of professional musicians in the nineteenth century to a musically talented woman in the same circumstances, or to a musically talented African American man born to farm laborers in the early twentieth century. The first musically talented man might be influenced most by an archetype directly connected to artistic expression; the woman might be connected to a "Heroine" archetype seeking to succeed in the face of adversity; and a heroic archetype might also characterize the early-twentieth-century African American man, whose road to artistic expression might be strewn with obstacles to be overcome. Predicting or explaining which archetypes will emerge in any individual is enormously complex. Archetypes are not givens that we actually see; rather, archetypes are *foundations* that give shape and meaning to events in our everyday lives. As Guggenbuhl-Craig explained, "We experience our activity as meaningful only when it is related to an archetypal foundation. A mother can never function with satisfaction as a mother, if her mothering is done only out of conscious reflection" (1977, p. 54). Thus a mother's relationship to her child is fundamentally archetypal. The personal mother-child relationship rests on this archetypal ground.

The Archetypes of Love Relationships

To understand people and their social structures requires a vision of the images
which are at work in the background. The phenomenon of marriage cannot be
grasped without considering the images which give marriage its form.

Adolf Guggenbuhl-Craig, *Marriage Dead or Alive*

We have been able to distinguish four archetypes of love that we
call *Soul Images*. These Soul Images give form and expression to our
love relationships. All four are available to each of us; however,
every individual tends to be characterized by only one of the four
Soul Images, which he or she expresses naturally, comfortably,
and regularly within a love relationship. You will be able to identify your own Soul Image and those of others as you review the
brief descriptions in this chapter and read the more detailed nar-
ratives in the chapters that follow.

The four Soul Images are the *Mercurial Lover*, the *Romantic Lover*,
the *Innocent Lover*, and the *Steadfast Lover*. We present them in this particular order as a way of highlighting their differences. Before we
describe them further, however, you need to be aware of some
important qualifications about the four Soul Images and how they
interact in love relationships.

- There are no better or worse Soul Images or combinations of
  Soul Images in love relationships. Each Soul Image is
  expressed in distinctive ways and interacts with each other
  Soul Image in a consistent manner. As a result, all the love
  relationships have their own unique qualities, strengths and
  weaknesses, and stresses and satisfactions.
- The Soul Images identify the way a person relates in love relationships (meaning, not a relationship between family mem-

bers or friends, but a relationship between lovers). Some people may behave in quite different ways in different relationships. For others, the Soul Image may be a global and consistent aspect of their character. In trying to determine your or another's Soul Image, it is best to focus on how you or the other person function *within a love relationship*. You may then be better able to see whether this Soul Image is used in other relationships and as a general worldview.

- As archetypal patterns, the Soul Images influence *all human love relationships*—those of unmarried as well as married couples, and those of gay and lesbian couples as well as heterosexual ones.

- The way a Soul Image is expressed can be modified by individual differences in personality. For example, an extraverted person may manifest a Mercurial Lover Soul Image somewhat differently than an introverted person; or an organized, careful, methodical Romantic Lover may express this Soul Image differently than a spontaneous, carefree, adventurous Romantic Lover. Similarly, the ages and genders of the partners, the presence or absence of children, the partners' physical and mental health, the longevity of the relationship, and other factors may contribute to the unique expression of the Soul Images within a particular relationship.

- The four Soul Images describe different patterns of perceiving, interpreting, and relating to the world and to others. When a particular Soul Image is central for a person, perceptions and expectations that fit in with the image usually seem right, necessary, and self-evident. If others do not share the same perceptions and expectations, they may be seen as misguided, wrong, different, or even weird. Tension, misunderstanding, and conflict may be the inevitable results. When you read about the different Soul Images, you may find it hard not to judge them—perhaps negatively—from the point of view of your own Soul Image. Try to avoid making such judgments if you can.

- In light of naturally occurring biases, some people may be tempted to see one or more of the Soul Images as immature or even pathological. *Such an appraisal is diametrically opposed to the point of view we are presenting in this book.* [2]

- No Soul Image is inherently better, more mature, or healthier than any other. For as Jung has succinctly stated, "The greatest danger that threatens psychology is one-sidedness and the insistence on a single standpoint. In order to do justice to the phenomena of the psyche, a variety of viewpoints is needed" (1970, p. 552).

The Mercurial Lover

The greatest sacrifice in marriage is the sacrifice of the adventurous attitude towards life.

George Bernard Shaw, *Getting Married*

For Mercurial Lovers, a love relationship is an opportunity for change, transformation, and fulfillment. They are in a perpetual state of becoming, forever evolving toward a future filled with possibility and the potential for change and development. They want to merge with their beloved and thereby evolve, expand, and enhance their sense of self. The process of change seems natural, exciting, necessary, and valuable. They believe it will inevitably lead to positive development. Mercurial Lovers see their love relationship as part of their "journey on the path of life."

Mercurial Lovers regard themselves and others as independent, autonomous, and separate—as having a distinct existence regardless of relationships to other people. They believe that one's identity and sense of self are unique. Their focus is on personal accomplishments and their ability to independently solve life's problems. Their beloved's independence and separateness from them is regarded as a fact that enables them to accept and encourage the beloved's interests and desires. They expect their own independence to be acknowledged and supported in the same way. They resist restrictions of their freedom and are sensitive to any hint of coercion from others, especially their beloved. Some partners may erroneously experience this resistance as a lack of love and commitment to the relationship.

An example of the importance of independence, autonomy, and separation is evident in an incident described by the writer Edward Abbey in his book *Desert Solitaire* (1968).[3] At the time of the following encounter, Abbey was a forest ranger at a national monument in the southwestern desert.

> "Oh ranger, do you live in that little house trailer down there?"
> "Yes madam, part of the time. Mostly I live out of it."
> "Are you married?"
> "Not seriously."
> "You must get awfully lonesome way out here."
> "No, I have good company."
> "Your wife?"
> "No, myself." (p. 263)

The focus for Mercurial Lovers is on *falling in love*.[4] They seek an ideal mate and delight in the anticipation and passion of being with their beloved. They want the passion of love to persist into the future, and believe that as long as they and the beloved are together, life will be wonderful. However, their desire to perpetuate the state of falling in love makes Mercurial Lovers easily discontented with the comfort and predictability of an established relationship. They can become bored and impatient with the details of maintaining the day-to-day aspects of a relationship. Once comfort and predictability set in, the demands of everyday life may appear confining, making Mercurial Lovers restless and irritable. They may then notice their beloved's faults and frailties and become critical and judgmental. They wonder what happened to the spark in the relationship. Because of their emphasis on change, they want to be free to experiment with and explore different modes of experiencing themselves and the world. For them, the future is open-ended, full of change and transformation. They are likely to energetically pursue many interests and a wide variety of friends.

For the Mercurial Lover, the central relationship question is, "If I am a separate, changing individual, how can I merge with a beloved in an intimate, loving relationship?" In elaborating on this question, a Mercurial Lover might explain as follows:

"Change and the flux of life sustain me with vigor, further my transformation, and engage me with life's possibilities. Yet, this isn't enough. I also need the exhilaration of love through merging with my beloved. As much as I desire the passion of love, however, I also fear my beloved's love. My fear is that my beloved may innocently entice me to a life of predictability, comfort, and routine that will end in a suffocating and deadly inertia. If this happens, I will indeed lose my soul and I will become like an automaton in a Kafka novel."

Chart I summarizes the important attributes of the Mercurial Lover Soul Image.

The Romantic Lover

> At what moment do lovers come into the most complete possession
> of themselves, if not when they are lost in each other?

Pierre Teilhard De Chardin, *The Phenomenon of Man*

Chart 1

Characteristics of Mercurial Lovers

Attribute	Theme
Transformation of Self	Focus on a future filled with the potential for change and transformation.
Separateness	View their identity and sense of self as unique and distinct from relationships.
Autonomy	Value independence and autonomy; resist restrictions on freedom and are sensitive to any hint of coercion from others.
Falling in Love	Revel in the intensity and novelty of the experience of love.

Romantic Lovers value constancy, permanence, and completeness in their relationship to their beloved. In contrast to Mercurial Lovers, their sense of identity or selfhood comes from relationships, giving them a feeling of wholeness and mutual reliance. As true "romantics," they strive to cultivate and refine their expression of relatedness. Romantic Lovers often assume that others share the belief in the "oneness" of all and the power of love. They tend to be idealistic, having faith that "love conquers all." They believe that if we love and respect each other, most if not all problems can be solved and differences resolved. They apply this principle not only to intimate relationships, but to social and communal ones as well. As a result of this approach, they may have difficulty accepting that people can place their individual desires above the needs of a relationship. Being motivated primarily by self-interest doesn't make sense to them. They are likely to judge people who behave in this way as selfish and uncaring. This is in sharp contrast to the Mercurial Lovers' assumption that everyone has a separate and independent sense of self.

Romantic Lovers focus on *being in love* and all the ways they can share the love experience with the beloved. They do not want to merge with their beloved as Mercurial Lovers do; they want to *share identities* with their beloved. Romantic Lovers strive to enhance their being in love almost to the exclusion of other relationships and concerns. They are content to "let the rest of the world go by." Because of the centrality of the love relationship, separations from the beloved can be experienced as a diminishment of love. They yearn for their beloved and resist interests and pulls from the outside world that may separate them from their beloved. Romantic lovers are therefore sensitive to any hint of separation, whether this is expressed in a partner's feelings or behavior. They regard separate and different interests of the beloved as potential threats to their love. They may therefore try to focus on or develop common interests, thereby ensuring the constancy of pleasure in a shared activity. This sensitivity to separation and difference may be erroneously seen by a partner as neediness, dependency, or childishness.

In contrast to the Mercurial Lovers, who fear losing their separate identity in a relationship, Romantic Lovers are concerned about maintaining a sense of themselves as individuals *through a relationship*. Sharing their identity with the beloved maintains a sense of self in the relationship in such a way that they risk having no sense of self outside the relationship. For the Romantic Lover, therefore, the central relationship question is, "If my sense of self and identity is constituted by my relationship with my beloved, can I have a sense of self and fulfillment when I am alone?" A Romantic Lover might elaborate the thinking behind this question as follows:

"I can only be a complete human being if I am in a loving relationship with my beloved. For only through our love can we each lose our separateness from the world and become one with the world. Only then can 'I' become a 'We,' and then another new and true 'Me.' What happens then if I am separated from my beloved?

Chart 2
Characteristics of Romantic Lovers

Attribute	Theme
Stability	Value constancy, permanence, and completeness in the relationship with the beloved.
Relatedness	Sense of identity or selfhood comes from the relationship with the beloved, resulting in a feeling of wholeness.
Togetherness	Emphasis is on participating in and sharing all aspects of their lives, from minutiae to everyday events to major occurrences, as expressions of togetherness.
Being in Love	Focus is on all the ways the love experience can be shared and enhanced with the beloved.

Do I still exist? Will I no longer feel joy and pleasure? Will I be devoid of any sense of who I am? That prospect truly frightens me. If it occurs, I will be truly afflicted with a lovesickness."

Chart 2 summarizes the important attributes of the Romantic Lover Soul Image.

The Innocent Lover

The opposite of love is indifference.

Rollo May, *Man's Search for Himself*

Innocent Lovers are similar to Mercurial Lovers in viewing the world as changing. In contrast to Mercurial Lovers, however, the Innocent Lovers' relationship with the beloved constitutes and confirms their sense of self. Innocent Lovers view change and growth as establishing their connection to other people and the world. They find that the comfort and certainty of their relationships leads to change and growth. Because their sense of self is sustained through relating within the flux of change, Innocent Lovers value all of the ways they receive love and affirmation from their beloved. Cherishing others and being cherished in return are both very important to them. They are therefore likely to be quite sensitive to signs of indifference and emotional distance. In contrast to Romantic Lovers, who are concerned about possible isolation, Innocent Lovers are sensitive to any signs that the beloved feels uninterested and detached from them. People with other Soul Images may erroneously see Innocent Lovers as dependent, insecure, and clinging—as sacrificing their separate identity for comfort and certainty.

Innocent Lovers are similar to Romantic Lovers in enjoying a common identity with their beloved. They differ, however, in that Romantic Lovers "share" in each others' identity—their formation of identity is mutual. The identity of Innocent Lovers, however, is essentially "bestowed" by each of them—*being loved* is therefore very important for the formation of a sense of self for Innocent Lovers. Oneness within the relationship occurs through maintaining continuity with the beloved. This continuity is strengthened and actualized by projecting the togetherness with the beloved into the future through shared memories, projects, and plans.

Like Romantic Lovers, Innocent Lovers acquire their sense of relatedness through their delight in sharing experiences with the beloved. The Innocent Lover, however, sees the beloved as part of the wholeness and flux of the world. Their emphasis on change leads them to a commitment to the growth of their relationship in the *future.* Romantic Lovers, in contrast, seek to *differentiate* their unique relationship from the world at large, perpetuating their *present* relationship into the future.

Chart 3
Characteristics of Innocent Lovers

Attribute	*Theme*
Change and Development	Change and growth toward a goal establish a connection to people and the world.
Relatedness	A sense of selfhood comes from the loving relationship with the beloved.
Togetherness	Togetherness with the beloved is maintained by sharing projects, plans, and dreams for the future.
Being Loved	The knowledge and comfort of being loved is the nourishment that will lead to change and growth.

Innocent Lovers want to share common interests with the beloved. They may take up an interest or activity in order to share it with the beloved. This is an important expression of love for them.

For the Innocent Lover, the central relationship question is, "If my sense of self is confirmed by my beloved in an intimate relationship, can I develop and have a sense of self when I am not being loved?" An Innocent Lover might elaborate on this concern as follows:

"It is an old adage that one only exists when one is loved. That's the way it is for me. My beloved's love for me is what sustains me and grants me the will and the energy to grow, develop, and be at one with the world. What I dread is the possibility that my beloved will no longer love me. If that happens, I will lose not only my sense of self, but also my dreams and goals for the future. It is for this reason that my beloved must confirm the love that sustains me. If not, I will truly be lost."

Chart 3 summarizes the important attributes of the Innocent Lover Soul Image.

The Steadfast Lover

Love does not consist in gazing at each other but in looking outward together in the same direction.

Antoine de Saint Exupéry, *Wind, Sand, and Stars*

Steadfast Lovers value constancy and continuity. In contrast to Mercurial Lovers, who are interested in change and transformation, Steadfast Lovers focus on differentiation—on the refinement and expression of all facets of their selfhood. They are concerned with how to differentiate themselves and how they can be unique and distinct from their interpersonal, social, and cultural environment. They place great value on individuality. Steadfast Lovers believe that a person's characteristics are stable, enduring, and coherent. They try to fulfill the potential that is latent within them. As a result, they cherish their independence. Like Mercurial Lovers, they see one's sense of self as independent of any and all relationships.

They accept their partners as separate, independent individuals, and they want that same kind of acceptance for themselves. They can therefore *appear* somewhat detached and emotionally distant in a relationship. Both Romantic and Innocent Lovers may misinterpret such an appearance of detachment as cold and uncaring. Romantic Lovers miss the sense of inseparability they expect in a love relationship, while Innocent Lovers are likely to feel isolated and unimportant to their beloved.

In contrast to Romantic Lovers, for whom being in love is central, *staying in love* is most important for Steadfast Lovers. Faithfulness and constancy are therefore highly valued. They strive to make their relationship more complex, differentiated, and complete while still maintaining a separate sense of self. Like

Mercurial Lovers, Steadfast Lovers accept and encourage their partners' independent interests and activities. When Steadfast Lovers cannot maintain the mutuality they expect in their relationship, they may fear that their independence, self-sufficiency, and separateness are in jeopardy. They may become forceful in their attempts to get what they expect in the relationship, and therefore risk being judged as autocratic and domineering. Some partners may interpret the Steadfast Lover's attempts to achieve equality in the relationship as the very opposite—as a one-sided and controlling use of power.

Steadfast Lovers may experience tension between their sense of self as separate individuals and the potential for losing part of that separateness through closeness and intimacy with another person. The central relationship question for Steadfast Lovers is, "How can I maintain my individuality and still be in a loving relationship?" A Steadfast Lover might elaborate on this question as follows:

"If I am a separate individual and I have a distinct identity, will I have to surrender or lose part of my identity and individuality to be in a loving relationship? After all, to be in a loving relationship means that I will have to take into consideration what my partner wishes and desires. I just can't do what I want without at least informing or consulting my partner. What's worse, suppose my partner objects to what I want or has a different preference? If I give in to that, doesn't that mean I will lose part of me?"

Chart 4 summarizes the important attributes of the Steadfast Lover Soul Image.

The Four Soul Images

Why are there four Soul Images, and why these particular ones? The answer is that these four have consistently appeared in relatively coherent form in our many years of experience working with

Chart 4
Characteristics of Steadfast Lovers

Attribute	*Theme*
Stability	Value is placed on constancy and continuity. Focus is on the refinement and expression of all facets of their selfhood.
Separateness	Accept their partners as separate, independent individuals and want that same kind of acceptance for themselves.
Autonomy	Value independence, uniqueness, and distinctness from social and cultural environments.
Staying in Love	Place high value on faithfulness and constancy in the love relationship.

individuals and couples. Even for those individuals and relationships where the Soul Images are less distinct and harder to identify, recognizing the attributes of the different Soul Images proves illuminating, clarifying, and useful.

How do these four Soul Images yield ten kinds of relationships? A person may be in a relationship with someone of the identical Soul Image—for example, two Innocent Lovers—or with someone of a different Soul Image—say, a Romantic Lover and a Steadfast Lover. All possible combinations of the four Soul Images produce ten different kinds of relationships.

Identifying the Soul Images

We have found that individuals and couples vary in the ease with which they are able to select the Soul Images that best fit them. As is the case with most attempts to characterize human beings, there are subtleties and variations that may not fit the description. To help in distinguishing the Soul Images, Chart 5 summarizes the important attributes of all four Soul Images for comparison and contrast.

Overview of This Book

The remainder of *True Loves* is divided into three parts. Part 1, "Images of Relationships," consists of Chapters 2 and 3. Chapter 2, "What Is Love?," discusses the background and rationale for the Soul Images that make up the ten love relationships. It presents an unbiased method to assess different kinds of intimacy and describes the nature of love for people with different Soul Images. The chapter also describes the important themes that form the basis for the Soul Images. Chapter 3, "Stress in Relationships," shows how the characteristics of each of the Soul Images emerge in exaggerated ways when a couple experiences stress. The conscious and unconscious processes that are involved in quarrels are shown to be directly connected to a couple's Soul Images.

Part 2, "The Ten Love Relationships," consists of the ten chapters that describe couples with particular combinations of Soul Images. Important features of the relationship are described. Examples illustrate the uniqueness of each particular love relationship as the couple deals with everyday issues such as household tasks, money, friendships, communication, extended family, work, sex, recreation, and childrearing. The effect of increasing stress in the relationship is described in a concluding scenario that presents an initial disagreement the couple have, followed by a more serious quarrel.

Chapters 4 through 7 present relationships where the partners in the couple relate to each other with the same Soul Image. Two

Chart 5

Characteristics of the Four Soul Images

Soul Image	Attribute	Theme
Mercurial Lover	Tranformation of Self	Focus on a future filled with the potential for change and transformation.
	Separateness	View their identity and sense of self as unique and distinct from relationships.
	Autonomy	Value independence and autonomy; resist restrictions on freedom and are sensitive to any hint of coercion from others.
	Falling in Love	Revel in the intensity and novelty of the experience of love.
Romantic Lover	Stability	Value constancy, permanence, and completeness in the relationship with the beloved.
	Relatedness	Sense of identity or selfhood comes from the relationship with the beloved, resulting in a feeling of wholeness.
	Togetherness	Emphasis is on participating in and sharing all aspects of their lives, from minutiae to everyday events to major occurrences, as expressions of togetherness.
	Being in Love	Focus is on all the ways the love experience can be shared and enhanced with the beloved.

Mercurial Lovers are described in Chapter 4, two Romantic Lovers in Chapter 5, two Innocent Lovers in Chapter 6, and two Steadfast Lovers in Chapter 7. Chapters 8 and 9 cover partner combinations with *opposite* Soul Images. Chapter 8 presents the Innocent Lover and Steadfast Lover combination, and Chapter 9 the Mercurial Lover and Romantic Lover combination. (The

Chart 5

Characteristics of the Four Soul Images (continued)

Soul Image	Attribute	Theme
Innocent Lover	Change and Development	Change and growth toward a goal establish a connection to people and the world.
	Relatedness	A sense of selfhood comes from the loving relationship with the beloved.
	Togetherness	Togetherness with the beloved is maintained by sharing projects, plans, and dreams for the future.
	Being Loved	The knowledge and comfort of being loved is the nourishment that will lead to change and growth.
Steadfast Lover	Stability	Value is placed on constancy and continuity. Focus is on the refinement and expression of all facets of their selfhood.
	Separateness	Accept their partners as separate, independent individuals and want that same kind of acceptance for themselves.
	Autonomy	Value independence, uniqueness, and distinctness from social and cultural environments.
	Staying in Love	Place high value on faithfulness and constancy in the love relationship.

rationale for the opposition of Mercurial Lover and Romantic Lover may not be immediately obvious to readers; we provide the basis for this conclusion in Chapter 2.) Chapters 10 through 13 cover relationships in which the partners are neither the same nor opposite in their Soul Images. We designate these relationships as similar. Chapter 10 presents the Mercurial Lover and Innocent Lover, Chapter 11 the Innocent Lover and Romantic Lover,

Chapter 12 the Mercurial Lover and Steadfast Lover, and Chapter 13 the Romantic Lover and Steadfast Lover.

Part 3, "Enduring Love Relationships," contains Chapter 14, "Love, Acceptance, and Compatibility," and a brief "Epilogue." Chapter 14 describes factors that affect the acceptance that is necessary for a lasting love relationship. The nature of compatibility and its relationship to acceptance is also discussed. The chapter includes examples showing how knowledge of the four Soul Images contributes to a couple's understanding and acceptance of themselves and each other. The Epilogue identifies two important areas that are not included in the discussion of the Soul Images and love relationships: the interaction of the Soul Images with personality attributes, and the way in which severe and persistent external and internal stress distort the expression of the Soul Images.

Part I) *Images of Relationships*

Part I establishes the foundation for our
approach to love relationships. Its aim is to
enable readers to view the ten love relationships from a new and unbiased point of
view. Both Chapter 2, "What Is Love?," and
Chapter 3, "Stress in Relationships," serve
this purpose, although in quite different ways.
Together, these chapters give readers the
foundation needed to fully appreciate the
nature of the different love relationships we
present in Part 2 of the book.

Chapter 2, "What Is Love?," provides the
context within which the Soul Images occur.
Included in the discussion is an explanation
of the different meanings of *intimacy* for the

four Soul Images. We suggest a way of avoiding bias in viewing the intimacy within any love relationship. The subsequent discussion of the *nature of love* further explores common personal and societal biases about mature love. We attempt to broaden the reader's perspective so that other views of love can be understood and accepted. This chapter also provides an explanation of the difference between the important life and relationship *themes* that characterize each of the Soul Images, and identifies these themes as psychological *complexes* that emerge in relationships.

Chapter 3, "Stress in Relationships," builds on the foundation created in the previous chapter. It shows how stress serves as a trigger for quarrels, and how the different meanings of intimacy, the biases about the nature of love, and the various life and relationship themes create distinctive dynamics in the quarrels of different kinds of couples. The chapter shows how both conscious and unconscious complexes characteristic of a couple's Soul Images emerge in predictable and consistent ways during the different stages of a quarrel. The scenario in the chapter serves as a specific model for the disagreements and quarrels included in each chapter of Part 2. Understanding the structure and stages of quarrels will enable readers to better understand and assess the content and style of quarrels typical of the ten love relationships.

2 ⟩ *What Is Love?*

> *"Love" is . . . together with hunger, the immemorial psychic driving-force of humanity. It is, psychologically considered, a function of relationship on the one hand and a feeling-toned psychic condition on the other. . . . There can be no doubt that love has an instinctual determinant; it is an activity peculiar to mankind.*
>
> C. G. Jung, *Symbols of Transformation*

The Soul Images are the foundational patterns that structure and give form to our most important activities, especially our love relationships. A Soul Image not only characterizes the significant and peculiar ways that we relate in a love relationship, but also constitutes the meaning and importance of an intimate relationship for us. As a result, people with different Soul Images may have views of relationships that differ considerably from those that are commonly held.

Love's Many Splendors

The basic assumptions underlying our view of love and intimate relationships are the following:

- Who and what we are defines how we love and what love means to us.
- Because there are many different kinds of people, there are many different kinds of love.
- If there are many different kinds of love, there are many different kinds of love relationships.

In other words, there isn't only one experience of love and only one true love relationship. The Soul Images give a unique character to each relationship. Therefore, all ten true loves have their own sources of pleasure and satisfaction, as well as their own difficulties and deficiencies.

This chapter places the Soul Images within a larger context that will help illuminate their profound influence on love relationships. To accomplish this, we will look at the relationship between the Soul Images and the following constructs:

- The different meanings of *intimacy*
- Differing views about the *nature of love*
- Important *life and relationship themes*

The Different Meanings of Intimacy

What we mean by a love relationship is one that includes the following elements:

- Constancy—It exists over time.
- Reciprocity—There is a mutuality in the relationship.
- Exclusivity—The love is not directed at anyone but the beloved.

- Intimacy—There is (or can be) a cognitive, emotional, physical, and sexual warmth or closeness in the relationship.

Note that there is no simple and straightforward definition of intimacy, as there is for constancy, reciprocity, and exclusivity. Our Soul Image determines what intimacy means to us and how we express it. From this standpoint, there can be many valid expressions of intimacy.

The Nature of Intimacy

If intimacy means different things to different couples, is there some unbiased way to talk about intimacy? We have found it helpful to explore intimacy in terms of a relationship's *temperature* and *proximity*.

Temperature This aspect is relevant when we describe a relationship as warm or cool, hot or cold. The temperature in a relationship may be indicated by the amount of physical and verbal contact between a couple. Using these descriptors, the standard in our society for intimate relationships clearly is to be warm. The following indicators may be helpful for understanding this dimension of intimacy:

- Hot—passionate sexual activity; kissing and caressing in public
- Warm—holding hands, touching, and physical closeness in private and public; use of terms of endearment
- Cool—minimal physical contact; nonverbal and nonphysical expressions of affection; politeness in public
- Cold—criticism, negating comments, bickering, or sarcasm in private and public

Proximity This dimension refers to the degree of closeness in a relationship. Some relationships may be described as close, others as more distant. Proximity reflects the "atmosphere" in the relationship; it is implicit in the extent to which a member of a couple is sensitive to the nonverbal indicators of the partner's well-being. Proximity may be difficult for observers to assess. The couple themselves, however, may be aware of some of the following cues that reflect the distance or closeness in their relationship:

- Distant—The couple (or one member) may be unaware of the unspoken distress or joy of the partner, unless directly affected by it; the well-being of one member of the couple has little effect on the well-being of the other.
- Close—The couple (or one member) is deeply affected by the other's unspoken distress; one member's well-being is a function of the other's well-being; they (or he or she) are sensitive to each other's moods and behavior.

Viewing intimacy in these two ways gives us an unbiased way of assessing different kinds of relationships. Satisfying relationships can vary from cold to hot and from distant to close. For example, there are relationships that are close and cold, as humorously shown in the movie *When Harry Met Sally*. Harry and Sally bicker a lot and criticize each other publicly as well as privately. But they are also quite close—sensitive to each other's innermost thoughts, moods, and feelings. Close and cold relationships can also be seen in some forty- or fifty-year marriages where the couples constantly criticize, chide, and disparage each other. At the same time, their connection to each other is so finely tuned that they can respond instinctively and nonverbally to each other's deepest needs. Although these apparently cold and acrimonious relationships are often difficult for others to appreciate, their stability and longevity often indicate the fulfillment they bring to the couples themselves.

Other relationships may be hot and distant. Perhaps the classic depiction of Don Juan is the prototype of a hot and distant relationship: there is a good deal of short-lived sexual passion with little or no awareness of the partner's thoughts and feelings. Excellent film examples of hot and distant intimacy appear in the various relationships shown in *Les Liaisons Dangereaux*. Their intense heat and distance constitute both the excitement and danger inherent in such relationships.

Warm and close intimacy is typical of couples in many American families portrayed on television programs in the 1950s and early 1960s. Think of such classics as *Leave It to Beaver, Father Knows Best,* and *The Dick Van Dyke Show.* The couples are verbally and physically demonstrative as well as remarkably in tune with each others' thoughts, feelings, and sense of well-being. It is not surprising that this kind of relationship served as the "ideal" against which TV viewers often judged their own or their parents' relationships.[1] There is a sense that this is the way intimate relationships "are supposed to be."

As seen in literature, classic hot and close relationships often end badly. Examples include Romeo and Juliet, Heloise and Abelard, Lancelot and Guinevere, and Antony and Cleopatra. A more recent example is the relationship between Count Ladislaus de Almásy and the married Katharine Clifton in the award-winning novel and film *The English Patient.* Such relationships can bring intense and all-consuming joy to the participants. But they also bring great heartbreak and sorrow, and often end prematurely in violent separation and death.

Stereotypical cold and distant relationships can be seen in the arranged marriages depicted in many nineteenth-century British novels. Such a relationship is captured in the image of a very long, formally set dining table, with the husband and wife at either end silently eating dinner. Although observers may judge such relationships negatively, the couple themselves often appear quite content and comfortable with this kind of intimacy. Such couples would agree with the notion that marriage is a social contract and has no necessary connection to love.

Warm and distant relationships may appear to others to be the same as warm and close ones. There can be a significant display of warmth, concern, and solicitude both privately and in public. In terms of closeness, however, the couple may be comfortably unaware of and unconcerned about each other's innermost thoughts and feelings. They may both prefer this approach and be quite satisfied with this aspect of their relationship.

Temperature, Proximity, and Soul Images

Each Soul Image has its own preferred temperature and proximity. Mercurial Lovers generally prefer relationships that are hot and somewhat distant; Romantic Lovers prefer those that are hot and close; Innocent Lovers prefer those that are warm and close; and Steadfast Lovers prefer those that are cool and close. Conflicts may emerge when a couple with different Soul Images have different relationship temperatures and proximities at which they feel comfortable. For example, a Romantic Lover may be rebuffed when trying to kiss a Steadfast Lover partner in public. Or an Innocent Lover may be deeply hurt when a Mercurial Lover partner fails to recognize that he is upset.

Chart 6 summarizes the relationship between the Soul Images and these two indicators of intimacy. In Chapters 4 through 13, we will see how these different perspectives on intimacy shed light on various issues in the ten love relationships.

The Dominant View of Love Relationships

Most if not all of the writings about love relationships take the view that intimacy can occur only between two separate and distinct individuals. Jung reflects this notion in his statement that "This identity, this clinging together, is a great hindrance to individual relationship. . . . Relationship is only possible when there is sep-

Chart 6
Relation of Soul Images to Temperature and Proximity

Soul Image	Temperature	Proximity
Mercurial Lover	Hot	Distant
Romantic Lover	Hot	Close
Innocent Lover	Warm	Close
Steadfast Lover	Cool	Close

arateness" (1960, p. 265). If Jung is correct, intimacy in a relationship cannot occur for lovers whose expression of love is a merging or sharing of their respective identities; this would not constitute a real relationship.

C. A. Meier (1995) identifies the assumption that underlies Jung's notion about separation and relationship:

> But what unconsciousness means in every relationship is non-differentiation, i.e., at least partial identity. A consequence of this is the well-known fact that one partner presupposes in the other the same psychological structure, the same interests, the same sexual functioning and feeling. In other words, there is an illusion of unity which seems to create "one heart and one soul." (p. 156)

Meier is saying that a love relationship in which the lovers feel a shared identity is unconscious and not "mature." If Jung and Meier are correct, this would mean that Romantic Lovers and Innocent Lovers are incapable of truly intimate love relationships. Steadfast Lovers would be the only exemplars of intimacy within a mature relationship. In the Jung/Meier view, Mercurial Lovers would be capable of intimacy, since they find their identity through separateness and independence. However, their Mercurial qualities may make them seem less "mature."

We strongly disagree with such a conclusion, for Jung and Meier are looking at relationships almost exclusively from the standpoint of the Steadfast Lover Soul Image. They are not alone in this, for as we mentioned earlier, the Jung/Meier assumption is implicit in most approaches to thinking and writing about love relationships. In such views, a merging or sharing of lovers' identities is incompatible with the shared life of a mature marriage.

Jung's dictum that there can be no relationship without separation may, however, be applicable to other, nonlove relationships. Remember, there is no necessary correspondence between a person's Soul Image in a love relationship and how he or she relates in other contexts. For example, a surgeon may be authoritative, directive, and businesslike at work, but may be an Innocent Lover in relation to his wife; or a business executive may create a relaxed and egalitarian team approach as a manager, but may be a Steadfast Lover in relation to her husband.

⎰ The Nature of Love

Love is a force of destiny whose power reaches from heaven to hell. . . . Love may be an ethical, a social, a psychological, a philosophical, an aesthetic, a religious, a medical, a legal, or a physiological problem, to name only a few aspects of this many-sided phenomenon. . . . This invasion of love into all the collective spheres of life is, however, only a minor difficulty in comparison with the fact that love is also an intensely individual problem.

C. G. Jung, *Civilization in Transition*

So many statements in poems, fiction, operas, folk and popular music, scholarly works, and everyday conversation begin with the same words used by Jung—*love is*. That it is a "many-sided phenomenon," as Jung states, is clear from the great variety of endings to this phrase. No single ending is likely to satisfy everyone. Nevertheless, it would be helpful in our exploration of differing love relationships to have a specific way to discuss the nature of love.

Jung's concept of *psychic energy*—the force that activates our psychological system—gives us a way of understanding love in all its many facets and expressions. It helps us to avoid talking about love as some "thing" that ends the sentence that begins *love is*. Instead, we can talk about love as a purposeful, goal-directed expression of who we are as human beings. For as we said at the beginning of this chapter, *who and what we are determines what love means to us and how we express it.*

Love as Energy

Even though energy is not a thing we can actually see, or even a concept we can define in anything but an abstract way, everyone seems to know what energy is. We talk about having more or less of it at different times; wanting to devote most or none of it to different interests and activities; feeling drained of it; feeling energetic; being energized by an activity, a person, or an idea; having our energy spread too thin; and so on. These kinds of ordinary and everyday expressions actually describe some very important characteristics of energy in general, and psychic energy in particular. Such characteristics lie at the heart of our understanding of the nature of love as an expression of psychic energy. Here are the characteristics of psychic energy that are implied by our everyday statements:

- Energy varies in its *intensity*—how much we have of it at any one time.

- Energy is typically directed or *focused* on or toward something.
- Energy is *finite*—we have only a certain amount of it available at any one time.

These three qualities of energy are useful and important for understanding how love is expressed as psychic energy. The *intensity* of the love that we express may vary from *mild* to *strong*. The *focus* of our love can vary from *narrow* to *broad*. And because energy is finite, we have only a certain amount of it available for any one way of expressing it. Because of this limit on the amount of available energy, its intensity and focus are related to each other in predictable ways.

Let's assume, for example, that we have one hundred units of psychic energy available for the expression of love. If we direct eighty units (*strong,* intense energy) to one particular way of expressing love—for example, sexual passion—the focus of that energy will be *narrow*. As a result, only twenty units of energy will be available for other ways of expressing love. This use of psychic energy would be described as *strong* and *narrow*.

Now suppose that someone has a variety of ways of expressing love—sexuality, shared interests and activities, providing economic security, and so on. The one hundred units of psychic energy available must be distributed among the many expressions of love. Therefore, each expression will receive a relatively small quantity and intensity of the available psychic energy. This focus of psychic energy will be *broad;* the intensity of energy for any one behavior will therefore be *mild*.

The Soul Images and Psychic Energy

You can see how love as psychic energy might be expressed differently by people with each of the four Soul Images. For example, Romantic Lovers' psychic energy is likely to be *strong* and *narrow*—being with the beloved would be the central goal. On the other hand, Steadfast Lovers, who are concerned with refinement and differentiation of the love relationship, may have a *broader* focus and therefore *milder* expression of psychic energy toward any one aspect. Whereas Mercurial Lovers and Innocent Lovers, with their interest in growth, development, and change, are likely to entertain a wide variety of ways of loving—sexual expression, shared interests, building a home together, devoting time to children, having heart-to-heart discussions, and so on. If they try to accommodate all of these, each one will be *mild* in its use of psychic energy. When love is expressed in only one or two ways, however, each will be *strong* in its use of psychic energy. In general, Mercurial and Innocent Lovers' use of psychic energy can vary from mild to strong.

The intensity and focus of love may vary *within* a relationship as well. For example, at the beginning of any love relationship there is likely to be a great deal of passion and persistent thoughts of the beloved. The psychic energy expressed here is likely to be *strong* and *narrow*. As the love relationship continues, the initial passion and spark may diminish, and there will inevitably be a *broader* focus in order to deal with the demands of daily living. There will now be more ways of expressing love in the relationship, so the expression of love in any one area is likely to be more *mild*.

The birth of children is often reported as heralding a change in the sexual expression of love. A couple may say something like "We made love very often before we had children, but after the children were born our love life became practically nil." Viewing love as energy provides insight into this lessening of lovemaking. For as the scope of our energy broadens—as different ways of expressing love emerge—this one aspect, sexual passion, will inevitably diminish in intensity. On the other hand, if the narrow and strong focus on the sexual expression of love is maintained, other aspects of the love relationship will inevitably be of lesser importance. For example, the couple may develop few common

Chart 7
Relation of Soul Images to Expressions of Psychic Energy

Soul Image	Focus	Intensity
Mercurial Lover	Broad	Mild to strong
Romantic Lover	Narrow	Strong
Innocent Lover	Broad	Mild to strong
Steadfast Lover	Broad	Mild

interests and friendships, and may have little interest in each other's lives outside of the bedroom.

Chart 7 summarizes the relationship of the Soul Images to expressions of psychic energy.

Important Life and Relationship Themes

We began this chapter with the statement that "The Soul Images are the foundational patterns that structure and give form to our most important activities, especially our love relationships." You have probably noticed that there are some similarities, differences, and contrasts in the characteristics of the four Soul Images. There are two opposite themes that encompass some of these similarities and differences, and each Soul Image embodies one of each of the two opposite themes. The two pairs of themes are the following:

1. *Stability* versus *change*
2. *Separateness* versus *relatedness*

As you read the following descriptions of these themes, you may recognize (or recall from Chapter 1) that the Mercurial Lover Soul Image reflects *change* and *separateness,* the Romantic Lover Soul Image involves *stability* and *relatedness,* the Innocent Lover Soul Image embodies *change* and *relatedness,* and the Steadfast Lover Soul Image encompasses *stability* and *separateness.* (See Chart 5 for a review.) If you have not yet identified which Soul Image best describes you in your love relationship, the following discussion of these themes may help.

The theme of *stability* involves the following aspects:

- Accepting constancy as a fact
- Valuing purposes and goals rather than processes
- Appreciating history and the past
- Having enduring values
- Placing a high value on stability
- Desiring completeness
- Wanting to become differentiated and distinct

People who are described by this theme believe that by becoming differentiated and distinct, their purpose in life can be actualized and their essential nature realized. The focus is on *being who and what you are* as opposed to *becoming or achieving an identity.* This theme is appealing to people who emphasize individuality and uniqueness in their love relationship. That is why the *Romantic Lover* and *Steadfast Lover* are located here.

The theme of *change* involves the following elements:

- Desiring change rather than stability
- Emphasizing transformation rather than differentiation
- Valuing the process more than the outcome
- Focusing on growth and development
- Assuming that everything and everyone is unique and constantly changing
- Looking toward the future and its possibilities

People who are described by this theme believe that the processes of change, growth, and development will permit them to be transformed—to become a unique individual, different from who they were before. The focus is on *growing toward an individual identity*. This theme is appealing to people who emphasize the limitless potential inherent in human nature and in their love relationship. For that reason, *Mercurial Lovers* and *Innocent Lovers* are located in this group.

The theme of *separateness* involves the following components:

- Establishing one's identity through separateness rather than relatedness
- Seeing one's basic sense of self as independent of relationships
- Focusing on how we are different and distinct from others
- Valuing detachment and objectivity
- Respecting courage and endurance
- Finding life's ultimate meaning through individual achievement
- Understanding and relating to others through the conscious process of *empathy*

People who are described by this theme see themselves as ultimately responsible for their own destiny ("I am the master of my fate . . . the captain of my soul," as the poet W. E. Henley so aptly put it). Their identity is tied to their separateness and even detachment from others. From their position of separateness and independence, they can identify with and understand another's situation, feelings, and motives. This capacity for empathy is a conscious choice for them and is their natural vehicle for relating to their beloved. *Steadfast Lovers* and *Mercurial Lovers* are included in this group.

The theme of *relatedness* involves the following components:

- Finding one's identity through relatedness rather than separateness

- Believing that relationships create, establish, and define our sense of self
- Feeling involved and connected to the world around us.
- Including everyone and everything in one's potential web of relationships—relatives, friends, intimates, strangers, society at large, and nature
- Finding life's ultimate meaning in the context of relationships.
- Understanding and relating to others through *sympathy*

People who are described by this theme see themselves as inseparable from their relationships with others and the world (think of John Donne's famous dictum that "No man is an island, entire of itself"). Meaning, identity, and selfhood are tied to these connections; without relationships, there is no sense of who a person is. They believe that whatever affects one person in a relationship also affects the other person. This is the basis for their use of sympathy to understand and relate to their beloved. Unlike the conscious act of empathy, sympathy occurs automatically and is not an intentional act. The Soul Images *Innocent Lover* and *Romantic Lover* are located in this group.

⎰ Soul Images and Complexes

The opposite themes we just described structure the four Soul Images. These building blocks help specify what is meaningful and important to us in a love relationship and what we expect of ourselves and our beloved. Such meanings, values, and expectations represent the *complexes* that are embedded in each Soul Image.

"Complexes" can be most simply defined as *those feelings, thoughts, images, and behaviors that are intensely and sometimes quietly important and meaningful to us.* Complexes are a natural, adaptive part of our personalities. They identify what we pay attention to in our lives and where we place our energies. Our interests, our passions, our likes and dislikes are all aspects of the complexes that make us unique, active individuals. A person with no complexes would be in a vegetative state. There would be no interests or values that would provide the energy to do anything.

Complexes in Everyday Life

There are some pretty reliable ways to know when we are experiencing one of our complexes. When we have an emotional, exaggerated, or uncompromising reaction to something, our emotion, excess, or inflexibility is a sign that something important to us has been aroused. That "something" is a complex. Here are two pithy examples:

1. Having just finished weeding the flower bed in the backyard, Will called to his wife, Courtney, to come look at the result. Courtney came to the back door and said amusedly, "Will, you don't need my approval." Will momentarily felt hurt but dismissed the feeling and continued weeding.

2. After dinner one evening Daniel said to his wife, Megan, "Let's go to a movie tonight." Megan replied, "Not tonight, I still have some work to do. But why don't you go, anyway?" Daniel said, "That's okay, I don't have to go." The following week, Megan had to attend a meeting after dinner. Daniel said, "Since you're going to a meeting, I think I'll go to a movie."

Some would regard Will's and Daniel's behavior as immature and needy. However, their Soul Images tell us a different story. Will, an Innocent Lover, and Daniel, a Romantic Lover, both value relatedness. For Will, sharing an experience is important and a sign of being loved, even if it is only the shared experience of a well-weeded garden. A shared activity and experience is also important for Daniel. For him to go to the movies when Megan was busy away from home was permissible because it didn't violate the togetherness of their love.

Courtney and Megan are not uncaring and insensitive wives. Rather, Courtney is a Steadfast Lover, and Megan is a Mercurial Lover. Their identity comes through separateness, so that shared experiences are relatively unimportant. It did not occur to Courtney that Will's request that she look at his weeding was an expression of love; in the context of her Steadfast Soul Image, Will's request was best explained as his rather childish need for approval. Similarly, Megan was unaware that "going to the movies together," is a meaningful way for Daniel to experience and share his love for her; in the context of her Mercurial Soul Image, Daniel's decision not to go to the movies the first week but to go the next week were independent of each other. She didn't understand that her availability or unavailability to go with him was the determining factor.

If complexes identify what is important and meaningful to people, then one could say that Daniel and Will have a "togetherness complex" and that Courtney and Megan have an "independence complex." It is these kinds of complexes that stir us and may cause many seemingly trivial difficulties for us. Remember, our Soul Image influences our perception of what is good and proper in a relationship. If one is either a Steadfast or a Mercurial Lover, the togetherness complex can be perceived as negative, especially when it is exaggerated. If one is either a Romantic or an Innocent Lover, however, the independence complex can be perceived negatively, especially when it is extreme.

Complexes may also be at work when we describe an acquaintance or co-worker. For example, a co-worker asks Daniel, "What's Armando like? I heard he was hard to get along with." Daniel replies, "He gets uptight about deadlines. Otherwise, though, he's pretty easygoing." Here Daniel is indicating what is meaningful and important to Armando; he's pointing out Armando's complex. Indeed, our descriptions of people often consist of a list of their complexes. We tend to describe those attributes and values that are important for that person.

Negative and Positive Complexes

As natural indicators of what is important and meaningful to us, complexes are neither good nor bad in and of themselves. Jung stated that complexes are "quite natural phenomena which develop along positive as well as negative lines" (1960, p. 101). Consequently, there can be both negative and positive complexes.

Negative Complexes When the colloquial phrase "hang-up" is used to describe a person's behavior, a negative complex is being described. This kind of complex disrupts relationships. Here's an example: Daniel is asked by a co-worker, "What's Jesse like? I've heard he's hard to get along with." Daniel replies, "He's not a bad sort, but he has a hang-up about bosses. He thinks all bosses are out to get you." Here Daniel is pointing out not only what is meaningful and important to Jesse, but also what disrupts his relationships. For another example, a *negative father complex* would entail a set of values and beliefs not only about a person's father, but about authority figures in general. These values and beliefs would interfere with relationships with people in authority and with all kinds of bureaucratic or authoritative institutions. *A negative complex is a set of meaningful values that makes the person hypersensitive and disrupts relationships.*

Positive Complexes When the colloquial phrase "turn-on" is used to describe a person's behavior, a positive complex is usually indicated. These complexes facilitate and enhance relationships. For example, Daniel continues to talk about Jesse: "There's another thing about him you ought to know. He gets turned on by deadlines. He's not at all like Armando in that way. When there's a deadline, Jesse gets on a high and is great to work with." Here Daniel is pointing out a positive complex. Jesse gets very task oriented and becomes cooperative and efficient. Similarly, a *positive father complex* permits a person to relate easily with her or his actual father as well as with people in authority and bureaucratic institutions. *Positive complexes, are a set of meaningful values that enhance and facilitate relationships.*

Conclusion

We have now explored the relationship between the Soul Images and the intimacy indicators of temperature and proximity; discussed the nature of love as an expression of psychic energy; defined and described the themes that are embedded in the complexes that characterize each of the four Soul Images (stability versus change and separateness versus relatedness); and identified some of the positive and negative complexes that are embedded in each Soul Image. Chart 8 on pages 46-49 summarizes all of these important characteristics for each of the Soul Images. In the next chapter, we will see how a clash of complexes can result in the stress, tensions, and misunderstandings that lead couples to quarrel and fight.

Chart 8
Characteristics of the Four Soul Images

Soul Image	Attribute	Theme	Kind of Intimacy		Expression of Psychic Energy	
			Temperature	Proximity	Focus	Intensity
Mercurial Lover	Transformation of Self	Focus on a future filled with the potential for change and transformation.	Hot	Distant	Broad	Mild to strong
	Separateness	View their identity and sense of self as unique and distinct from relationships.				
	Autonomy	Value independence and autonomy; resist restrictions on freedom and are sensitive to any hint of coercion from others.				
	Falling in Love	Revel in the intensity and novelty of the experience of love.				

Soul Image	Attribute	Theme	Kind of Intimacy		Expression of Psychic Energy	
			Temperature	Proximity	Focus	Intensity
Romantic Lover	Stability	Value constancy, permanence, and completeness in the relationship with the beloved.	Hot	Close	Narrow	Strong
	Relatedness	Sense of identity or selfhood comes from the relationship with the beloved, resulting in a feeling of wholeness.				
	Togetherness	Emphasis is on participating in and sharing all aspects of their lives.				
	Being in Love	Focus is on all the ways the love experience can be shared and enhanced with the beloved.				

Chart 8

Characteristics of the Four Soul Images (continued)

Soul Image	Attribute	Theme	Temperature	Kind of Intimacy / Proximity	Focus	Expression of Psychic Energy / Intensity
Innocent Lover	Change and Development	Change and growth toward a goal establish a connection to people and the world.	Warm	Close	Broad	Mild to strong
	Relatedness	A sense of selfhood comes from the loving relationship with the beloved.				
	Togetherness	Togetherness with the beloved is maintained by sharing projects, plans, and dreams for the future.				
	Being Loved	The knowledge and comfort of being loved is the nourishment that will lead to change and growth.				

| Soul Image | Attribute | Theme | Kind of Intimacy | | Expression of Psychic Energy | |
			Temperature	Proximity	Focus	Intensity
Steadfast Lover	Stability	Value is placed on constancy and continuity. Focus is on the refinement and expression of all facets of their selfhood.	Cool	Close	Broad	Mild
	Separateness	Accept their partners as separate, independent individuals and want that same kind of acceptance for themselves.				
	Autonomy	Value independence, uniqueness, and distinctness from social and cultural environments.				
	Staying in Love	Place high value on faithfulness and constancy in the love relationship.				

3 | *Stress in Relationships*

> *Just as we tend to assume that the world is as we see it, we naively sup-*
> *pose that people are as we imagine them to be. . . . In this way everyone*
> *creates for himself a series of more or less imaginary relationships. . . .*
> *Excellent examples of this are to be found in all personal quarrels. . . . It*
> *is the natural and given thing for unconscious contents to be projected.*
>
> C. G. Jung, *The Structure and Dynamics of the Psyche*

Misunderstandings, disagreements, and hurt feelings are com-
monplace in any love relationship. Often they result in tension
and stress that cause quarrels. In this chapter we will discuss three
scenarios illustrating different degrees of relationship stress:

1. The relationship at its best, when there is mutual understand-
    ing and reciprocal needs are satisfied.
2. The relationship under transient stress; how a couple con-
    tends with hurt feelings, disappointments, and disagreements.

3. The relationship at its worst, when the stress is persistent and reciprocal.

The Structure and Causes of Quarrels

Each of the following scenarios illustrates the different stages of a disagreement in which tension and stress may cause quarrels. To understand quarrels, we will look at them from two perspectives, their *structure* and their *causes*.

The Structure of Quarrels

Examining the structure of quarrels focuses our attention on the sequence and patterns that occur in most quarrels. This perspective shows how an expression of annoyance can progress from a disagreement to a severe quarrel.

Phase One: The Disagreement

- As a disagreement continues with no resolution, tension increases.
- The persistence and increase of tension cause misunderstanding.
- Sustained tension and misunderstanding cause stress.

This stage in the disagreement is crucial. If a resolution does not occur, the disagreement intensifies and a quarrel ensues. The following scenario illustrates an easy resolution to a disagreement.

Carlos and Gina have been married for four years. They have no children. Carlos is a successful real estate broker. His Soul Image is a Mercurial Lover. He has many friends and a large extended family. He was previously married and has remained friendly with his ex-wife, Natalie. Gina is a competent administrator who recently obtained a major promotion as a public relations supervisor. This is her first marriage. None of her family lives close by, although she frequently talks with them over the phone. Her Soul Image is an Innocent Lover. Often on his way to and from errands, Carlos visits Mario and Julie, his brother and sister-in-law. On his return, Gina asks him indirect questions about his errands. His replies are vague and offhand. Gina becomes persistent and asks why the errands have taken so long. Carlos stumbles and makes excuses. Finally, Gina catches him in a lie. She becomes upset, and they have the following conversation:

Gina: I wish you wouldn't lie to me. It hurts me.

Carlos: I know, hon, but you don't like my visiting Mario and Julie.

Gina: I know I don't like it. But what makes it worse is that you lie about it. It's the lying that really gets me upset.

Carlos: I know you get upset; I just want to avoid the hassle. You give me a hard time every time I want to go over there.

Gina: I know that they're important to you, and I know I get annoyed with your frequent visits, but I'll get over it, it's my little crazy. Please don't get all bent out of shape when I get a little pissed. I'll get over it. It's no big deal. Just don't lie about it. You know you're a lousy liar.

Carlos: Okay, hon. I'll try not to lie anymore.... I love you. You know I'm sorry.

Gina: I love you, too.

Here they recognized their differences, acknowledged their respective parts in them, and resolved the disagreement. It is important to note that from Gina's point of view, Carlos lies not because he is dishonest, but because he doesn't love her. It is her fear that he doesn't love her that causes her inquisitive behavior. However, when she confronts him about his lying, she doesn't accuse him of not loving her. Rather, she simply states that it hurts her. Also, she doesn't demand; she *asks* that he not lie again. Thus Carlos has no need to be defensive; he doesn't want to hurt her, so he agrees. In this scenario, their respective Soul Image attributes become visible: Gina is concerned about commitment, and Carlos is fearful of losing his autonomy.

Phase Two: The Quarrel

- Persistent misunderstanding and stress consume large amounts of energy and can be exhausting.

- Sustained fatigue and stress jeopardize the ability to integrate and respond to the issues.

- Fatigue and stress continue to consume more energy.

- Negative aspects of the participants' Soul Images are evoked.

In this scenario, the quarrel between Carlos and Gina is not easily resolved. Anger and hurt feelings emerge, and the tension increases as they become more adamant in defending their position. After Gina catches Carlos in a lie, the following dialogue ensues:

Gina (plaintively): If you really loved me, you wouldn't lie to me.

Carlos (exasperated): But I do love you. The reason I lie is because you get possessive and complain that I spend more time with my brother than with you. That's ridiculous!

Gina: I am not ridiculous! Whenever I express my feelings, you tell me that I shouldn't have them. If you feel that way, why do you even want to be with me?

Carlos: I'm sorry. I do want to be with you, but it's also important to me to visit my brother and his wife. You know I like them very much.

Gina: Well, how can we grow together with you spending time with your family and friends? Don't I count?

Carlos: Gina, I love you very much, just don't crowd me, okay? Everything will be all right between us. Trust me.

Gina: Honey, how can I trust you and believe that you love me if you lie to me?

Carlos: All right! I'll promise that I won't lie to you. But please let me visit Mario and Julie. I can like them and still love you, can't I?

Gina: Do you really love me?

Carlos: Yes! Of course! You know I do. You're the only one that really counts for me.

Gina: Then, Carlos, please don't lie. It hurts me very much.

Carlos: Okay, honey, I promise. I love you, Gina.

Gina: I love you, too.

In the above scenario, Gina accuses Carlos of not loving her. Carlos then has to justify his behavior by accusing Gina of possessiveness. Both express hurt feelings as well as informing the other of what is important to them. Their acceptance of each other prevents the quarrel from escalating, and they are able to reach a resolution. This, however, is not the case in the next phase.

Phase Three: The Fight[1]

- As the polarization continues, the complexities of the issues become one-dimensional; each sees them from an opposite point of view.
- Escalating polarization results in extreme opposition in which the partners affirm the validity and righteousness of their own side.
- Emotionality increases as anger and hurt feelings become intense.
- The high stress reduces the disagreement to *either-or* and *nothing-but* accusations.
- A severe quarrel ensues, full of accusations and counteraccusations.
- Attempting to achieve a happy resolution becomes problematic.

For this scenario, let's go back to some of the events that preceded Gina and Carlos's quarrel. Recently, Gina was experiencing external stress: She was promoted to a supervisory position at work. Because of her added responsibilities, she spent more time at work and was tired at the end of her long workday. Gina also experienced internal stress within the relationship: She frequently felt ignored by Carlos. His work in real estate entailed irregular hours. Many times he had to work evenings and weekends. Gina, on the other hand, worked a regular 9-to-5 schedule. In addition, Carlos attended a "men's group" twice a month. Gina at times felt lonely even though she had friends and many interests. She tried to suppress her feelings because she felt that Carlos' absences were part of his career. Every time he worked late, every time he was away on a weekend, and every time he visited his brother, she tried to be understanding and accepting of his activities. She even stopped talking to him about her own work-related concerns.

Carlos experienced similar external stress. He, too, was busy at work as well as having many social commitments. He viewed Gina as a "homebody" who enjoyed being with him. He felt that this was part of her charm. He suppressed his resentment when she became irritable and complained about his activities. Carlos knew that Gina didn't like him to work evenings and weekends. He endeavored not to be offended and to accept her annoyance and need to be in control.

The disagreement between Gina and Carlos is the result of the accumulation of these annoyances, slights, and unfulfilled expectations. The stage is now set for a severe quarrel. For both Carlos and Gina, tension is very high and emotions are running strong. Now when Gina finally catches Carlos in a lie, the following quarrel ensues:

Gina (plaintively): If you really loved me, you wouldn't lie to me.

Carlos (exasperated): But I do love you. I lie because you get possessive and bitch about how much time I spend with Mario and Julie, and that I'd rather be with them than with you. That's ridiculous!

Gina: I am not ridiculous! If you feel that way, why do you even want to be with me? (Sobbing; accusingly) Are you seeing another woman? Are you still seeing Natalie? [Natalie is his ex-wife.]

Carlos: Natalie and I are just friends.

Gina: Well, I'm your wife. You're married to me.

Carlos: Quit crowding me!

Gina: Well, why don't you just leave if I'm crowding you? Go to Natalie! Go to Mario! Go to your friends! You'd rather be with them anyway!

(Gina is sobbing bitterly now, and Carlos is feeling exasperated and helpless.)

Carlos: I don't want to leave you, just give me some space, okay?

Gina: How can I believe you? You lie all the time. I can never trust you!

Carlos: You're just a possessive bitch!

Gina (sobbing): If you feel that way, I might as well leave.

(She goes to the bedroom and begins packing her bags. Carlos follows her.)

Carlos: Honey, please don't be this way.

Gina (furious): You're just selfish. Nobody can tolerate you.

(Gina leaves the house. Carlos remains feeling helpless, furious, and despairing. He says to himself, "This is the story of my life." Then he adds, "That bitch, I hope she doesn't come back." However, a few hours later, Gina returns. Carlos apologizes, but she responds with silence. Both are cool and distant. There is still much tension between them.)

In contrast to the first two scenarios, this one is fraught with tension and stress. The quarrel between Carlos and Gina illustrates a pattern that emerges as stress persists or increases in intensity. When disagreements continue with no resolution, the tension also persists. This is certainly what has happened. The persistence of tension also caused considerable internal stress between them.

Now that we have looked at the structure of a quarrel, let's look at its causes.

The Causes of Quarrels

Examining the causes of a quarrel assumes that it is the result of several preceding events. Examining the content of a quarrel often reveals its cause or causes. Why are some issues important to some couples but trivial to others? Here the importance of the Soul Images comes into play.

To some readers, the quarrel between Gina and Carlos may seem trivial. Why would any wife or husband be hurt and angry if their partner visited a relative? Obviously, the injured spouse must be sick, codependent, or neurotic and in need of therapy. However, other readers may sympathize with Gina and regard her hurt and anger as an appropriate response to a partner's selfish dishonesty. Both of these judgments about the cause of the quarrel are *biased appraisals* and *valid appraisals*. The different appraisals are due to the different *complexes* that result from the Soul Images. *It is the clash between these complexes that is the unbiased cause of our quarrels.*

Our complexes determine how we evaluate the behavior of our partner. If Gina and Carlos were operating from different Soul Images, different complexes would be evoked for them, and the content of their quarrels would be quite different. For example, suppose the Soul Images were reversed: Carlos is the Innocent Lover and Gina the Mercurial Lover. In this instance, Carlos would be hurt because Gina wouldn't be home when he finished work in the evenings. She'd be out having coffee with her friends. When he'd work weekends, she might be playing golf or horseback riding with one of her female or male friends. Carlos would try to be understanding, and would suppress his annoyance at her indifference to him. He would complain occasionally about having leftovers for dinner and eating alone. Gina would try to be understanding and suppress her annoyance with his "little boy" neediness and occasional possessiveness.

In Chapter 2 we gave some examples of the apparently trivial, everyday complexes that come out in love and work relationships. The quarrel of Carlos and Gina seems different not only in its intensity, but in the character and extremeness of the statements made. Are "stronger" or "more important" complexes at play for Gina and Carlos?

Complexes, like other aspects of our psyches, can be either *conscious* or *unconscious*. What accounts for the difference between relatively "mild" complexes and those that appear more seriously disruptive of relationships is whether the complex that is activated is conscious or unconscious. The following discussion of consciousness and unconsciousness will help you understand the differences involved.

Consciousness and Unconsciousness

Since everybody believes or, at least, tries to believe in the unequivocal
superiority of rational consciousness, I have to emphasize the importance
of the unconscious irrational forces, to establish a sort of balance.

C. G. Jung, *The Symbolic Life*

Many of us understand and use the words *conscious* and *unconscious* in an everyday, colloquial way. And the way we use these terms is often quite accurate. The following definitions, however, will sharpen your understanding and accurate application of these terms.

Consciousness

Consciousness includes all the psychological contents of which we are aware and which we are able to control and direct at will. We are behaving *consciously* when we can adapt to changing circumstances and discriminate among events that occurred in the past, those occurring in the present, and those that may occur in the future. We see events in shades of gray and in differing nuances of meaning, not just in black-and-white. When we say what we want to say and are aware of directing our energies toward or away from something, our *consciousness* is operating. We can reflect on the past, act in the present, and anticipate and plan for the future while maintaining an awareness of the relationships between and among the past, the present, and the future.

Unconsciousness

Unconsciousness, on the other hand, refers to the part of our psyche that is outside of our awareness and cannot be controlled and directed by us. When we respond to changing circumstances in a rigid, unvarying, stereotypical manner, and when we do not discriminate between events from the past, those occurring in the present, and those that might happen in the future, we are behaving *unconsciously.* We are responding to ourselves, others, and life situations in an all-or-none, black-and-white manner.

Jung described the central attribute of the unconscious—that it is outside of our awareness—most completely in the following statement:

> The unconscious depicts an extremely fluid state of affairs: everything of which I know, but of which I am not at the moment thinking; everything of which I was once conscious but have now forgotten; everything perceived by my senses, but not noted by my conscious mind; everything which, involuntarily and without paying

attention to it, I feel, think, remember, want, and do; all the future things that are taking shape in me and will sometime come to consciousness: all this is the content of the unconscious. These contents are all more or less capable, so to speak, of consciousness, or were once conscious and may become conscious again the next moment. (1960, p. 185)

For Jung, the unconscious is not just the repository of forbidden, conflicted, or painful events. *The unconscious is simply being unaware.* The absence of awareness may be for a moment, a few days, weeks, and sometimes years. In the third phase of Gina and Carlos's fight, their usual mode of relating to each other was disrupted. They exhibited intense anger and a polarization of their points of view—signs that unconscious complexes had intruded into the quarrel.

) Unconscious Complexes

Unconscious complexes are ideas or images that are charged with value and importance and are denied or rejected by us. The two indicators that signal when unconscious complexes have been activated are *inflexibility* and *emotionality*.

Inflexibility

Inflexibility can be expressed in two important ways: through "always" or "never" statements and through "nothing-but" statements.

Always or Never Statements   When we make an *always* or *never* statement, an unconscious part of ourselves is doing the talking. "How can I believe you? You lie all the time. I can never trust you!" These statements by Gina indicate an intrusion of her unconscious into the disagreement. Suppose she had said instead, "You often lie," or "Frequently I question whether I can trust you." There is no hint of a categorical *always* or *never* in these statements. When we are aware of exactly what we intend to say—that is, when we are behaving consciously—our statements are *probabilistic*. This means we explicitly or implicitly use such qualifiers as *rarely, sometimes, often,* or *frequently*.

Nothing-But Statements   An example of a *nothing-but* statement is Carlos's blurting out, "You're just a possessive bitch!,", meaning, "You have no qualities other than being a possessive bitch." This is a *literalism* that restricts Gina to only one quality, thereby diminishing her. Even if the *nothing-but* statement were intended as a compliment instead of an insult, it might still be offensive. For example, some persons would take offense if their partner or spouse said to them, "You're just my sweetheart," or "You're simply great in bed." Whenever a *nothing-but* comment is directed at us, we are momentarily surprised, and if we reflect on it, we are often vaguely bothered by the statement.

Emotionality

Emotionality is a secondary sign of an activation of unconscious complexes. Mild or intense emotions may or may not accompany the inflexibility indicators. The more intimate the relationship involved, the more likely it is that emotionality will be present. For example, a person may display a negative unconscious complex about a stranger, an institution, or a class of people without displaying any emotion. The person may calmly say, "I have no respect for politicians. They're all dishonest." In a quarrel with a loved one, however, we are likely to be intensely emotional in addition to being inflexible. Both of these indicators of unconscious complexes were prominent in the fight (phase three) between Gina and Carlos.

The Paradox of Love

The clash of unconscious complexes and their intrusion into a relationship involve a paradox. Our psyches operate by the principle that for every amount of conscious energy, there is an equal and opposite amount of unconscious energy.[2] Applying this principle to our behavior means that the more accepting we are of our partner, the more we become unconsciously rejecting. This seems to be an unhappy paradox. Does this mean that the love we experience is false? Is a love relationship always doomed? Is there no such thing as true love?

Fortunately, such dismal conclusions are not warranted. Instead, we can use this paradox to understand why it is not what we *say* to our loved ones but rather what we *do not say*—the trivia that we shrug off, minimize, and reject—that creates the difficulties in our relationships.

The origin of the word *trivia* helps us understand this paradox: In ancient Rome there was a crossing of three roads that was called the *trivia*. At the intersection was a statue of a goddess. As people crossed the trivia, they would pay homage to the goddess. As the trivia became a busy intersection, however, people didn't take the time to pay homage to the goddess; they ignored her. The "trivia" in our lives, therefore, are those things that we have divested of the sacred, of their true meaning. They must be endowed again with the sacred in order for us to be aware of their meaning and importance.[3]

It is the trivia in our relationships that cause problems. It is the small slights, too *trivial* to mention, that increase our distress. Divesting these slights of their importance relegates them to the unconscious part of ourselves. We ignore their importance and meaning in our lives until they reappear as the unconscious complexes that intrude into our quarrels.

It is admittedly very hard to notice something that isn't there, but that is what paying attention to our unconscious entails. Austin speaks of unconsciousness as the "missing" aspect of our psyches in his statement that "The unconscious presents itself not so much as a completeness in itself, but as something that demands to be completed. It manifests itself by absence, yet this is a strange absence, which stains everything in the objective mode with its presence" (1990, p. 18).

The more Gina and Carlos try to be accepting and loving, the more they become unconsciously rejecting and angry. The paradox is that because of their love, they try to ignore the small hurts that they inflict on each other. As the disparity between their conscious and unconscious feelings grows, so does the tension. The stronger the tension, the more conscious energy is required for them to be accepting and loving. The greater the tension, the harder it is for them to maintain a balance within themselves and in their relationship.

As a result of this kind of dynamic, when partners are under stress they are in a profound muddle. The paradox of love is that only by endowing the trivial slights with importance and mentioning them to the beloved can the love be sustained. In the absence or failure of such an approach, we must depend on our inevitable quarrels to bring forth our complexes and remind us of those things that are important, meaningful, and sacred to us. Looked at in this way, quarreling is a necessary, adaptive, and effective way of reestablishing our connection to ourselves and our beloved.

Summary

In summary, the three stages in the dynamics of a quarrel are as follows:

Phase One: The Disagreement

- As a disagreement continues with no resolution, tension increases.

- The persistence and increase of tension cause misunderstanding.

- Sustained tension and misunderstanding cause stress.

Phase Two: The Quarrel

- Persistent misunderstanding and stress consume large amounts of energy and can be exhausting.

- Sustained fatigue and stress jeopardize the ability to integrate and respond to the issues.

- Fatigue and stress continue to consume more energy.

- Negative aspects of the participants' Soul Images are evoked.

Phase Three: The Fight

- As the polarization continues, the complexities of the issues become one-dimensional; each sees them from an opposite point of view.

- Escalating polarization results in extreme opposition in which the partners affirm the validity and righteousness of their own side.

- Emotionality increases as anger and hurt feelings become intense.

- The high stress reduces the disagreement to *either-or* and *nothing-but* accusations.

- Negative complexes are evoked.

- A severe quarrel ensues, full of accusations and counteraccusations.

- Attempting to achieve a happy resolution becomes problematic.

This sequence describes patterns and dynamics repeated in most lovers' quarrels. Even though the structure is the same, however, the themes and complexes evoked are determined by a couple's particular Soul Images. For example, the Mercurial Lover and Innocent Lover Soul Images put their unique stamp on a quarrel. In the next ten chapters, which describe each of the ten different love relationships, we will see that the different kinds of quarrels that occur are a function of the different Soul Image combinations. It will be evident why

- Couples argue about the same issues throughout their relationship
- Couples seem to argue about "trivial" concerns
- Relationships can be unstable and even volatile, and at the same time, satisfying
- Relationships may be stable, comfortable, and unhappy

Part 2 〉 *The Ten Love Relationships*

The aim of the following ten chapters in Part 2 is to provide you with an understanding of the ten love relationships as they are likely to be experienced by couples who:

- Are "normal"—meaning that they are not suffering from any psychologically dys- functional state
- Experience the kind of stress that is typical of everyday life
- May be married or unmarried
- May be either heterosexual or homosexual

These ten chapters are arranged in three groups. The first group, consisting of Chapters 4 through 7, describes couples who share the *same* Soul Image. The second group, consisting of Chapters 8 and 9, describes couples who have *opposite* Soul Images (an Innocent Lover with a Steadfast Lover, and a Mercurial Lover with a Romantic Lover). The third group, consisting of Chapters 10 through 13, describes couples who have *similar* or *related* Soul Images: Some of their important life and relationship themes (see Chapter 2) may be the same, but some are different.

We discuss couples with the same Soul Image first because these combinations most clearly define the characteristics of the four Soul Images. We discuss couples with opposite Soul Images second to highlight the contrasts between opposing Soul Images and themes. And we discuss couples with similar or related Soul Images last because the combination of similarities and differences involved in these relationships makes them appear somewhat more complicated.

Each chapter begins with a quotation intended to capture the point of view characteristic of couples in that kind of relationship. The discussion that follows identifies the distinctive feature(s) of the relationship, the particular complexes that each partner brings to the relationship, and the ways in which these complexes influence the everyday lives of the partners in that love relationship. The effects of stress on the relationship are then depicted in a scenario of a disagreement and subsequent quarrel. The development of the disagreement and quarrel is based on the detailed explanation of disagreements, quarrels, and fights included in Chapter 3. The specific complexes and indications of unconscious complexes are noted where they occur in the account of the couple's interaction. Finally, a summary titled "The

Nature of This Love Relationship" highlights the everyday areas that typically elicit specific complexes.

The order in which aspects of daily life are presented within the chapters varies considerably, as does the amount of space devoted to different aspects of the couple's lives. Such variability is a reflection of the distinctiveness of the relationships. For example, embedded in each chapter is the same brief description of a precipitating life situation. This is followed by a discussion of the manner in which each of the ten different couples responds to it. However, the placement of the precipitating situation within the text and what it illustrates about the couple's relationship vary from chapter to chapter.

One caveat: In reading the descriptions of the ten true love relationships, keep in mind that human beings and the way they relate can be subject to many different interacting factors. Therefore, it is unlikely that the descriptions we give will apply in every respect or at all times to couples characterized by the ten relationships.

4 ⟩ *Two Mercurial Lovers*

Marriage is that relation between man and woman in
which the independence is equal, the dependence mutual,
and the obligation reciprocal.

Louis K. Anspacher, Address, Boston

The distinctive feature of the relationship of two Mercurial Lovers is its high energy. This energy is the result of the partners' belief in the intrinsic worth of change, autonomy, and independence. There are certain risks associated with the energy of their relationship, however. The high energy may increase their distance, make them less involved, and lead them to live separate lives. In order to lessen the risk of becoming permanently separate or estranged, the couple engage in many disagreements, arguments, and discussions. These frequent intense interactions are important and serve a constructive end: they enable the couple to regenerate their relationship in order to gain access to the transformative aspect of change and autonomy in their lives.

Jung stated that "The greater the tension between the pairs of opposites, the greater will be the energy that comes from them" (1953, p. 290). It is through the Mercurial Lovers' disagreements that tension is converted to useful energy. This is why their discussions and disagreements are important for sustaining their relationship and their love for each other. The Mercurial expression of love can fluctuate from mild to strong and is broad in focus. The nature of intimacy for Mercurial Lovers is distant and hot. As a result, the lovemaking of two Mercurial Lovers can sometimes be very strong, intense, and passionate and at other times less passionate and even perfunctory. This fluctuating character in their expressions of love and intimacy is another unique aspect of the relationship for two Mercurial Lovers. Viewed from the outside, it may lead others to regard their relationship as unstable and even chaotic. For the couple themselves, however, it is a natural and congruent expression of true love.

Couples who share the same Soul Image have similar perspectives about many things, including their biases and sources of irritation. For two Mercurial Lovers, the complexes we expect to see in their day-to-day relationships are as follows: the intrinsic value of change that contributes to the transformation of self, a focus on separateness and autonomy as the vehicles for forming a personal identity, discussing as the natural way of resolving conflict, and perpetuating the state of falling in love as the central aspect of the love relationship.

The characteristics of Mercurial Lovers are summarized in Chart 9. The next section describes how the complexes listed in the chart are expressed in the everyday lives of Mercurial Lover couples. To highlight the complexes being discussed, they are identified in the margin beside the relevant descriptions.

Chart 9
Characteristics of Mercurial Lovers

Central Relationship Question

"If I am a separate, changing individual, how can I merge with a beloved in an intimate, loving relationship? Change and the flux of life sustain me with vigor, further my transformation, and engage me with life's possibilities. Yet this isn't enough. I also need the exhilaration of love through merging with my beloved. As much as I desire the passion of love, however, I also fear my beloved's love. My fear is that my beloved may innocently entice me to a life of predictability, comfort, and routine that will end in a suffocating and deadly inertia. If this happens, I will indeed lose my soul and I will become like an automaton in a Kafka novel."

Attributes, Themes, and Complexes

Change	Feel that any change is good in itself. Change has intrinsic value.
Transformation of Self	Focus on a future filled with the potential for change and transformation.
Separateness	View their identity and sense of self as unique and distinct from relationships.
Autonomy	Value independence and autonomy; resist restrictions on freedom and are sensitive to any hint of coercion from others.
Discussing	Value explorative communication and discussing the relationship and what it means.
Falling in Love	Revel in the intensity and novelty of the experience of love.

Kind of Intimacy

Temperature	Hot—passionate sexual activity; kissing and caressing in public.
Proximity	Distant—unawareness of the unspoken distress or joy of the partner.

Expression of Psychic Energy

Focus	Broad—many expressions of love.
Intensity	Mild to strong expressions of love.

The Mercurial Lover—Mercurial Lover Relationship

Every couple must deal with issues around household responsibilities. For a Mercurial Lover couple, the requirements of running a household may seem to be burdensome but inevitable restrictions of their freedom of choice and action. As a result, there is considerable tension and concern about the equal assignment of tasks so that each partner will do his or her fair share. The part-ners prefer to be individually responsible for things rather than working on them together. For example, one may take on cooking and the other cleaning up; one may be responsible for outside chores and the other for helping the children with homework. Because household routine takes time and energy away from more satisfying pursuits, there may be dissatisfaction, complaints, and criticisms of each other's effort and performance. Maintaining a balance between individual freedom and shared responsibilities can be a continual source of disagreement for them. Frequent discussions that lead to trying out different approaches are therefore common. On occasion, a couple may choose to work together on routine chores as an efficient way to free up time to do other things. They may also help each other out when asked, and assume that the other person will reciprocate at another time.

This general approach to household tasks seems to characterize Mercurial Lover couples regardless of how old they are, how long they have been together, or their style of relationship. Mercurial Lover couples in more traditional marriages may abide by gender expectations in task assignments, but the issues of equity and restriction of spontaneity and freedom are likely to surface in one way or another. For example, a Mercurial Lover wife in a more traditional marriage may harbor resentment and envy toward her husband's greater freedom to pursue his career and outside interests. However, this issue would not be as important to "traditional" wives with the other three Soul Images.

Mercurial Lovers devote a great deal of energy to activities that are outside the love relationship. They see work and friendships as an important source of joy and fulfillment. Work is a particularly important way to experience their own individuality and to encourage that of the beloved as well. They are interested in and support each other's concerns, successes, satisfactions, and work aspirations. If one partner feels

Complexes
Autonomy
Transformation of Self

dissatisfied and unfulfilled in his or her work, the other is likely to favor the dissatisfied partner changing jobs. Even if the change results in a diminished income or altered lifestyle, both will willingly bear such hardships to achieve their own and each other's goals. They are likely to agree that personal and work fulfillment are well worth the effort and any accompanying hardships. Mercurial Lover couples may even agree to live apart for extended periods of time if this is necessary or beneficial to one or the other's career. Of all the love relationships, a Mercurial Lover–Mercurial Lover couple's relationship is most likely to tolerate and even thrive within such a living arrangement.

Mercurial Lover couples also tend to agree that increased self-knowledge will enhance their own satisfaction as well as their enjoyment of each other. They may be attracted to books, lectures, and workshops with a focus on growth and development. Sometimes their interest can be an important opportunity for a shared experience; at other times, one partner may be encouraged by the other to take time for individual self-exploration. For example, a forty-five-year-old Mercurial Lover wife became increasingly dissatisfied and unmotivated in her work, with the couple's lifestyle, and with her own prospects for the future. She wondered if she was experiencing a midlife crisis. Her Mercurial Lover husband encouraged her to take the time to explore her unsettling feelings. When a weeklong retreat about midlife transitions was advertised, he signed her up for it and paid for it. She was delighted and appreciative.

It is consistent with their complexes for a Mercurial Lover couple to keep their finances separate, with each contributing as equally as possible to their mutual support. Such an approach satisfies their values around equality, independence, freedom, and personal accomplishment. Separate checking accounts allow each to keep track of his or her individual money and the amount each provides for joint responsibilities. In couples in which one partner is the primary financial contributor, a similar approach to equity and independence is followed to the degree possible.[1]

Complexes are also evident in the tendency of Mercurial Lover couples to have a broad spectrum of friendships. Usually, each maintains friendships both outside the relationship and also as a couple with other couples. In general, the partners are accepting of each other's opposite-sex friendships and usually do not see them as a cause for distrust or jealousy. Such friendships are viewed as separate from the couple's love relationship. One partner's friends may or may not eventually become friends of both Mercurial Lover partners. In either case, including each other's friends in social invitations and family events is considered natural and enhancing for the couple.

Complexes
Separateness
Autonomy

Mercurial Lovers are also likely to have friends with a wide variety of lifestyles, beliefs, and attitudes, as they are interested in and respectful of others' individuality and autonomy. Though uncompromising and outspoken about their own values, they rarely make disparaging remarks about other people's ways of living their lives. For example, the son of one Mercurial Lover couple told his parents that his sixteen-year-old girlfriend was going to be traveling around Europe by herself during the summer. According to their son, the girl's parents allowed her to do anything she wanted with little or no guidance. The Mercurial Lover couple told their son that they would be uncomfortable allowing him the latitude given to his girlfriend, although they respected the judgment of her parents.

People with different Soul Images may wonder about a Mercurial Lover couple's acceptance of each other's outside friendships, especially opposite-sex relationships. Others may judge one partner or the other as naive, if not blind to the dangers involved in such relationships. They may also worry about the couple's commitment to each other. This is especially true when the observer is an Innocent or Romantic Lover, for whom identity occurs within the love relationship. For people with these Soul Images, such outside friendships can seem threatening. This is illustrated in an incident that occurred when a Mercurial Lover couple, Laura and Keith, were invited to a dinner party at the home of friends. Both looked forward to going, as some of their good friends would be there along with some people they didn't know. However, on the morning of the day of the dinner, Laura felt ill.

"I'm really disappointed to miss it," she said. "Maybe if I rest all day I'll be well enough to go. What bad timing!"

"It sure is. I was really looking forward to the drive up there together. It'll be boring without you along. Try to get better so you can go."

However, Laura's symptoms worsened during the day, and she told Keith that she felt too sick to go to the party. "You'll just have to tell me all about it, and especially if any of the new people are interesting," she said.

"Okay," said Keith, "but I really wish you could go, too."

Keith went to the party alone. One of the guests was a single woman who worked in the same field as Keith. They spent most of the evening in animated conversation. On their way home from the party, one of the other couples talked about their discomfort with Keith's behavior.

"First of all," said the husband (an Innocent Lover), "he should have stayed home with Laura."

"And on top of that," said his wife (a Romantic Lover), "he shouldn't have talked to that woman all night. I really feel sorry for Laura. I worry that their relationship is in trouble."

When Keith arrived home after the party, he told Laura all about it and about the new friend he had made.

"I was sure it would be okay with you because I know you'll have a lot in common with her, too," he said. "So I invited her to the barbecue we're having next weekend. That way you won't have missed so much from the party."

"That's terrific. I'm anxious to meet her," said Laura. "Now I'm going to get some sleep."

Mercurial Lovers are also likely to be quite tolerant and supportive of each other's outside interests and recreational preferences, even when they don't share them. They neither expect nor want to have all their interests in common. Separate vacations are therefore acceptable, even encouraged. The value placed on their mutual autonomy and independence permits and encourages this, especially if one person senses that the other needs time away for replenishment. (Innocent and Romantic Lovers, whose sense of self comes from relatedness, would likely view separate vacations as a negation of their love. And separate vacations may be acceptable for Steadfast Lovers, but only under certain circumstances.)

In spite of their emphasis on separateness, Mercurial Lover–Mercurial Lover couples enjoy being together for recreation and vacations. However, for couples who have few recreational interests in common, finding mutually interesting activities can be a problem. There may be a shared concern about their difficulty in finding ways to spend satisfying "quality time" together. This may stimulate vague doubts about the substance and commitment in their relationship, which can become a serious issue if no satisfactory resolution is found.

For example, one couple in their fifties found that they could not agree about what to do for a long-awaited two-week vacation together. In the past, their recreation time together had been either family-oriented or a brief extension of a work-

Complex
Separateness

related trip for one or the other. They worried that perhaps they had "become strangers to each other." They had read in magazine articles that this could happen to busy, two-career couples when their children had grown. After several intense discussions with each other and several trusted friends, however, they realized that what they really enjoyed doing together hadn't changed—they liked to talk to each other! They decided to take their vacation time at a retreat center that had speakers and discussion groups on topics of mutual interest to them.

Independence from and acceptance by their parents is a frequent issue for Mercurial Lovers. Contacts with family are often stressful for both of them. They can be quite critical of their own and each other's families. Phone calls and family visits may be anticipated with some reluctance. The

Complexes
Autonomy
Transformation of Self

source of the distress usually centers around both Mercurial Lovers' complexes of autonomy and transformation of self, which include a strong desire for self-determination. This makes them sensitive to perceived criticism from both sets of parents. They may accuse their own and each other's parents of not appreciating and respecting their lifestyle, values, and individual accomplishments. They are therefore quick to take offense when parents offer unsolicited advice or appear intrusive and judgmental. If the "offending" parents have Soul Images other than that of a Mercurial Lover, they are likely to be hurt and puzzled at their adult child's negative reactions. Parents who are themselves

Mercurial Lovers may be more understanding of this aspect of their adult children and therefore try to avoid any hint of interference.

Depending on their particular family constellations, two Mercurial Lovers may have close relationships with their own and each other's siblings. A favorite topic of conversation with siblings is how hard it is to get their parents to respect the adult status of their children. If a sibling has a different Soul Image, he or she may not be as concerned about this. An Innocent Lover sibling may welcome parental advice, while a Steadfast Lover sibling is likely to be comfortable giving advice to parents as well as receiving it.[2]

With the birth of children, Mercurial Lovers anticipate a restriction of their freedom and autonomy. There is minimal disruption when they succeed in *adding* the child to their lives rather than eliminating important activities because of the child. This enables Mercurial Lovers to retain valued activities and prevents them from feeling burdened, resentful, and constrained. Mercurial Lovers favor an egalitarian, flexible attitude toward their children, permitting and encouraging a wide latitude for exploration and autonomy. They encourage their children to make their own life choices and may criticize their child's school if it is seen as rigidly limiting their child's development.

Complexes
Autonomy
Change (Intrinsic)

When Mercurial Lovers have a child whose natural Soul Image or personality is quite different from theirs, they may wonder about the effectiveness of their childrearing. For example, a couple may worry when their son (who may favor an Innocent Soul Image) lets other children choose games and activities and wants his parents' approval all the time. They may be similarly concerned and puzzled if their (possibly Steadfast) daughter seems "too conscientious and helpful to other people instead of pursuing her own passions."

Open communication is very important to Mercurial Lovers. The partners share an expectation that their personal growth, self-knowledge, individuality, and independence will be enhanced by their relationship. They believe these goals can be achieved through explorative communication and dedicate a lot of energy to discussing their relationship and what it means to them. They treat each other as valued friends and partners. Talking candidly about their hopes, fears, doubts, and dissatisfactions seems not only natural but also necessary for the well-being of the relationship. They warmheartedly engage in frequent and intense examinations of the nature of their relationship as well as the individual progress of each toward autonomy and self-hood. Inasmuch as they share the same sensitivity to limitations and restrictions, each is quick to point out the other's "excessive or unjustified" demands and intrusions. Of all of the relationships, that of two Mercurial Lovers probably comes closest to following the tongue-in-cheek advice of comedienne Phyllis Diller, who reportedly said, "Never go to bed angry. Stay up and fight."

Complexes
Change (Intrinsic)
Transformation of Self
Separateness
Falling in Love

Mercurial Lovers welcome their partner's honest confrontation, even when they are hurt or offended by it. They interpret such involvement as an indication of interest and understanding. They do not find being asked to change something about themselves objectionable. Rather than taking such a request as criticism or rejection (as might occur for someone with a different Soul Image), a Mercurial Lover will likely accept it as caring concern. Without understanding the underlying values that motivate Mercurial Lovers, others may entirely misjudge and overlook the genuine closeness, intimacy, and love in this aspect of their relationship.

Similarly, the seeming instability of such relationships reflects the couples' attempt to balance the need for individual autonomy with the desire for closeness and intimacy. What seems to others to be instability may reflect the appropriate form of stability we might expect between two Mercurial Lovers. Sameness, routine, regularity, and predictability would lead to discomfort and dissatisfaction—and therefore function as the equivalent of "instability" for Mercurial Lover—Mercurial Lover relationships. This kind of Mercurial Lover "instability" is probably the reason for the frequent appearance of magazine articles with such titles as "How to Rekindle the Spark in Your Marriage."

More than other same—Soul Image couples, Mercurial Lover couples don't feel a need to communicate with each other when they are away on a trip unless there is some specific reason to do so. Just having contact with each other isn't that important. They may be content to wait until they get home to tell the partner anything interesting that happened. When both partners are Mercurial Lovers, this is accepted as natural and desirable, for it validates each person's freedom from burdensome obligations. A partner whose Soul Image is different, however, may react negatively to this approach to communicating.

The change and evolution of their sexual relationship are important to Mercurial Lovers both for their individual and for their mutual development. They consider pleasure from sex as

Complexes
Falling in Love
Separateness

their separate responsibility. They freely discuss their sexual relationship with each other and are very tolerant and patient when one or the other has a period of lack of interest and/or enjoyment of sex. However, persistent sexual problems would be seen as a sign of failure to evolve together toward greater intimacy and would therefore have a major impact on their overall satisfaction with the relationship. Indeed, persistent absence of sexual passion would be intolerable and would provide a strong motivation to end the relationship.[3]

When two Mercurial Lovers divorce, they may easily maintain a friendly relationship; they may get together, talk on the phone, and continue to be interested in and inform each other about various aspects of their lives. If one or both remarry, friendships can be formed between former and new spouses. For example, a teenager was invited by her best friend to go to the opera with her family. The "family" in this case consisted of the friend's mother and stepfather, as well as her father and stepmother. People with other Soul Images might find this level of friendship between ex-spouses quite puzzling and perhaps "too modern."

The Clash of Complexes

The life of two Mercurial Lovers can be exciting, open, and full of energy. Their shared values and complexes are in accord with many contemporary expectations of a "good relationship." With their emphasis on open communication and confrontation, we might expect few quarrels. In fact, quarrels and fights are likely to be minimal in relationships where partners have the same Soul Images, as long as the external stresses are minimal. In actively pursuing change, autonomy, and independence, however, Mercurial Lovers are likely to encounter many stressors. Consequently, their clash of complexes will most likely be initiated by external stress.

Monique and Aaron have been married for almost seven years. They met at a party in San Francisco while Aaron was a graduate student in biology at Stanford and Monique was a struggling ceramics artist in San Francisco who also had a degree in art history and worked part-time at an art gallery. They were immediately attracted to each other and maintained a dating relationship until Aaron received his doctorate two years later. Aaron didn't want to teach, so he accepted a job at a privately endowed research institute in Santa Fe, New Mexico. It was then that they decided to marry. Monique was excited by the prospect of living in the

Southwest amidst Native American art and culture. Aaron was excited about the area because of the easy availability of hiking and skiing. Soon after their arrival, Monique got a job at a gallery. She gave up her ceramics work because of the newness and excitement of southwestern art.

They were both happy and very active. Aaron was engaged with his research and especially enjoyed the rugged southwestern landscape. Several years later, Monique became a buyer for a major graphic arts gallery. As a buyer, she travels a lot and seeks out established and new artists who have potential. Aaron admires Monique for her aesthetic eye and keen talent for recognizing new artists. At times he envies her work because it allows her to be immersed in the world of art and artists. He frequently complains of the comparative dullness of his work as an applied research biologist. For her part, Monique admires and envies Aaron for his academic credentials.

Phase One: The Disagreement

- As a disagreement continues with no resolution, tension increases.
- The persistence and increase of tension cause misunderstanding.
- Sustained tension and misunderstanding cause stress.

One evening when Aaron came home from work, Monique initiated the following conversation:

Monique: Honey, I'm so excited. I'm going to the international art show in Montreal. I'll have a chance to meet some great artists. I'm getting quite a reputation.

Aaron: Gee, that's nice.

Monique: Nice? It's fantastic!

Aaron: I think I'll take a few days off and go along with you.

Monique: Actually, I don't think that would be a good idea.

Aaron: What do you mean by that?

Monique: Well, you'd cramp my style. I'll be very busy and meeting new people, and I don't want to have to worry about you.

Aaron: Since when have I been a worry to you? We usually have a great time.

Monique: Well, frankly, you've been a little down in the dumps lately, and you're not always so easy to be with.

Aaron: Oh, really? I didn't think you noticed.

Monique: Please don't get sarcastic. You've been mumbling about how boring your project at work is. Maybe you should see a therapist.

Aaron (sarcastically): Maybe I should see my wife once in a while.

Monique: What the hell does that mean? I'm busting my buns trying to bring in my share of the money!

Aaron: Do you have to brag all the time? I still make more money than you, and I do more of the work around the house, too.

Monique: Honey, there's something going on here. I really mean it. You should see a therapist. You've never been this sarcastic. What's wrong? Is it really getting bad at work?

Aaron: I'm bored stiff. There's nothing to do that's creative. I feel like a technician just cranking the wheels. I look at the rats in the lab and think that at least there's something new every time they go through that maze. I feel like I'm on a treadmill going nowhere.

Monique: Look, honey, don't feel so bad. Why don't you take a few days off, and we'll talk about you maybe quitting and finding a new job. It'll be a nice getaway in Montreal. The change will be good for you.

Aaron: Actually, I've been considering some options.

Monique: Let's talk about them after dinner—then go to bed early and have a party.

Aaron: Okay, hon.

(They kiss and that night they have a great "party"—their code word for sex.)

It is apparent from this exchange between Monique and Aaron that many complexes were activated. There is one indicator of an unconscious complex—Aaron's implicit accusation that Monique is *always* bragging. It was at this point that their disagreement could have become a quarrel. However, Monique's excitement and lack of stress enabled her to respond empathetically to Aaron, and a comfortable resolution occurred, resulting in reduced tension between them. This is not the case in the next scenario, in which the tension increases.

Phase Two: The Quarrel

- Persistent misunderstanding and stress consume large amounts of energy and can be exhausting.

- Sustained fatigue and stress jeopardize the ability to integrate and respond to the issues.

- Fatigue and stress continue to consume more energy.

- Negative aspects of the participants' Soul Images are evoked.

Monique has an added external stress that she didn't mention to Aaron: The gallery where she works is considering her for a promotion. She would be in charge of setting up a new gallery in another state. She is both excited and apprehensive about the prospect. She has questions about the impact this change would have on her marriage and her career. She enjoys the challenge and variety of her present job and wonders whether managing a gallery would become routine after a while. The pending decision has caused her considerable stress. The following exchange between Monique and Aaron follows from the comment of Aaron's that contained an activated unconscious complex:

Aaron: Do you have to brag all the time? I still make more money than you, and I do more of the work around the house, too.

Monique: Not for long, you won't!

Aaron: What's that supposed to mean? Do you think I'm so incompetent that I'll lose my job?

Monique (sarcastically): Well, that could happen. But that wasn't what I meant. I was thinking—

Aaron (interrupting): What do you mean, "that could happen"? Is that what you really think of me?

Monique: Wait a minute. You think I brag all the time and don't do my share. But I work hard and I certainly do my share in spite of what you think. All you do is complain about me and whine. Sometimes I think that you'd like it if I wasn't around at all!

Aaron: You aren't around much anyway. Most of the time you're traveling. And when you do get back, you're grouchy.

Monique: Look who's calling the kettle black! You're not always a pleasure to be around! As soon as I walk in the house, you start whining.

Aaron: Look! I don't whine! I just try to tell you how I feel. Isn't that what men are supposed to do?

Monique: They're supposed to be interested in and care for their wives and not act like little boys.

Aaron: I don't have to take this crap! I'm leaving!!

(Aaron leaves the house, slamming the front door behind him. Monique goes into the living room and turns on the TV just for some distraction. She begins to weep and thinks to herself, "Why do we always end up fighting about these things?" Aaron goes for a walk in the neighborhood. He's angry and upset.[4] He says to himself, "Why do we always end up in a fight?" After half an hour, he returns home.)

Aaron: Monique, I've been thinking. Something's wrong here. I don't know what's going on. Why are we fighting? You're upset and I'm upset. We're supposed to listen to each other. Honey, what's wrong?

Monique: It's something I haven't told you—

Aaron (interrupting): Are you having an affair?

Monique (laughing): Don't be silly. I don't have time for an affair.

Aaron: Then what's wrong?

Monique: I have a chance to open a new gallery in Phoenix.

Aaron: That's great! Isn't it?

Monique: It's not only setting it up. They want me to run it. It would mean I'd have to live there.

Aaron: I see. That's why you've been so irritable! What are you going to do?

Monique: What do you want me to do?

Aaron: That's a loaded question! The important question is, What's the best thing for you? I really mean it.

Monique: I really want the job. I'd make almost twice as much as I'm making now.

Aaron: That's a lot of money. But could we manage being apart that much?

Monique: It's only a one-hour flight. I'd come home on the weekends, and you could come out whenever you're free. We could afford that and a housekeeper, too.

Aaron: It has some possibilities. I have an idea. Let's go to Roberto's. We'll talk about it over a glass of wine and dinner.

Aaron and Monique were then able to have a productive conversation. During their earlier interaction, however, their unconscious complexes were evident. Aaron accused Monique of *always* bragging, and Monique accused Aaron of *always* complaining and of being *nothing but* a whiner. Aaron's rejoinder to Monique's *nothing-but* accusation was that she was *nothing but* a grouch. Finally, Monique's unconscious complex emerged in accusing Aaron of being *nothing but* a little boy. The identified complexes activated in their quarrel are characteristic of Mercurial Lover Soul Images. Recall Aaron's change complex and the boredom he was experiencing at work. We also saw Monique's autonomy and change complexes emerge.

Quarrels have the same structure and cause no matter what Soul Images the couple may have: They are caused by a clash of complexes. Aaron and Monique valued the independence and equality in their relationship, and their mutual complexes created conflicts for them. In this case, stress can be caused by any situation that puts their commitment to the relationship and their need for independence in opposition. Aaron's dissatisfactions with his job and Monique's opportunity to enhance the meaningfulness of her work were in direct opposition to their commitment to each other. Their clash of complexes created their quarrel.

The Nature of This Love Relationship

It is quite apparent that the life of two Mercurial Lovers is one of high energy and change. The value they place on autonomy, independence, change, and transformation necessitates frequent discussions. They talk a great deal about their needs for independence, equality, and change. Such discussions are likely to be prolonged and intense when one or more of their complexes are in jeopardy. Focusing on where they are in the relationship and whether there is equality in the relationship permits Mercurial Lover–Mercurial Lover couples to reaffirm their love for each other. Experiencing the joys of falling in love is central to their love relationship. They eagerly pursue situations and activities that help maintain the vitality and excitement of their love.

Complexes were evident in the quarrel of the Mercurial Lovers Monique and Aaron. Both the desire for change and the absence of change were central issues in the couple's interaction. Also critical to the couple's discussion was their respect for their own and each other's desires for separation, autonomy, independence, and falling in love. Moreover, unconscious complexes were evident in several *always* or *never* and *nothing-but* statements they made.

Individual histories and circumstances may vary widely among Mercurial Lover–Mercurial Lover couples, but these same complexes can be seen in their daily lives and in their quarrels. We hope you now have a better and deeper understanding of, appreciation for, and ability to appraise this kind of true love.

5 | *Two Romantic Lovers*

*At what moment do lovers come into the most complete possession
of themselves, if not when they are lost in each other?*

Pierre Teilhard de Chardin, *The Spirit of Loving*

Two Romantic Lovers are true soul mates. They are likely to be ardent, affectionate, attentive, and contented with each other. They express their love spontaneously and tend to enclose their lives in their love relationship. As a result, they strive to maintain and enhance their experience of being in love to the relative exclusion of other things. For Romantic Lovers, every activity is rich with meaning when they experience it together. They share a confidence and optimism about their lives that is subject to their continuing experience of being in love. As idealists, they expect that love will "conquer all." Their love relationship itself enables Romantic Lovers to comfortably deal with life's uncertainties as individuals and as a couple. Being in love strengthens them and their relationship. This is reflected in their *strong* and *narrow* expression of love and in the *hot* and *close* nature of their intimacy. Along with the general characteristics of the Romantic Lover Soul Image, these combine to form the complexes we typically see expressed in the everyday lives of two Romantic Lovers.

Couples who share the same Soul Image have similar perspectives about many things, including their biases and sources of irritation. For two Romantic Lovers, the complexes we expect to see in their day-to-day relationships are as follows: an emphasis on stability and enhancement of relationship in their lives, a focus on relatedness and togetherness as the vehicles for forming a personal identity, accommodating as the natural way of resolving conflict, and perpetuating the state of being in love as the central aspect of the love relationship.

The characteristics of Romantic Lovers are summarized in Chart 10. The next section describes how the complexes listed in the chart are expressed in the everyday lives of Romantic Lover couples. To highlight the complexes being discussed, they are identified in the margin beside the relevant descriptions.

The Romantic Lover–Romantic Lover Relationship

Romantic Lovers share the complex of forming a sense of self through relatedness. They are therefore at risk of being considered overly dependent on each other. Their particular expression

Complexes
Relatedness
Togetherness
Stability

of this theme also makes them appear to others as unrealistic and "hopelessly romantic" in their expectations of the relationship. Their relationship is central to forming and enhancing their sense of self. It is through the differentiation of their relationship that their mutual sense of self emerges. By experiencing the many

Chart 10

Characteristics of Romantic Lovers

Central Relationship Question

"If my sense of self and identity is constituted by my relationship with my beloved, can I have a sense of self and fulfillment when I am alone? I can only be a complete human being if I am in a loving relationship with my beloved. For only through our love can we each lose our separateness from the world and become one with the world. Only then can 'I' become a 'We,' and then another new and true 'Me.' What happens then if I am separated from my beloved? Do I still exist? Will I no longer feel joy and pleasure? Will I be devoid of any sense of who I am? That prospect truly frightens me. If it occurs, I will be truly afflicted with a lovesickness."

Attributes, Themes, and Complexes

Stability	Value constancy, permanence, and completeness in the relationship with the beloved.
Enhancement of Relationship	Focus on differentiation of the relationship with the beloved.
Relatedness	Sense of identity or selfhood comes from the relationship with the beloved, resulting in a feeling of wholeness.
Togetherness	Emphasis is on participating in and sharing all aspects of their lives as expressions of togetherness.
Accommodating	Accommodation is the natural way of resolving conflicts and preserving the state of Being in Love.
Being in Love	Focus is on all the ways the love experience can be shared and enhanced with the beloved.

Kind of Intimacy

Temperature	Hot—passionate sexual activity; kissing and caressing in public.
Proximity	Close—deeply affected by the other's unspoken distress.

Expression of Psychic Energy

Focus	Narrow—focused expressions of love.
Intensity	Strong expressions of love.

facets of their relationship, they also express the facets of their selfhood.

The influence of finding one's sense of self through relatedness is especially evident in the way a Romantic Lover couple approaches communication. Romantic Lovers are extremely sensitive to nuances of speech and body language. In the context of selfhood through relatedness, they know themselves and each other through their refined sympathetic interconnectedness. A touch, a glance, a word spoken at just the right or wrong moment, or an object belonging to the beloved—all can be filled with significance. This Romantic Lover style of communication is reflected in every medium we associate with romantic love—love songs, love poems, and love scenes in novels, dramas, and films.

It is their way of communicating that causes Romantic Lovers to be judged, if not ridiculed, as "hopeless romantics," "lovesick," "lovelorn," or "blinded by love." As a culture, we find romantic love to be an appealing fantasy, a charming expression of youthful naiveté, and something the "victims" will, we hope, "get over." In fact, however, this communication style of Romantic Lovers is not restricted to youth, nor is it merely a sign of an overly sentimental nature. Such a level of sensitivity to each other appropriately reflects a shared focus on the relationship as the source of one's awareness and knowledge of oneself.

Complexes
Being in Love
Relatedness
Togetherness

Romantic Lovers want to tell each other about important occurrences in their daily lives. They like to stay in touch when they are apart just to enjoy the intimacy of their relationship. Daily phone calls may be the norm when one of them is out of town. If something special, exciting, or unusual happens while they are apart, each usually thinks first to share the news with their beloved. If the partner can't be reached for some reason, extreme disappointment and a sense of loss may ensue.

Of all the relationships, two Romantic Lovers are the most likely to have an agreement that they will never go to bed

Complex
Accommodating

angry. Their concurrence on the complex of accommodating to resolve disagreements is the vehicle for setting aside their conflicts and focusing on areas that promote and restore harmony.

An incident that happened to Lindsay and Eric illustrates the importance of togetherness for a Romantic Lover couple. They were invited to a dinner party at the home of friends. Both of them were looking forward to going. However, on the morning of the day of the party, Lindsay felt ill. Her symptoms worsened during the day, and she told Eric that she felt too sick to go to the party.

Eric said, "I know you must be feeling really awful. I wish there were something I could do to make you feel better. Do you feel like watching a good movie?"

Lindsay replied, "Maybe that would help some."

Eric went out and rented their favorite romantic fantasy, *Somewhere in Time.* They both resonated with the film's theme of overcoming the obstacle of time and place to fulfill the inevitability of their love for each other. Since Lindsay didn't feel much like eating, Eric just had a sandwich for dinner. They both got into bed, enjoyed the movie together, and then went to sleep. Lindsay felt much better the next morning. She told Eric, "I was really disappointed that we missed the dinner party, but the comfort and closeness of our evening together made up for it."

Agreement on the importance of togetherness affects all aspects of a Romantic Lover–Romantic Lover relationship but is especially evident in their approach to household responsibilities. Routine chores and household projects can become special and meaning-

Complexes
Relatedness
Togetherness
Stability

ful ways for the couple to experience and enrich their love. The simplest activity can take on heightened significance and pleasure—cleaning the house, bringing the car to be serviced in preparation for a trip, even creating a budget. When done either together or as an individual effort to please the beloved, such seemingly mundane acts serve as expressions of love and devotion. They give the relationship stability, permanence, durability, and comfort. And when household tasks interfere with a Romantic Lover couple's ability to enjoy each other, the partners are likely to hire other people to do them.

The everyday requirements of sharing a household also serve to enhance the relationship. The greater the breadth, variety, and number of shared experiences, the greater the opportunity for knowing and defining themselves within the intermingled whole that constitutes their true love relationship. Thus, the more Romantic Lovers do with and for each other, the more each of them experiences wholeness. This is in sharp contrast to their opposites, the Mercurial Lovers, for whom wholeness comes from their own individuality and autonomy. Sharing the accomplishment of otherwise meaningless goals would therefore not appeal to Mercurial Lovers. One Romantic Lover couple agreed that tending their flower garden together on weekends was the best way for them to reconnect with the intensity of their love for each other, especially when their busy work lives forced them to be apart for much of the workweek.

Complexes
Enhancement of Relationship
Stability

Relating to parents and other family members is likely to be unimportant to Romantic Lovers compared to other aspects of their lives. Since their focus as a couple is primarily on each other, family obligations like holiday and vacation visits may be treated as necessary but undesirable duties. Relating to their families as a couple may not be a central concern, though each may have close rela-

Complexes
Togetherness
Relatedness
Being in Love

tionships with his or her own family or even with members of each other's families. Contacts with extended family are likely to be more welcomed when the Romantic Lover couple has children. Even then, however, they may take advantage of the child-care opportunities available during family visits to spend some time alone together. One young Romantic Lover couple and their four-year-old daughter habitually spent one week during the summer visiting with the wife's large family at her grandparents' farm. They would then leave the child with the willing relatives while the two went camping by themselves in the nearby mountains. Some of the other members of the family were amused and charmed by the Romantic Lover couple's eagerness to go off together away from everyone else.

In contrast to Mercurial Lover couples, Romantic Lover couples seem quite independent from their families of origin. They neither demand nor want the approval of parents, and some couples may appear to their families as somewhat distant, unin-

Complex
Enhancement of Relationship

terested, and unconcerned. Separation from family is important to Mercurial Lovers in their emphasis on becoming distinct and autonomous individuals. Romantic Lovers create their own security and distinctiveness within their love relationship.

Romantic Lover couples use money to enhance the passion in their relationship. They are likely to buy sentimental gifts, go on exotic vacations, and plan thoughtful and elegant celebrations of anniversaries and birthdays. They may agreeably forgo material possessions and even future financial security in favor of expensive but

Complexes
Being in Love
Stability
Accommodating

meaningful romantic expressions. They are most at ease when there is sufficient money to allow important expressions of their love for each other. When budgeting is necessary, neither may feel comfortable restricting themselves and each other. At times they may avoid the task, so that managing and budgeting their finances can be somewhat haphazard. However, they can zealously scrimp and save when the goal is a meaningful expenditure in the service of their love relationship.

There is little direct influence of the Romantic Lover Soul Image on the kind of work and commitment to work of Romantic Lovers. However, like everything else in their lives, work demands may clash with their relationship needs. When this happens, a good deal of internal and external conflict may result. If one partner's work conflicts with planned time together for the couple, the other may express resentment and hurt. This may come out in demands that the situation be fixed somehow, or accusations that the other doesn't really value the relationship. In response, the accused Romantic Lover may be intensely apologetic as well as annoyed at the beloved's lack of understanding. When a coveted six-month-long training opportunity in Germany was offered to one Romantic Lover, she struggled with the prospect of being separated from her lover for that length of time. Both of them were finally able to accept the situation when her partner found that she was financially able to make two visits abroad during the six months.

Complexes
Relatedness
Togetherness
Enhancement of Relationship

The combined complexes of enhancement of relationship and relatedness lead to some of the intense yearning and passion that are classically associated with romantic love. Love songs again illustrate features of Romantic Lovers that result from their complexes. For example, the theme of many country and western songs is the lover's despair at being separated from the loved one and the accompanying longing for the intense feeling of being in love. These same complexes are expressed in the way the couple approaches friendships, recreation, sex, and childrearing.

Complexes
Enhancement of Relationship
Relatedness
Togetherness
Stability

Romantic Lover—Romantic Lover couples enjoy friendships with like-minded couples, often couples who are either Romantic Lovers, Innocent Lovers (see Chapter 6) or a combination of the two (see Chapter 11). Together with one or several couples, they may enjoy planning for and spending time together during vacation trips. They are likely to enjoy being together with such friends for celebrations of their own and their friends' birthdays and anniversaries. Celebrating holidays with close friends is often preferable to being with family. However, when possible, a Romantic Lover couple may prefer a holiday trip alone to spending time with either family or friends.

The partners in a Romantic Lover couple may have individual friendships, but these are likely to be relatively few and unimportant compared to, for example, the friendships of Mercurial Lovers. In general, given the choice of spending time with a friend versus being with the beloved, the love relationship wins out. Friends whose Soul Images are either Mercurial Lovers or Steadfast

Complexes
Relatedness
Togetherness
Being in Love

Lovers may become annoyed and critical when a Romantic Lover refuses an invitation or backs out of one—especially if the reason given is the partner's wishes. One Mercurial Lover tried to get his Romantic Lover colleague at work to play tennis with him one night a week. He finally gave up after most requests were met by the Romantic Lover saying, "Gee, I'm sorry. Amy and I were planning to spend the evening together."

Romantic Lovers tend to be wary of each other's opposite-sex friendships and even necessary work relationships. Both experience anxiety about the potential for the transfer of the partner's love to an appealing other person. And both may sometimes have a concern that they themselves might be vulnerable to the romantic persuasion of someone

Complexes
Stability
Being in Love

else. Some Romantic Lovers find themselves prone to intense, though usually brief, fantasies of passion with a real or imagined person who is not their beloved. One Romantic Lover wife was distressed to find herself obsessed with fantasies of passionately kissing her best friend's husband. She felt so guilty and uncomfortable that for several months she made excuses to avoid being with him, even when others were present. She energetically renewed her attentions to her husband, and after a time, her feelings for the other man dissipated.

As an opportunity to be together in a meaningful way, recreational activities are very important to Romantic Lovers. The most desirable activities are those that allow the couple to be close to each other. Favorite ways to do this include dancing, candlelit dinners at home or in an elegant restaurant, a long walk on a deserted beach, a weekend in a cabin in the woods, or a vacation cruise. For the most part, Romantic Lover couples enjoy being by themselves. However, they will include other couples in some of their recreational activities as long as sufficient time alone is guaranteed. It probably would not occur to Romantic Lovers to consider taking separate vacations. Even necessary business trips by one or the other partner are only reluctantly tolerated. When a business trip allows the beloved to go along, the couple are pleased to take advantage of the opportunity.

Complexes
Accommodating
Being in Love

Romantic Lover couples enjoy creating their own meaningful and special recreational activities, and these may take on the importance and regularity of private rituals. For example, several times a week when their busy schedules permitted, Ryan and Sharon would prepare a gourmet dinner together and dine by candlelight. After the dinner, they would make love. These evenings were invariably the high point of their week.

The pleasure of lovemaking is mutual and reciprocal for a Romantic Lover couple. Each is sensitive to whether the partner is enjoying sex. Their sexual passion is interdependent, so if one of them isn't enjoying it, both of their experiences are diminished. When a partner isn't satisfied, the beloved may express concern about the other's mood, health, or some other transient factor. Romantic Lovers enjoy the mutuality of feeling profoundly and inseparably connected to each other

Complexes
Being in Love
Accommodating

before they make love. If this feeling is absent, making love is neither desired nor capable of correcting the absence of unanimity. They are not likely to have a passionate and satisfying sexual connection with each other when there is discord in other aspects of their relationship. This is not necessarily the case, however, when a Romantic Lover is paired with someone with a different Soul Image. The rationale for this difference will become clear when the particular nature of those love relationships is discussed in later chapters.

With their value of harmonious cooperation and their sympathetic connection to each other, Romantic Lovers can "read" each other's sexual desires so there isn't need for discussion of their sexual relationships. In fact, talking about lovemaking may be experienced as a disconnection from the intimacy of sex as an expression of love.

The bearing and raising of children is seen by Romantic Lover couples as an integral part of their love for each other. Giving birth to a child and sharing in its care is an important way of further enhancing themselves within the context of their love relationship. However, the actual presence of a child in their lives can stimulate some ambivalence for Romantic Lovers, particularly for a new father. He may be unprepared for and resentful of the diminished

Complexes
Relatedness
Being in Love
Accommodating

attention he receives from his beloved, and may fear a permanent distance and separation from her. The new mother is also likely to feel some concern and anxiety as she feels her energies pulled toward loving and caring for her child.

The birth of a child can add to the ways Romantic Lovers can experience their love for each other. What both partners acquire is a broadening of the ways their love is expressed. Therefore, there is a modification of the *strong* and *narrow* expression of love

Complex
Enhancement of Relationship

that is typical of Romantic Lovers. For the most part, the partners adapt to the addition of a child to their relationship, and the child eventually occupies a comfortable niche within the Romantic Lovers' relationship. At times, however, Romantic Lovers may resent the interference of children in activities that are important to their love relationship. They may miss the way things were before they had children. Should a grown child wish to return home for an extended period of time, they may be displeased and resistant to the intrusion, and are likely to be firm in setting a limit on the length of stay.

When two Romantic Lovers divorce, they prefer minimizing contact with each other; seeing each other can stimulate memories of the good parts of the relationship and a reexperiencing of the pain of their loss. They may therefore handle the necessary collab-

Complexes
Stability
Being in Love
Enhancement of Relationship

oration about children without having to see each other whenever this is possible. Over time, whatever negative factors contributed to the breakup of the relationship tend to fade somewhat, and are replaced by a nostalgia for the romance and what might have been. With both partners sharing a propensity for fantasizing and perhaps embellishing the positive qualities of the relationship, two divorced Romantic Lovers may reconcile and remarry. If the same factors that led to the divorce resurface, they are likely to divorce yet again. Sometimes, however, being apart for a time, especially if one or both try relationships with other people, can help the couple find greater satisfaction "the second time around."

The Clash of Complexes

The life of two Romantic Lovers can be intense in its intimacy and shared passion. As with Mercurial Lovers and Innocent Lovers, the tensions leading to disagreements and quarrels are likely to be precipitated by external stressors.

Susan met Timothy while she was a student in a sculpturing class he taught. Timothy was a charismatic teacher, and Susan an enthusiastic pupil. She learned his neoclassical style of sculpture and became very adept at it. There was an immediate attraction between them, and after the workshop ended, they began dating. They were married a year later. Timothy was a widower and ten years older than Susan. His previous wife had died after a long and painful illness. This was Susan's first marriage.

Susan was attracted to Timothy because, as she described it, "He was the first man who made me feel like a woman." Susan's teenage years had been very unhappy. She was a tall, gawky teenager, and did not date often. She recalled that her mother frequently tried to "dress her up" so that she would be more attractive to boys. Susan's mother didn't encourage her athletic interests and natural artistic abilities. Secretly, Susan had crushes on some of the boys at school. She recalled that she was profoundly hurt when one of them jeeringly said, "You look like a female hockey player."

Science was Timothy's main interest during his youth, and he earned a science degree at college. He married his high school sweetheart, Allison. They were deeply in love, devoted to each other, and very happy. Several years after they married, however, Alison was diagnosed with leukemia. After several remissions and recurrences, the illness became chronic. Allison died four years later. Her death had a profound effect on Timothy. He became depressed and contemplated suicide. He quit his job and became an artist. A family inheritance allowed him to live modestly, and he devoted his energies to his artistic work. Discovering he had a natural flair for teaching, he began holding workshops.

What attracted Timothy to Susan was her energy and wistfulness. He said, "It's as if Susan and I share an unspoken deep sorrow." They began traveling around the country giving workshops together, and soon developed a reputation as excellent teachers. She enjoyed the challenge of the workshops and the feeling that she and Timothy were in tune with each other. Timothy savored the workshops as times for them to be together. Timothy's devotion to Susan was fulfilling for her. She was quite happy following his neoclassical sculpturing style because they were able to be together and travel to interesting places. However, her curiosity and natural proclivity for a different style engendered an impatience with his unwillingness to explore new techniques.

Phase One: The Disagreement

- As a disagreement continues with no resolution, tension increases.
- The persistence and increase of tension cause misunderstanding.
- Sustained tension and misunderstanding cause stress.

An ostensibly minor occurrence caused considerable tension in Susan and Timothy's heretofore idyllic relationship. Susan received a commission to create a large sculpture. One day while Timothy was working in their studio, Susan hesitantly entered and initiated the following conversation:

Susan: Sweetie, I want to talk to you. I've been keeping something from you.

Timothy (still working): What, dear?

Susan: Tim, I'm serious. Stop working and listen to me.

Timothy (smiling): Honey, what's wrong?

Susan: Nothing. I've received a commission to do a piece for a new office building.

Timothy (puzzled): How did they know about our work?

Susan: It's not "our work." It's *my* work they're interested in.

Timothy: But you know we work together.

Susan: I submitted a drawing of an abstract piece, and they liked it.

Timothy: Why didn't you submit one of our pieces?

Susan: Sweetie, abstract expressionism is important to me. I don't know how to explain it. Imaging this way just flows, and it seems effortless. You know how you feel when you get an idea for a piece? Well, I envied you because I never really felt that way. But now I feel it with abstract expressionism.

Timothy: I never knew that. This is very important for you.

Susan: Yes, it's very meaningful for me.

Timothy: Well, Susan, I have a confession to make, too, and I have to apologize to you because I wasn't able to say it before.

Susan: What is it? You're scaring me.

Timothy: I've always sensed that you never got as excited as I did with a new piece, and I felt that maybe you were shallow. Now I know why, and I apologize.

(He embraces her.)

Susan: Oh, hon, I love you.

(They kiss.)

Timothy: We'll still have a great time doing things together, won't we?

Susan: Yes, we will. I have a feel for abstract design. Just because I do things differently doesn't mean we'll become separate. We'll still be together; we'll still work together.

Timothy: We'll still do the workshops?

Susan (reassuringly): Of course we will. After I finish this piece. I figure it'll take about three months. We'll survive a little bit of loneliness.

Timothy: Okay, sweetheart. I'm glad we had this conversation.

Susan: Me too.

Susan's commission was an external stressor that caused a potential clash of their complexes. For both Timothy and Susan, the complex of enhancement of relationship is very important. Susan's commission brought to the surface her tension between relatedness and togetherness. The commission elicited her feelings of being constrained artistically. It enabled her to experience a richness and fullness of expression that were very precious to her. However, Timothy feared that Susan's interest in exploring new artistic styles was a way of distancing herself from him. In their disagreement, no indicators of unconscious complexes emerged. They were able to resolve their minor disagreement and maintain their closeness.

Phase Two: The Quarrel

- Persistent misunderstanding and stress consume large amounts of energy, and can be exhausting.
- Sustained fatigue and stress jeopardize the ability to integrate and respond to the issues.
- Fatigue and stress continue to consume more energy.
- Negative aspects of the participants' Soul Images are evoked.

In order to complete the commissioned sculpture on schedule, Susan was unable to travel with Timothy for about three months. Both of them were unhappy about this. While Timothy was gone, Susan remained in their studio and worked on the sculpture. Although they talked to each other every night on the phone, they were both lonely and missed each other deeply.

One day, the company that commissioned the sculpture sent their architect, Jeffrey, to inquire about the sculpture and to determine its location on the building site. Susan felt an immediate kinship with Jeffrey, though she also experienced a disquietude that puzzled her. He liked her sculpture very much and expressed a sensitivity for her abstract expressionistic style. Susan was surprised and quite pleased by Jeffrey's response, as Timothy was only mildly complimentary of her new style. (Indeed, Susan felt somewhat patronized by her husband.) She and Jeffrey chatted for quite a while. When he asked her out for lunch, she at first refused, claiming that she had a lot of work to do, and then impulsively accepted his invitation. They lunched at a nearby restaurant and talked for over two hours. The remainder of the day, Susan was energetic and happy. That evening after Timothy's telephone call, however, she felt guilty because she had not mentioned her lunch with Jeffrey. The following week, Susan had lunch with Jeffrey three times, ostensibly to discuss the placement of her sculpture. Susan was surprised and pleased with how close and open she felt with Jeffrey. They both expressed their comfort with each other.

When Timothy returned from his trip, he sensed a distance and coldness from Susan, and was hurt and bewildered. Although he tried to be accepting of her work, his tension was already high because of the separation they had both just experienced. Susan was tense because of her attraction to Jeffrey. Consequently, they were both susceptible to any hints of distance and rancor, when Timothy began the following conversation:

Timothy: Is anything wrong? You've been distant and preoccupied.

Susan: Nothing's wrong. I just don't feel well. I've been working very hard to finish the commission.

Timothy: Well, maybe you need a break. I have another workshop in San Francisco in two weeks. We can be together and have great seafood dinners on the wharf. Remember how much we liked the sourdough bread?

Susan (curtly): I won't be able to go.

Timothy: Why? You'll be finished with the sculpture by then.

Susan: Yes, but I'll have to supervise the placement. Jeffrey and I will have to work together on this.

Timothy: Who's Jeffrey?

Susan (trying to appear casual): Oh! Didn't I tell you? He's the architect who designed the building. Jeffrey and I have been discussing the placement of my piece. He really likes it.

Timothy (suspiciously): What's to discuss? How often have you been meeting with him?

Susan: Not often.

(She walks away, but Timothy follows her.)

Timothy: You're so distant—what's wrong? Are you upset with me?

Susan: I'm not distant. I told you I was busy and overworked. Why do you have to think of yourself all the time?

Timothy: I'm not thinking of myself, I'm thinking of us. Is there something wrong with us? We've always been so close.

Susan: So close that I feel smothered.

Timothy: What do you mean by that?

Susan: I have to do everything your way. You think I'm shallow, so I have to do everything your way.

Timothy (angrily): I knew you shouldn't have accepted this commission. It's separating us.

Susan (shouting): I knew it! You don't want me to be successful!

Timothy (shouting): That's not so. You just don't want us to be together. You're the selfish one.

Susan: (shouting): You don't understand me at all! I don't know why we're even together! We have nothing in common, and sometimes I think you don't even like me!

Timothy (shouting): You're the one who wants to be separate, not me!

(A full-blown quarrel results. Susan storms out of the studio, leaving Timothy in a despairing rage.)

The quarrels of Romantic Lovers are distinctly different from those of Mercurial Lovers. Whereas the Mercurial Lovers value independence and equality, Romantic Lovers value togetherness and harmony. Timothy wanted Susan to do everything his way so that he could experience an enhancement of relationship within his relatedness to her. She, however, became aware that she was providing the means through which Timothy could be fulfilled in the relationship. Through her friendship with Jeffrey, she discovered that her relationship with Timothy was restraining her sense of herself. She felt that the relationship was discordant and out of harmony. In their quarrel, the unconscious complexes that were evoked were different from those in the Mercurial Lovers' quarrel. Timothy accused Susan of being *nothing but* distant, and Susan accused Timothy of *always* thinking of himself. Each accused the other of being *nothing but* selfish.

One of the difficulties that two Romantic Lovers face is dealing with the question, "Can I be who I am and be fulfilled outside of the relationship?" Even though a Romantic Lover may be unhappy and unfulfilled, to leave the relationship would risk isolation and a diminution of self. That is why Romantic Lovers usually stay in a relationship that is unfulfilling; unhappiness is more tolerable than isolation and a loss of self.

Romantic Lovers are likely to leave an unfulfilling relationship only if there is another person with whom they may fulfill their sense of themselves. Timothy's incompleteness in the relationship was not as profound as Susan's because he had previously experienced a fulfilling relationship in his first marriage. His work also now gave his life meaning that Susan could only partly share. She became attracted to Jeffrey because her interaction with him brought to awareness her unhappiness and lack of fulfillment. The task for both Timothy and Susan now is to see if they can find a way to be fulfilled within their marriage.

The Nature of This Love Relationship

Two Romantic Lovers experience a sense of rightness in their being together as true soul mates. There is an intensity and passion in their devotion to maintaining and enhancing their experience of being in love. They are strengthened and affirmed through their relationship, so accommodating each other's needs and desires comes naturally to them. Because of this focus on accommodating, each partner tends to develop a sensitivity to the unspoken wishes of the beloved. Their ultimate goal is to create and maintain a stable and dependable relationship that will both fulfill their sense of themselves as individuals and ensure cohesiveness within the relationship.

These complexes were revealed in the disagreement and quarrel between Susan and Timothy. Their quarrel stimulated many unconscious complexes for both of them, as shown in the many *always, never,* and *nothing-but* statements they made.

Individual histories and circumstances may vary widely among Romantic Lover–Romantic Lover couples, but these same complexes can be seen in their daily lives and in their quarrels. We hope you now have a better and deeper understanding of, appreciation for, and ability to appraise this kind of true love.

6 | *Two Innocent Lovers*

To love is to discover and complete [one's self] in someone other than oneself.

Pierre Teilhard de Chardin, *The Future of Man*

The relationship of two Innocent Lovers is uniquely optimistic. The couple approach their life together with the profound belief that through love, cooperation, and togetherness their sense of self will be fulfilled. Playfulness, attentiveness, and affection characterize their planned optimism. They want to feel that as a couple they are part of a relationship, a family, a community, and the world at large. They are most content when everything is meaningfully interrelated and in harmony, and often prefer a lifestyle that reflects their values of cooperation and altruism.

Innocent Lovers favor a way of living that is compatible with their personal values. They are partial to environments in which cooperation and fellowship are valued. Because of this, others may mistakenly regard them as unassertive, and even dependent or immature. Contrary to others' perceptions, however, the assurance of being together with and loved by their partners strengthens Innocent Lovers both individually and as a couple. This is consistent with their way of expressing love, which can vary from *mild* to *strong,* with a typically broad focus. The *warm* and *close* nature of their intimacy also adds to the togetherness of their love relationship. Along with the general characteristics of the Innocent Lover Soul Image, these combine to form the typical complexes we see expressed in the everyday lives of two Innocent Lovers.

Couples who share the same Soul Image have similar perspectives about many things, including their biases and sources of irritation. For two Innocent Lovers, the complexes we expect to see in their day-to-day relationships are as follows: an emphasis on change and its contribution to the development of the relationship, a focus on relatedness and togetherness as the vehicles for forming a personal identity, cooperating as the natural way of resolving conflict, and perpetuating the state of being loved as the central aspect of the love relationship.

The characteristics of Innocent Lovers are summarized in Chart II. The next section describes how the complexes listed in the chart are expressed in the everyday lives of Innocent Lover couples. To highlight the complexes being discussed, they are identified in the margin beside the relevant descriptions.

⟩ The Innocent Lover—Innocent Lover Relationship

The spontaneity and fun in Innocent Lover partnerships come from change and its importance for the development of the relationship. The partners share an expectation that through change, the relationship and each partner will grow. The complex of change for Innocent Lovers is *instrumental* to this goal. The

Chart II

Characteristics of Innocent Lovers

Central Relationship Question

"If my sense of self is confirmed by my beloved in an intimate relationship, can I develop and have a sense of self when I am not being loved? It is an old adage that one exists only when one is loved. That's the way it is for me. My beloved's love for me is what sustains me and grants me the will and the energy to grow, develop, and be at one with the world. What I dread is the possibility that my beloved will no longer love me. If that happens, I will lose not only my sense of self, but also my dreams and goals for the future. It is for this reason that my beloved must confirm the love that sustains me. If not, I will truly be lost."

Attributes, Themes, and Complexes

Change	A focus on change and growth toward a goal establishes a connection to people and the world. Change has instrumental value.
Development of Relationship	Relationship results in the assurance that development toward mutual wholeness will occur.
Relatedness	A sense of selfhood comes from the relationship with the beloved.
Togetherness	Togetherness with the beloved is maintained by sharing projects, plans, and dreams for the future.
Cooperating	Cooperating is the natural way of resolving conflict and preserving the state of Being Loved.
Being Loved	The knowledge and comfort of being loved is the nourishment that will lead to change and growth.

Kind of Intimacy

Temperature	Warm—holding hands, touching, and physical closeness in private and public; use of terms of endearment.
Proximity	Close—deeply affected by the other's unspoken distress.

Expression of Psychic Energy

Focus	Broad—many expressions of love.
Intensity	Mild to strong expressions of love.

Innocent Lover's notion of change contrasts with the Mercurial Lover's, for whom change is *intrinsic*—natural and good in itself.

> **Complexes**
> *Change (Instrumental)*
> *Development of Relationship*

Innocent Lovers are therefore likely to approach the world with anticipation and optimism about their future. Planning for future goals is a frequent topic of discussion: Their focus is on an ideal state that will occur sometime in the future.

Concentrating on a future ideal may make an Innocent Lover couple somewhat dissatisfied with the present. They may complain to each other about things they want and do not yet have, and are most content when anticipating positive future goals. However, if they disagree on how to achieve those goals, each may be disappointed and begin to doubt their connectedness within the relationship. For example, an Innocent Lover couple in their late twenties shared a desire to have a vacation cabin near a lake. They often talked about how happy they would be once they were able to fulfill this dream. The wife was determined to first make sure that their home in the city was comfortable and that they could meet all their financial obligations before they looked seriously at lakeside property. Her husband, on the other hand, was convinced that if they waited too long, other pressures would distract them from this goal. He wanted to look for and even buy something soon, even if it meant doing without some other things. The couple argued frequently about this, especially when they were both feeling frustrated with their work or with their financial situation.

Innocent Lovers are less likely to disagree about the ways they enjoy being with each other. They often take pleasure in doing

> **Complexes**
> *Cooperating*
> *Togetherness*

household tasks together, making their togetherness an end in itself. They work cooperatively and are not competitive or self-centered in what they do. Even routine and repetitive activities can be done with a spirit of lighthearted fun, especially if getting the tasks out of the way means that they can then share something that really excites them. Outside pressure or conflicting demands can make it harder for Innocent Lovers to work together cooperatively. Enjoyable activities can then become tedious chores, and the couple may try to get through them by dividing them up and working on them independently.

Doing things in a nonpreferred way can lead them to push tasks off on each other, which adds to the displeasure and resentment they experience. One couple promised to help neighbors build a fence one Saturday, but wanted to finish cleaning the house first, as Saturday morning was their usual day for household chores. To save time, they each worked on a separate room instead of doing different tasks in the same room. By the time they finished, both were quite irritable and criticized the way the other had cleaned. In the course of their accusations and counteraccusations, they both acknowledged that they regretted their promise to help the neighbors and would rather do something else with their afternoon. Knowing they both felt the same way resolved their bickering. They helped their neighbors build the fence all afternoon, and treated themselves to a restaurant dinner afterward.

Innocent Lovers view money as instrumental to achieving their objectives, and not as something intrinsically desirable. For example, they would prefer not to work hard just to make a lot of money if they would not have the time to spend and enjoy it. They are also likely to pool the money each earns rather than keeping it separate. In this way they are similar to Romantic Lovers and different from Mercurial Lovers. They are also similar to Romantic Lovers in preferring not to be responsible for creating and maintaining a budget, since Innocent Lovers prefer to be free to accept life with as little restriction as possible.

Complexes
Development of Relationship
Cooperating

They are most content when there is enough money so that they don't have to limit their spending. Neither is likely to enjoy the constraints of a budget, and stress around this may lead to arguments and mutual accusations of mismanagement. Usually, one of the pair is more naturally adept at attending to financial matters, and will therefore reluctantly assume the responsibilities for overseeing the family finances. He or she may then be accused by the partner of being controlling, unreasonable, and overly cautious. This occurred with the couple described earlier who wanted to have a lakeside vacation home. The wife, who kept the budget and paid the bills, favored delaying action; in the heat of arguments, the husband would accuse her of being a "withholding dictator."

Innocent Lovers' natural tendency to relate to others through sympathy influences their style of unspoken communication with each other. They share an expectation that each will be sensitive to the desires and feelings of the other. Each is likely to notice when the other needs help or encouragement and will willingly provide sympathy and relief. Having the beloved know without being told what is needed or desired is seen as a sign of love, caring, and shared values. When such sensitivity is absent, it is taken as a sign of distance and lack of caring.

Complexes
Relatedness
Being Loved

Misreading or failing to pick up on a beloved's subtle, nonverbal cues of distress or displeasure can result in anger and hurt accusations. Because the relationship is central to the Innocent Lover's identity, seemingly trivial misunderstandings can yield rather intense reactions. The "misread" partner may feel devalued and misunderstood, and may see his or her partner as uncooperative and uncaring. Meeting the needs of an Innocent Lover is the most important way for the beloved to ensure that an Innocent Lover partner feels loved. The following story illustrates how one Innocent Lover couple dealt with a minor misunderstanding and thereby prevented it from escalating into a quarrel.

Kimberley and Seth were invited to a dinner party at the home of friends. They were both looking forward to going. However, the morning of the day of the party, Kimberley felt ill. Her symptoms worsened during the day, and she told Seth she felt too sick to go to the party.

"I guess I'll call them and say we can't come," he said. "Are you really sure you're too sick? Maybe I should wait in case you feel better."

"I'm really just too sick," said Kimberley with some annoyance. "I wish you'd be a little more sympathetic. It's not that I don't want to go. You're not thinking of going without me, are you?"

"Of course not!" said Seth. "And I *was* being sympathetic. I was just trying to make you feel better by suggesting you might not really be as sick as you feel now. Then we could go and have a good time. But we'll be okay at home. I would never even think of going without you. Maybe we can watch a movie together to get your mind off being sick."

"Okay," said Kimberley. "I know you wouldn't go without me, and I'm sorry I jumped down your throat."

Innocent Lovers' selfhood and fulfillment are enhanced and strengthened through the closeness and cooperative spirit in their relationship, so that each emerges as able to meet life's challenges with confidence.[1]

More than any of the other Soul Images, Innocent Lovers seek a congruence between the world of work and their love relationships. An Innocent Lover will probably be more distressed if the demands of work interfere with the love relationship than if the demands of the love relationship clash with work goals.[2] As a result, choosing a career and staying in a work situation may be influenced by how much freedom it allows the partners for each other. Innocent

Complexes
Cooperating
Relatedness
Togetherness

Lovers seek work circumstances that allow the couple sufficient time together. They also appreciate goodwill and cooperation in the workplace.

Innocent Lovers seek a harmonious balance between work and home life. If this proves impossible, work may become the means to an end of providing enough free time and money for enjoyable outside activities. Retiring early may become an important goal. Innocent Lover–Innocent Lover couples who have saved or inherited money may choose to work in an enjoyable avocation rather than the job or career for which they were trained. For example, a couple who were both trained as professionals left their professional jobs after their tenth wedding anniversary. After exploring various alternatives, they started a small mail-order business for specialty foods, a long-standing shared interest.

When there is moderate stress in an Innocent Lover relationship, work demands can become a source of distress. Each may see

Complexes
Togetherness
Cooperating
Being Loved

the other's involvement in work as indifference, disinterest, and a withdrawal of love. Regardless of the Soul Image of the partner, Innocent Lovers tend to see their beloved as *choosing between* being with the Innocent Lover or being with someone or something else. With the high priority an Innocent Lover couple puts on being together, it can be especially upsetting when a beloved seems to be choosing work over the relationship. An Innocent Lover who supervised a large dental equipment laboratory had to spend many extra hours at work learning and training others on a new electronic device. Her Innocent Lover partner was at first supportive and helpful, offering to take on extra household tasks while the assignment lasted. However, when the dental supervisor announced that she had to work on a Saturday when they had already planned a day trip, an argument ensued. "Just tell them no!" he said. "You've had lots of practice the past few weeks saying no to me whenever I needed you!" "I'm not doing it because I want to but because I have to," the woman replied. "If you loved me, you would be more understanding. I'm doing this for us, not for me."

Friendships are also influenced by the value Innocent Lovers place on their unity as a couple. Each may have a few close friends, but they tend to be most content when they do things together with other couples. At times, close individual friendships may lead the noninvolved partner to

Complexes
Togetherness
Cooperating

feel like an outsider. More often, however, a close friend of one will end up being close to both members of the couple. For example, an Innocent Lover husband played racquetball with a single friend from work and often invited him home afterward. The husband, the wife, and their friend enjoyed these visits greatly, and the Innocent Lover couple began including him in family gatherings. When the single friend married a year later, the two couples continued a warm connection with each other.

Similar outcomes can occur with an Innocent Lover couple's family relationships. For Innocent Lovers, family members are part of the web of relationships that are important to their comfort, security, and identity as a couple. Both generally enjoy a good deal of contact with their own and each other's families. They tend to use vacation time for family visits and like spending holidays, birthdays, and other special events with their parents and siblings. Being accepted

Complexes
Development of Relationship
Relatedness
Being Loved

by and close to their own and each other's families enhances and affirms the two Innocent Lovers' relationships with each other and with the community at large. If one of the Innocent Lovers is not particularly close to his or her parents and family, the spouse's family is likely to be "adopted" wholeheartedly instead. This importance of family closeness makes Innocent Lovers markedly different from Mercurial Lovers, who strive for independence and separateness from their families. Innocent Lovers are also distinct from Romantic Lovers, whose focus on differentiating and refining their love relationship leads to their placing relatively little emphasis on extended family relationships.

Innocent Lovers also enjoy the closeness and playfulness that comes with having children. At times, however, a new mother may seem excessively involved with the child, and the new father may feel

Complexes
Development of Relationship
Relatedness
Being Loved

excluded and unloved. In this regard, Innocent Lover parents are similar to Romantic Lover parents, as both Soul Images value affirmation within the relationship itself. "Competition" with children can therefore potentially jeopardize the security and comfort of these relationships.

As parents, Innocent Lovers are notable for their ability to understand and relate at their children's level of experience. They can participate in the games and activities of their children as if they were children themselves. People with an Innocent Lover Soul Image are often the favorites of their nieces, nephews, and friends' children. Active participation in their own children's sports, dance lessons, and informal play with friends is common. Consequently, children and their Innocent Lover parents are able to share an enviable warmth, closeness, and lightheartedness.

Some Innocent Lovers may at times feel overburdened by childrearing, especially when many other external responsibilities demand their attention. It may be difficult for them to maintain

Complexes
Cooperating
Being Loved

a consistent parental role: They may vacillate between overindulgence and excessive attempts at control. If a child reacts to such wavering by expressing anger, the Innocent Lover parent may accuse the child of hurting the parent's feelings, being uncooperative, or being disobedient. The child's behavior is seen as a failure on the parent's part to communicate the value of connecting to and cooperating with others.

Innocent Lovers tend to miss their children very much when they are gone, and may be reluctant to be separated from them for long periods, especially when the children are young. When children leave for college or move out to be on their own, Innocent Lover parents may react with great sadness and a sense of loss. However, once adjusted to their absence, they are likely to thoroughly enjoy the renewed closeness of their love relationship with each other. Similarly to Romantic Lovers, they may not welcome any lengthy return home of their adult children.

In their sexual relationship, Innocent Lovers share an emphasis on the direct experience of sensual pleasure. They therefore typically enjoy a passionate and uninhibited sexual relationship. They enjoy being able to please each other sexually but are even more focused on their own individual sexual fulfillment. Each may assume that his or her own sexual desire will be matched by that of the partner. Innocent Lovers

Complexes
Being Loved
Togetherness

can therefore be unaware of a partner's occasional lack of interest in sex. However, their own pleasure will not usually be diminished by a partner's lack of interest. Unlike Romantic Lovers, it isn't necessary for them to feel connected to each other to make love.

Innocent Lovers' enjoyment of sex can be quite independent of what is going on in other aspects of their relationship. If they have been arguing and are angry at each other, they can still come together sexually. A passionate and satisfying sexual relationship can exist even though there are major difficulties in other parts of an Innocent Lover–Innocent Lover relationship. Innocent Lovers are similar to Romantic Lovers in that they usually don't discuss sex and their sexual relationship. Nevertheless, it is often the glue that keeps an otherwise dissatisfied couple together. It isn't that good sex heals or even improves their relationship; rather, the pleasure they get from their lovemaking makes their distresses and dissatisfactions tolerable. Neither is willing to give up the intensity and passion of their sexual life together.

Sometimes Innocent Lovers may withhold sex as a way of emphasizing their displeasure with each other. This can result in quite lengthy periods of sleeping apart with no sexual activity at all. If the relationship in general is not satisfying to the partners, this long absence of connection through sexuality may lead the partners to end the relationship.

Two Innocent Lovers are probably at their best when they are free to enjoy life without impediments. They look forward to

Complexes
Change (Instrumental)
Development of Relationship

weekends and vacations, ready to experience new or favorite activities together. Their shared attraction to the natural world of plants, animals, and nature may influence their choices of common recreational interests. They may volunteer together for organizations that promote social and animal welfare and the preservation of the natural world or a particular way of life. For example, an Innocent Lover couple were distressed when they found out that a forest near both their parents' homes was destined for clear-cutting. They devoted their upcoming vacation to participating in actively protesting the plan.

Innocent Lovers may enjoy surprising each other in ways that express how much they care for and love each other. For example,

Complex
Being Loved

one may call the other at work to say he or she has made a reservation for dinner at a nice restaurant. The pleasure received from being the one surprised is consistent with a focus on being loved. Because Innocent Lover couples share this value, neither is likely to neglect this part of their relationship. For both, it is the thought behind the effort that counts, not the expense or elegance of what is offered. This is in contrast to Romantic Lover couples, for whom a romantic setting or nostalgic association greatly adds to the pleasure of a gift or a surprise outing.

Even Innocent Lover couples who don't get along well in their everyday relationship often report that their difficulties are left behind when they go on vacation. This occurs regardless of whether they go on a sightseeing trip or visit family members. Their capacity to have fun together seems similar to their ability to enjoy sex in spite

Complexes
Togetherness
Relatedness
Being Loved

of other dissatisfactions in their relationship. Both sex and recreation seem to exist apart from everything else. The independence of these two relationship features can be somewhat puzzling, even to the couple themselves. They may wonder why their good feelings about each other on vacation don't "spill over" into their everyday lives. Often daily stress and work demands are blamed for the discrepancy.

Their conclusion is understandable, for Innocent Lovers confirm their sense of self through their connection to the beloved. When the demands of work, children, and finances take their attention away from each other, each experiences a loss of togetherness, relatedness, and trust that they are loved. However, when they are free to focus exclusively on each other (as when on vacation or during lovemaking), their interrelatedness and sense of self are affirmed.

In addition to other ways of satisfying recreational needs, Innocent Lovers, especially men, tend to enjoy collecting things. Their collection may consist of coins, figurines, cars, antiques, classic comic books, tools, and the like. The meaning

Complex
Development of Relationship

and value of these collections lie in the connection they make between the past, the present, and the future. For example, a comic book collection provides continuity with the past of childhood, the presence of adulthood, and the future of retirement.

Collecting silk flowers for one woman was an implicit part of her plan to eventually start a small gift shop. Innocent Lover partners are usually quite accepting and encouraging of each other's collecting interests, as long as expenditures for them don't strain their financial situation.

When two Innocent Lovers divorce, their hurt, anger, and feelings of rejection are likely to persist for a long time. Of particular distress is the cessation of their shared goals for their future together. Their divorce relationship can remain acrimonious for years, and maintaining civility with each other may be difficult, even for the benefit of their children. They therefore prefer to have as little direct contact with each other as possible, sometimes using their children as go-betweens and message-bearers. In spite of intentions to the contrary, Innocent Lover parents may be unable to resist saying negative things to their children about the other parent. This can be eventually mitigated by their mutual desire to cooperate in raising their children. In their personal interactions, it may be hard for both to accept a divorced partner dating or remarrying. Regardless of the circumstances of the divorce or which partner initiated it, knowing the former beloved is with someone else can rekindle and intensify feelings of rejection and being unloved.

Complexes
Development of Relationship
Cooperating
Being Loved

The Clash of Complexes

Two Innocent Lovers fill their lives with the satisfaction and joy that comes of shared values and a commitment to cooperative problem solving. Their shared values and complexes lead to their desire to be together as much as possible and to rely on each other's support and affirmation. With their emphasis on related-

ness, togetherness, and cooperation, they expect to resolve difficulties with a minimum of quarreling. This is likely to be true as
long as external stress is at a minimum. Similar to other couples
who share the same Soul Image, Innocent Lovers most likely
become involved in a clash of complexes due to stress from the
outside world. Since Innocent Lovers often prefer a simple
lifestyle free from external stress, even moderate outside pressures
may activate their particular complexes.

Max and Annie have been married for twenty years and have
three sons aged sixteen, fourteen, and ten. Max is an electrical
engineer who has worked for a firm of consulting engineers for
the past ten years. He enjoys his work and his work situation,
which is flexible enough to permit him a good deal of time with
Annie and the boys. He enjoys coaching his youngest son's soccer
team. Some of his colleagues at work and their wives have become
good friends of both Max and Annie, and the families do quite a
bit of socializing together. Annie is head of the accounting
department at a large department store. She resumed her career
five years ago after the youngest child entered school. Though at
times the demands of work and home make her life more stressful
than she would like, she enjoys her work and her reputation as an
excellent supervisor and problem solver. Several of her colleagues
are also close friends with whom she and Max socialize.

Max and Annie are quite content. They enjoy having both
their sets of parents close by and do many things with them and
with other family members who also live nearby. They like the
sense of community that family and civic activities bring them.
Over the years they have developed a cooperative and comfortable
way of dealing with the normal, everyday stresses in their lives.
However, they sometimes complain about the outside pressures
that interfere with family time and commitments. Arguments
occur when one or the other feels overwhelmed by work and home
responsibilities, but for the most part their disagreements are

easily resolved. Their friends and family describe them as very caring, warm, and attentive to each other.

The two have a plan of retiring in ten years, moving to the farm where Annie grew up and that she will inherit, and converting the farm to a rustic weekend retreat center. They have been putting money aside to help finance their dream. When they visit Annie's elderly parents, who still live on the farm, they enjoy walking around and planning where different buildings and recreational facilities will go.

Phase One: The Disagreement

- As a disagreement continues with no resolution, tension increases.

- The persistence and increase of tension cause misunderstanding.

- Sustained tension and misunderstanding cause stress.

One evening, Max came home a bit later than usual. Annie sensed that something was wrong, even though he kissed her warmly and asked how her day was.

Annie: It was okay, but did you have a bad day? I can tell something is upsetting you.

Max: Well, I was hoping to wait until we had some time to relax and unwind before discussing this with you. I know you're not going to like it. I don't like it. But it could be exciting to go around to different places, although I usually don't like being away from home that much. Even so, I don't think I can really say no to Phil. He's counting on me. I'm really in a pickle.

Annie (heatedly): Will you stop having a conversation with yourself, and tell me what this is all about? It's not like you to keep things from me. Seems to me you've known about whatever is going on longer than just today!

Max: No, honey! I swear this just came up this afternoon. That's why I was late getting home, because Phil called me into his office and told me about a new contract we got to train engineers in South America. Since I'm the senior person on the systems they need, he wants me to be in charge. It means I'd have to go to Lima, Buenos Aires, and some other place in Brazil to set up the training and supervise. I'm afraid I'd have to be away for a week or two at a time.

Annie: You're right, I don't like it. It will really be hard on me and the kids. And you've never really liked traveling. Why don't you just tell Phil to get someone else? Isn't your family more important? What's he going to do, fire you? He knows we're a very close family.

Max: Don't be so unreasonable. Sure, he knows I like to be near my family, but sometimes he kind of teases me about it and maybe thinks I'm not committed enough to work. That bothers me. You know what's important to me, but my job is important for our future together and the kids. I don't like this either, and I think you could be a little more sympathetic instead of attacking me!

Annie: I'm not attacking you, I'm just upset. How long is this contract for, anyway? And how many trips would there be?

Max: It's only for eight months, but I'd probably have to make five or six trips during that time.

Annie: Well, I wish you could say no to Phil, but I don't want you to if it doesn't feel right to you. I know how happy you are at work. I guess we'll manage. The boys will just have to help more.

Max: You're great, Annie, and I love you. By the way, did I mention I'll get a big bonus at the end of the project?

Annie: You will? That's terrific! We can use some of it to do some special things to make up for your being gone.

Max: And we can put the rest toward the retreat center. When we miss each other when I'm away, we'll be able to look forward to all the time we'll have together once we move to the farm.

In the absence of external stressors, the life Max and Annie enjoyed with their family and friends was quite satisfying to both of them. The need to respond to the new work demand put stress on the couple's comfortable way of living. Max's uneasiness about how his boss perceived him also emerged as a more serious concern as a result of the request that he take on added responsibility. The couple adequately resolved the potential conflict between work and family by redefining the situation. They were able to view it as contributing to their shared values of togetherness and relatedness. The bonus would contribute to their enjoyment of each other in the near future and enhance their long-range plan for retirement as well.

Phase Two: The Quarrel

- Persistent misunderstanding and stress consume large amounts of energy, and can be exhausting.
- Sustained fatigue and stress jeopardize the ability to integrate and respond to the issues.
- Fatigue and stress continue to consume more energy.
- Negative aspects of the participants' Soul Images are evoked.

Three months later Max has made four trips, each ten days long. It has been difficult for both of them and for their children, especially the youngest, who becomes uncharacteristically needy and demanding when Max is gone. Though the novelty of the situation made the children cooperative the first two times Max was away, they now complain about the extra things they have to do. Annie is quite harried working full-time, chauffeuring the kids around, and helping them with their homework as well. She also worries about their oldest son, Zach, who is about to get his driver's license; she doesn't think he's had enough practice time with her and Max. While he is away, Max complains about missing Annie and the family, and when home, often expresses his joy to be there. He has many interesting stories to tell about the places and people he's visited, and everyone is eager to hear about his trips. Right now they are enjoying Max being home for three weeks, and life seems to have returned to normal. His next trip is two weeks away.

On Tuesday morning, Max calls Annie at work and asks her to go to lunch. The following conversation ensues:

Annie: I'd love to, honey, but we have a working lunch today. It's an important board meeting.

Max: Oh, gee. I really wanted to have lunch with you. Is there any way you can get out of it?

Annie: I can't. I have to present the financial report. Is something wrong?

Max (lightly): No, no, it can wait. It's just that things are going badly at the Lima facility, and I have to go back there before the scheduled trip to Brazil.

Annie (her voice rising): How much before, Max?

Max: I have to leave the day after tomorrow.

Annie (angrily): You can't go! You promised you'd be here another two weeks. You've already been gone more than you were supposed to. I think you *want* to be away from us. You just don't seem to care anymore!

Max (shouting): Look who's talking! What happened to "We'll be able to manage," and "The extra money will be nice for the future"? I'm stressed out enough about what's happening in Lima. You could be understanding, but you just attack me and accuse me! If you loved me, you wouldn't be like that.

Annie: If you loved me, you wouldn't be putting me through this hell! Well, I just don't care anymore. Go have your exciting career abroad! Stay away as long as you want! Your family will just have to learn to go it alone!

(She slams down the phone and breaks down sobbing. When Max calls back several times she refuses his phone calls. Both come home after work and barely speak to each other during the evening, though they make an attempt to act normal around the children. They go to bed still hurt and angry and lie at extreme opposite sides of the bed. Later in the night, however, they make passionate love, and in the morning they have breakfast together and commiserate about their mutual distress over the present situation. They comfort each other by talking about the farm and how it will be in ten years. They both express the hope that their love for each other will see them through this hard time.)

The external stress of being apart with both partners having to adapt to unwanted demands set the stage for the eruption of the unconscious complexes evident in their quarrel. Each sees the other as uncaring, uncooperative, and unappreciative of the other's stressful situation. Implicit in their *always* or *never* and *nothing-but* statements is fear about whether they are truly loved. The longer the partners are apart, the greater the feeling of disconnection, and the more each feels at a disadvantage in handling life's challenges. Unconscious complexes emerged in their mutual accusations of being uncaring and unloving. Blame and hurt feelings were the result for Max and Annie. Their lovemaking allowed them to reconnect and experience the strength of their relationship. This gave both of them renewed energy and resolve.

Innocent Lover couples are similar to Romantic Lover couples in finding their sense of self through relating and being together. Through a cooperative approach, they strive to grow together toward a fulfilling future. As a result, when one of them faces demands that force separation from their common goals, they both suffer. Becoming separate human beings while maintaining their relatedness can be a continuing dilemma for them.

Quarrels have the same structure and cause no matter what Soul Images the couple may have: They are caused by a clash of complexes specific to the Soul Images involved. Max and Annie value the unity that comes from their relationship, and when togetherness and relatedness are in jeopardy, their mutual complexes can create conflicts for them. Stress can be caused by any situation that pulls them apart. Max's desire to satisfy his boss and enhance the family's goals for the future conflicted with both his own and Annie's desire for a cooperative and close family situation. The clash of complexes created their quarrel.

The Nature of This Love Relationship

The uniquely optimistic relationship of two Innocent Lovers comes from their belief that being together in their love for each other and cooperating to achieve shared goals will promote and maintain their sense of self within a changing world. The experience of being loved is central for both partners, so they are sensitive to behaviors and verbal expressions that affirm that they are loved. Innocent Lovers place high value on being part of a family, a community, and the world, and many of their goals for the future are directed at such relationships. Cooperating with their beloved and with others is the natural and comfortable way to achieve the warmth and closeness that is an important part of being loved.

The quarrel between Max and Annie elicited many of their shared complexes and led both to make extreme, unconscious *always* or *never* and *nothing-but* statements. Although individual histories and circumstances may vary widely among Innocent Lover—Innocent Lover couples, these same complexes can be observed in their daily lives and in their quarrels. We hope you now have a better and deeper understanding of, appreciation for, and ability to appraise this kind of true love.

7 | *Two Steadfast Lovers*

Love is union under the condition of one's integrity, one's individuality.

Erich Fromm, *The Art of Loving*

The distinctive character of the relationship of two Steadfast Lovers is their mutual avowal of and respect for each other's interests, beliefs, and values. This egalitarian outlook enables them to be relaxed, amiable, helpful, and cooperative with each other. They share a comfortable confidence in their way of relating to each other, perhaps because their natural style corresponds to society's expectations of "mature" love. They enjoy the intimacy that results from refining and extending their knowledge of themselves, each other, and the nuances of their relationship. They tend to be effortlessly aware of each other's thoughts and feelings, but in a different way than is true for Romantic Lovers. Romantic Lovers use *sympathy* as the vehicle for knowing each other intimately, whereas *empathic* awareness is the medium for Steadfast Lovers.

Steadfast Lovers don't experience each other's thoughts and feelings; they are connected to each other through understanding and acceptance of the other's way of being. This kind of connection with each other may not be very apparent to others.

From the point of view of any of the other three Soul Images, the relationship of two Steadfast Lovers can be seen as stodgy, routine, and lacking in passion. For the Steadfast Lover couple themselves, however, the depth of satisfaction embodied in their relationship continues to increase over time. This is consistent with their way of expressing love, which is typically *mild* and *broad*. The *cool* and *close* nature of their intimacy also adds to the character of their love relationship. Along with the general characteristics of the Steadfast Lover Soul Image, these combine to form the typical complexes we see expressed in the everyday lives of two Steadfast Lovers.

Couples who share the same Soul Image have similar perspectives about many things, including their biases and sources of irritation. For two Steadfast Lovers, the complexes we expect to see in their day-to-day relationships are as follows: the importance of Stability and Differentiation of Self in their lives, a focus on Separateness and Autonomy as the vehicles for forming a personal identity, Negotiating as the natural way of resolving conflict, and perpetuating the state of Staying in Love as the central aspect of the love relationship.

The characteristics of Steadfast Lovers are summarized in Chart 12. The next section describes how the complexes listed in the chart are expressed in the everyday lives of Steadfast Lover couples. To highlight the complexes being discussed, they are identified in the margin beside the relevant descriptions.

⎰ The Steadfast Lover–Steadfast Lover Relationship

Two Steadfast Lovers value constancy in their relationship and agree on the importance of negotiation and perseverance in

Chart 12
Characteristics of Steadfast Lovers

Central Relationship Question

"How can I maintain my individuality and still be in a loving relationship? If I am a separate individual and I have a distinct identity, will I have to surrender or lose part of my identity and individuality to be in a loving relationship? After all, to be in a loving relationship means that I will have to take into consideration what my partner wishes and desires. I can't just do what I want without at least informing or consulting my partner. What's worse, suppose my partner objects to what I want or has a different preference? If I give in to that, doesn't that mean I will lose part of me?"

Attributes, Themes, and Complexes

Stability	Value is placed on constancy and continuity.
Differentiation of Self	Focus is on differentiation—on the refinement and expression of all facets of their selfhood.
Separateness	Accept their partners as separate, independent individuals and want that same kind of acceptance for themselves.
Autonomy	Value independence, uniqueness, and distinctness from social and cultural environments.
Negotiating	Negotiating is the natural way of resolving differences and conflicts.
Staying in Love	Place high value on faithfulness and constancy in the love relationship.

Kind of Intimacy

Temperature	Cool—minimal physical contact, nonverbal and non-physical expressions of affection, politeness in public.
Proximity	Close—deeply affected by the other's unspoken distress.

Expression of Psychic Energy

Focus	Broad—many expressions of love.
Intensity	Mild expressions of love.

dealing with life issues. Decisions about household tasks are therefore driven primarily by practicalities. The

Complexes

Stability

Negotiating

Differentiation of Self

division of labor may be based on capability, availability, and individual preferences
and interests. Regardless of who does what,
the goal is efficiency: They want sufficient
time to be available for important individual and joint activities.

In contrast to what is true for two Mercurial Lovers, equity in the
division of labor isn't necessarily the central consideration for two
Steadfast Lovers. If one partner is on occasion unable to perform
some usual task, the other partner will take care of it. No reciprocity is expected; it is simply assumed that when the need arises, the
other partner will willingly do the same. However, if the contribution of one persistently exceeds that of the other, resentment is
likely. The one doing most of the work may start keeping a mental
record of the inequity and eventually bring it to the partner's attention, sometimes with added annoyance because the partner failed to
notice it. Often, the couple enjoys working on many tasks together,
such as moving furniture, cleaning the garage, building a fence, or
making major household improvements. They also typically make
joint decisions about things they need to create a comfortable home.

In more traditional relationships, household tasks are likely to
be gender-driven. However, even in these marriages, the partners
may have a rather relaxed and flexible attitude toward gender-
related activities. For example, in one couple, the husband does
most of the cooking because he enjoys it and his wife does not; she
is content to clean up after meals. In another couple, the wife does
the cooking and her husband cleans up.

Steadfast Lover couples are often seen by family members as
responsible and mature. The couple's parents, siblings, children,
and other extended family members often seek their advice. The
Steadfast Lover couple may at times feel overburdened by such
family obligations. However, they generally go along with them,

acknowledging their natural suitability for such roles.[1] They will thus take charge of the care of their own and each other's parents and provide financial help to family members when they are in a position to do so. They consider both families as their shared responsibility. For example, a couple had an adolescent niece live with them for a year while her parents completed a difficult divorce. When another Steadfast Lover couple found that the elderly parents of both could no longer manage alone, they moved both sets of parents to a retirement facility close to their home. They were then able to oversee their care and maintain a close relationship with them.

Complexes

Stability

Negotiating

Steadfast Lovers regard children as part of the natural order of things and do not see them as disrupting their relationship. They believe that it is their responsibility as parents to transmit accepted values to their children so that they will grow up to be responsible and independent members of society. Their involvement in their children's activities helps encourage this outcome. They enjoy playing with their young children, but unlike Innocent Lover parents, do not play primarily for enjoyment. For Steadfast Lover parents, play is educational as well as fun, so they may guide and advise rather than actively participate in playing.

Complexes

Separateness

Autonomy

Stability

It may be difficult for Steadfast Lover parents to appreciate their Mercurial- and Romantic-natured children. They might worry about the seeming irresponsibility and lack of direction of Mercurials; they would be concerned that their "unrealistic" Romantic child could be disappointed and unfulfilled. With an Innocent child they are likely to be protective. Both they and their Innocent children enjoy their close, warm, and trusting relationship. Steadfast Lover parents are most likely to clash with their Mercurial children, and to a lesser extent, with Romantic children. They are, however, quite likely to be "traditional" grandparents—willingly providing childcare and advice, and happily "spoiling" the grandkids.

Steadfast Lover grandparents are perhaps the most likely of all the Soul Images to actually raise their grandchildren in situations where the children's parents cannot fulfill their parental role. One Steadfast Lover couple temporarily took over the rearing of their two granddaughters when their daughter, the children's mother, got divorced and became involved in a series of unfortunate relationships. The temporary arrangement eventually became permanent, and though the couple were ambivalent about giving up their freedom and independence, they accepted the inevitability of the situation.

Steadfast Lovers are similar to Mercurial Lovers in sharing the complex of Separateness. As a result, a Steadfast Lover–Steadfast Lover couple may be seen by Innocent and Romantic Lovers as disconnected from each other and not affectionate. Romantic and Innocent Lovers will see Steadfast Lover partners as dedicating too much energy to their separate interests instead of to the relationship. In fact, Steadfast Lovers risk overemphasizing their separateness and individuality to the possible detriment of the intimacy of their love relationship. If this happens, they may experience each other as cold, rigid, and distant, and their attention to each other may seem empty and perfunctory.

Devoting sufficient time and energy to social relationships can help mitigate Steadfast Lovers' tendency to overdo their individuality. Although each partner may have separate friendships formed around their independent interests, the Steadfast Lover couple may become friends with a couple one of them knows independently. If one partner is highly involved in political activities, for example, he or she may get to know couples with similar interests.

Social contacts with some of these couples may result in long-lasting friendships for a Steadfast Lover couple.

Like Mercurial Lovers, who also value their separateness, Steadfast Lovers are accepting of each other's opposite-sex friendships. For the most part, such friendships are formed around individual interests or work projects. For example, a Steadfast Lover wife may have a close friendship with a male colleague at work and may travel

Complexes
Stability
Autonomy
Staying in Love

and socialize with him during business trips. Her Steadfast Lover husband will typically regard such relationships as unavoidable and won't see them as threats to the love relationship. The partners in one Steadfast Lover couple each maintained a close work relationship with a colleague of the opposite sex. They discovered that some of their friends who knew of these relationships speculated about the state of their marriage and each one's "true" relationship with their colleagues. The couple were at first quite surprised and then later amused to be the subject of romantic gossip.

Two Steadfast Lovers approach money in a manner similar to their division of labor around household responsibilities: They generally like to have money matters well in control and try to figure out the best way to accomplish this. For example, in a more traditional relationship, the wife may do household budgeting while the husband may take care of long-range planning. In a less traditional situation, the division of labor may not be made along gender

Complexes
Negotiating
Differentiation of Self
Separateness

lines, but according to interest and skills. In any case, major expenditures are usually decided jointly. In a two-income couple, money is generally pooled and treated as family money, unless circumstances like second marriages prevail. If only one partner works outside the home, money is still likely to be viewed as a joint responsibility. However, some couples may agree on a division of responsibility where one partner takes over the major role in dealing with money. Whether it is the person who stays at home or the spouse who brings in the income will depend on factors such as personal preferences, time availability, and the like.

For Steadfast Lover–Steadfast Lover couples, career and work are accepted as central to differentiation and fulfillment. They don't see their independent work lives as competing with their love relationship. Rather, satisfaction and fulfillment in their work lives enhance their happiness in the relationship. They enjoy talking to each other about their work and at times may ask the other for advice. For example, a Steadfast Lover engineer frequently sought her husband's input about personnel matters at her work. He was able to give her a helpful perspective about sensitive situations involving people.

Complexes
Differentiation of Self
Separateness
Autonomy

The form and amount of communication between Steadfast Lover couples is contingent upon their shared interests rather than their shared Soul Image. How much of their individual lives and interests they discuss with each other will be highly individual. Some couples may treat each other as best friends and confidantes, while others may have only certain areas that they discuss with each other. Sometimes these are matters of shared family interest, like household affairs and childrearing; for other couples, a wide range of topics can be involved. If their work interests are similar, they enjoy discussing their work days and consulting each other on relevant career issues. Even when the kind of work they do is quite different, Steadfast Lover couples like keeping each other informed of their problems and successes in the work arena. Because both value their own and each other's independent pursuits, such discussions strengthen their affiliation, which adds depth and fullness to their relationship.

Complexes
Differentiation of Self
Separateness
Staying in Love

Enjoying recreational activities together is another way that depth and fullness can be added to their relationship. They like taking vacations together and try to accommodate the specific preferences of each partner within the same vacation. For example, if one person enjoys going to museums and the other prefers hiking, they'll figure out a way to compromise and accommodate both interests. However, if one partner really enjoys something that the other greatly dislikes, pursuing the activity is undesirable for both. The closeness of their intimacy would make each painfully aware of the other's distress or lack of enjoyment. For example, if the partner who liked museums absolutely hated hiking but agreed to hike anyway, neither partner would enjoy it. They would probably agree to omit hiking from their shared recreational time, and the hiker would hike at other times with friends.

Complexes
Differentiation of Self
Negotiating
Autonomy

In one couple, the husband liked jazz while his wife was indifferent to it. They therefore listened together to other music for which they had similar tastes. The husband satisfied his jazz interests whenever he went out of town without his wife by taking advantage of available jazz events on his own.

In situations where neither partner has a strong inclination toward a particular social or recreational activity, bypassing it and pursuing their individual interests may be preferred. For example, Simon and Michelle were invited to a dinner party at the home of friends. They were both planning on going. However, on the morning of the day of the party, Michelle felt ill. Her symptoms worsened during the day, and she told Simon she felt too sick to go to the party.

"I don't mind if you go anyway," she said. "I'm just going to take a hot shower and get into bed with my book."

"No, that's okay," Simon replied. "I'm not that interested in going, and anyway, I'd be a little uncomfortable without you there."

Michelle and Simon both stayed home. Michelle went to bed with her book, and Simon spent some time straightening out the tools in the garage and then watched television for a while before joining Michelle in bed.

Steadfast Lovers maintain an attitude toward sex that is similar to their approach to recreation: They don't tend to feel responsible for each other's sexual enjoyment and are unlikely to take it personally when their partner doesn't enjoy lovemaking from time to time. In this they are similar to Mercurial Lovers. However, if one partner persistently lacks pleasure in the sexual relationship, the other also suffers. Sensitivity to the nuances of each other's state of being is a central factor in this.

Complexes
Differentiation of Self
Autonomy
Staying in Love

The *mild* and *broad* expression of love that is characteristic of Steadfast Lovers can be seen in their sexual relationship. Sexual passion serves as only one among many expressions of their love. Its importance is therefore likely to vary considerably. For example, for a period of several weeks, a husband and wife were both devoting twelve-hour days to interesting work projects. They very much enjoyed giving each other progress reports during the few hours they were able to spend together each evening. But neither had much energy for or interest in sex during that time.

When two Steadfast Lovers divorce, they strive for a cordial but businesslike relationship focused exclusively on the needs of their continuing relationship—usually, the welfare of any children involved. They tend to be careful to respect and validate the children's relationship with the other spouse and take pains to ensure that the divorce is minimally disruptive to them. In their relationship to each other, two divorced Steadfast Lovers will maintain an emotional distance and are very unlikely to have a friendship with each other.

The Clash of Complexes

Freud was once asked, "What is a healthy person supposed to do?" His answer was simply "To love and to work." However, Freud did not stipulate the relative importance of love and work. Perhaps more than for any other Soul Image, for Steadfast Lovers maintaining a balance between love and work serves as an external stress. Because separateness, autonomy, and differentiation of self are central complexes, they can present a stressor that may result in a clash of complexes. The central question posed by their complex of separateness is, "How can I maintain my individuality and still be in a loving relationship?"

Linda and Michael met in college while working at the university library. They enjoyed books and shared a fantasy of one day owning a bookstore. Upon graduation, they married and, with the help of their parents, bought a small bookstore close to the university.

They were quite happy with the bookstore; they enjoyed the students and faculty who became their regular customers. The store provided them with a modest income, and they both became adept at and knowledgeable about the business and financial aspects of being retailers. They negotiated their duties as partners: Michael was in charge of the bookkeeping and accounting, and Linda took care of purchases and dealing with book distributors. A couple of students helped part-time with the selling. When Linda became pregnant with their first child, they purchased a small home in anticipation of becoming a family. They were happy and content. Several years later they had another child.

Phase One: The Disagreement

- As a disagreement continues with no resolution, tension increases.

- The persistence and increase of tension cause misunderstanding.

- Sustained tension and misunderstanding cause stress.

Reaching the age of thirty was an unwelcome event for both Linda and Michael, especially for Michael. They felt that their frivolous youth was over and that they had better make a commitment to life. Although they were contented being bookstore owners, they both felt that it was vaguely dissatisfying. Several weeks after Michael's thirtieth birthday, he told Linda that he wanted to discuss some ideas he had about their future. After the children went to bed, they sat at the kitchen table and had the following discussion:

Linda: What's up, Mike?

Michael: Linda, I've been thinking about our future. In ten years Brittany [their oldest daughter] will be a senior in high school getting ready to go to college, and in a few years after that, Josh will be ready. I don't think the store is going to provide enough money for us.

Linda: I know. I've been thinking about that, too.

Michael: Also, the enjoyment I get from the store isn't that great. I think turning thirty made me realize I'm unhappy.

Linda: I feel the same way. The store is getting to be just a job. So, what do you propose we do?

Michael: Well, I thought I'd apply to law school. What do you think?

Linda: Why law? Do you plan to become another John Grisham?

Michael (laughing): No, no! I wish. But I'm not a writer. I was thinking more of corporate law. Since I've been doing the books for the store, I've gotten interested in the business end of things. I think it would be interesting and challenging. Also, there's good money in it.

Linda (getting tense): But—what about me? What am I supposed to do? I can't see running the store by myself. And what about the children?

Michael: First things first. What do you think about my plan? Let's assume we can both manage it and that it will minimally disrupt the children.

Linda: If going to law school will make you happy, fine. But maybe I'd like to go back to school and have a new career, too. I can't run the store, run the household, *and* take classes. And you won't be any help! Law school is pretty demanding!

Michael: Please don't get upset, honey. Of course I want you to find a new career, too. Do you know what you'd like to do?

Linda: Not really. Right now there isn't anything that especially appeals to me.

Michael: Well, then, maybe you could figure it out while I'm in law school. What I thought is we should sell the store and use the equity as backup income if we get a little short on cash. I could also work weekends as a waiter to help.

Linda: And after you finish, I might want to get a graduate degree. But if we sell the store, I'm going to have to get an interim job or we won't have enough money to live on.

Michael: Is that okay? I could come home to study and be there for the kids while you're at work. Do you think we could manage all this?

Linda: I think so. The idea of getting a job isn't so bad.

Michael: It will only be for a few years, anyway.

Linda: Okay then. Let's do it!

Here, both Linda and Michael expressed unhappiness and experienced tension around both their issues as a couple and individual desires to differentiate themselves. There were several points in their discussion where the tension could have increased and resulted in a quarrel. Fortunately, they were able to maintain their ability to listen to and negotiate with each other.

Phase Two: The Quarrel

- Persistent misunderstanding and stress consume large amounts of energy, and can be exhausting.

- Sustained fatigue and stress jeopardize the ability to integrate and respond to the issues.

- Fatigue and stress continue to consume more energy.

- Negative aspects of the participants' Soul Images are evoked.

Within the year, Michael and Linda had sold the store, and the following year, Michael enrolled in law school. Linda got a job as an office manager in a hospital. Michael's studies were more time-consuming than he had anticipated. He enjoyed the classwork but found it difficult to study at home while attending to the children's needs. He was increasingly on edge when Linda came home from work, especially when she complained about her job and the way the hospital was run. Linda and Michael had little time for themselves because of the demands of his studies, Linda's work, and the needs of the children. Two years later, both of them were stressed out and exhausted.

One day Michael had a particularly difficult test on torts, and he was worried that he had performed poorly. That evening Linda came home infuriated. She complained to Michael about a disagreement with an uncooperative co-worker and how the co-worker wasn't doing his share. "Bob really infuriates me," she said. "He's just a male chauvinist pig. He thinks that women exist only to serve men. He treats me like I'm his secretary, and expects me to do his filing. He just tosses stuff on my desk and tells me to take care of it. He doesn't even *ask*; he *tells* me to do it. I've just about had it with him." Michael's response was, "Well, in a couple of years, after I get my degree, you'll be able to quit."

With this reply, Michael is responding to the indicators of Linda's unconscious complex—she made several *nothing-but* and implicit *always* statements directed toward her co-worker, Bob. Michael is trying to placate Linda because he infers that Linda is actually upset with *him*. He is tense and fatigued, so he is prone to hear Linda's complaints as directed at him because she believes he doesn't appreciate her efforts on his behalf. This erroneous assumption initiates a series of misunderstandings that activate unconscious complexes in both Michael and Linda.

Linda: Mike, you're not listening to me. Who said anything about quitting? I like my job.

Michael: I know, I know. Why don't you just take it easy, and I'll put the kids to bed.

Linda: Don't treat me as if I'm a child! I get enough of that patronizing crap at work.

Michael: Every time I try to be helpful, you give me a hard time!

Linda: When are you helpful? All you do is patronize me. You men are all alike.

Michael: Look, I come home and take care of the kids whenever I can! I cook! I'm up after midnight studying! I work on weekends! You've got it easy! All you do is come home, sit on your ass, and bitch!

Linda: I'll have you know I work very hard! And I do a lot around here, too. You're the one who bitches all the time. You always complain about law school, how hard it is. I'm afraid you're going to quit and tell me that it's not fulfilling for you or some crap like that.

Michael: Okay! Okay! I won't say another word about law school.

Linda: Now who's acting like a child?

(At this point, Michael walks away, goes to his desk, and opens a book. Linda goes to the bathroom and gets ready for bed. After a couple of hours of trying to study, Michael goes to bed also.)

As their exchange indicated, both Linda and Michael were tired and stressed out and felt falsely accused and unappreciated. Their fatigue and stress made them prone to getting caught in unconscious complexes reflecting lack of autonomy, stability, and differentiation of self in their lives. Their unconscious complexes emerged as *always* or *never* and *nothing-but* statements. They both accused each other of *always* complaining. Linda accused Michael of *always* patronizing her, and Michael accused Linda of being *nothing but* lazy and indolent. This is evident in his statement that "All you do is come home, sit on your ass, and bitch!" This seriously impaired their ability to negotiate their disagreement. The increased stress after two years of enacting their decisions led to the misunderstanding that caused their quarrel. Also evident was the heightened emotionality that typically accompanies the expression of unconscious complexes.

Quarrels have the same structure and cause no matter what Soul Images the couple may have: They are caused by a clash of complexes. Michael and Linda valued the separateness and autonomy in their relationship, and their mutual complexes created conflicts for them. Stress can be caused by any situation that threatens the stability of the relationship and the couple's ability to differentiate themselves within it. For Michael and Linda, the reality of the stresses of school and work caused them to misunderstand and misjudge each other. Their clash of complexes created their quarrel.

The Nature of This Love Relationship

It is easy to see why two Steadfast Lovers can be readily seen as prototypes for a mature love relationship. Their distinctive combination of stability, differentiation of self, and separateness, and their central focus on staying in love, are the mainstays of such an impression. Even their natural tendency to negotiate is in accord with the prevalent view of mature and adaptive relating. These Steadfast Lover qualities emerge in the love relationship as mutual affirmation and respect for each other's interests, beliefs, and values. Such an egalitarian outlook enables them to be relaxed, amiable, helpful, and cooperative with each other. At the same time, each partner is very attentive to and focused on fulfilling independent and autonomous desires and goals. It is important to remember, however, that Steadfast Lover–Steadfast Lover couples cannot be considered the prototype for a mature love relationship. Rather, theirs is one among *many* mature love relationships.

Steadfast Lover complexes emerged in the disagreement between Michael and Linda. Both were concerned about stability as well as finding a satisfying way of differentiating themselves. Their separateness and autonomy were central concerns in their plans for changing careers. The tense moments that occurred as the stress of an ambiguous future was discussed were successfully dealt with through negotiating with each other. This enabled them to maintain their important commitment to staying in love. With increased stress, however, their ability to negotiate was less successful.

Individual histories and circumstances may vary widely among Steadfast Lover couples, but the same complexes can be seen in their daily lives and in their quarrels. We hope you now have a better and deeper understanding of, appreciation for, and ability to appraise this kind of true love.

8 | *Innocent Lover and Steadfast Lover*

One works out a relationship, but one cultivates love.

R. C. Solomon, *About Love: Reinventing Romance in Our Times*

Although the Soul Images of Innocent and Steadfast Lovers are in most respects opposite, their complexes tend to complete and complement each other. For example, the Innocent Lover's desire to be loved and cherished fits comfortably with the Steadfast Lover's desire for the constancy of staying in love. Similarly, the Innocent Lover tends to identify important goals for the relationship, and the Steadfast Lover determines how these goals can be expressed. It is this balancing quality that gives the Innocent Lover–Steadfast Lover relationship its distinctiveness. The partners are typically comfortable, cooperative, caring, and secure. As a result, their different approaches to life can lead each to fulfill the other's hopes and expectations. There is often a clear differentiation of roles and responsibilities and a good deal of warmth, respect, and mutual caring in these relationships.

People who are in other kinds of relationships may mistakenly believe that Steadfast Lover–Innocent Lover relationships rest on a "power" difference—with the Steadfast Lover directing and dominating the couple's life and the Innocent Lover supporting and accommodating the partner's wishes. However, power—in the sense of one person dominating or controlling another—is irrelevant in this kind of relationship. Instead, there is a mutually gratifying conjunction of the complexes that emerge from each partner's Soul Image. Their complexes complement each other rather than being in opposition.

Couples whose Soul Images are opposite have quite different perspectives about many things. They do not share the same biases and sources of irritation, as do couples in which both partners have the same Soul Image. The differences in the sensitivities and hang-ups of Steadfast Lover–Innocent Lover couples are usually well known to both partners, who may learn to appreciate and benefit from each other's perspective. When this doesn't happen, their opposite focus can be the source of misunderstandings that may result in a clash of complexes leading to disagreements and quarrels.

The complexes that can be observed in these couples' day-to-day relationships are as follows: an emphasis on change and development of relationship for the Innocent Lover, as compared with stability and differentiation of self for the Steadfast Lover; relatedness and togetherness as the vehicles for forming personal identity for the Innocent Lover, contrasted with separateness and autonomy for the Steadfast Lover; cooperating as the natural way of resolving disagreements for the Innocent Lover and negotiating as the natural mode for the Steadfast Lover; and a focus on being loved as the central aspect of the love relationship for the

Innocent Lover, compared with staying in love for the Steadfast Lover.

A comparison of the characteristics of Innocent and Steadfast Lovers is provided in Chart 13 on pages 154 and 155. The next section describes how the complexes listed in the chart are expressed in the everyday lives of Innocent Lover–Steadfast Lover couples. To highlight the complexes being discussed, they are identified in the margin beside the relevant descriptions.

⟩ The Innocent Lover–Steadfast Lover Relationship

Of particular importance in understanding the sources of misperception and misunderstanding between Innocent and Steadfast Lovers is the fact that each person's way of looking at things seems so natural and self-evident that he or she assumes the beloved is operating from the same point of view. It isn't that they don't recognize that they and the beloved are different; rather, it's what they think the differences mean that is the issue. Each will interpret the meaning of the other person's behavior from his or her own perspective, implicitly asking, "What would *I mean* if I said or did that?"

For example, Innocent Lovers are likely to focus on future possibilities for change and development in their relationship. Such change and development occurs for them in the context of togetherness and relatedness with the beloved. Being valued and cherished by the beloved is therefore essential, and they want to have their partner's love for them demonstrated frequently. If their beloved seems distant or indifferent, an Innocent Lover can easily feel devalued and rejected.

In contrast, Steadfast Lovers focus on stability and differentiation of self in their relationship. Stability and differentiation occur within the context of the separateness and autonomy of each partner.

Chart 13

Comparison of Innocent and Steadfast Lovers

Central Relationship Question: Innocent Lovers

"If my sense of self is confirmed by my beloved in an intimate relationship, can I develop and have a sense of self when I am not being loved? It is an old adage that one only exists when one is loved. That's the way it is for me. My beloved's love for me is what sustains me and grants me the will and the energy to grow, develop, and be at one with the world. What I dread is the possibility that my beloved will no longer love me. If that happens, I will lose not only my sense of self, but also my dreams and goals for the future. It is for this reason that my beloved must confirm the love that sustains me. If not, I will truly be lost."

Attributes, Themes, and Complexes

Change	Change and growth toward a goal establish a connection to people and the world. Change has instrumental value.
Development of Relationship	Relationship results in the assurance that development toward mutual wholeness will occur.
Relatedness	A sense of selfhood comes from the relationship with the beloved.
Togetherness	Togetherness with the beloved is maintained by sharing projects, plans, and dreams for the future.
Cooperating	Cooperating is the natural way of resolving conflict and preserving the state of Being Loved.
Being Loved	The knowledge and comfort of being loved is the nourishment that will lead to change and growth.

Kind of Intimacy

Temperature	Warm—holding hands, touching, and physical closeness in private and public; use of terms of endearment.
Proximity	Close—deeply affected by the other's unspoken distress.

Expression of Psychic Energy

Focus	Broad—many expressions of love.
Intensity	Mild to strong expressions of love.

Chart 13

Comparison of Innocent and Steadfast Lovers (cont.)

Central Relationship Question: Steadfast Lovers

"How can I maintain my individuality and still be in a loving relationship? If I am a separate individual and I have a distinct identity, will I have to surrender or lose part of my identity and individuality to be in a loving relationship? After all, to be in a loving relationship means that I will have to take into consideration what my partner wishes and desires. I can't just do what I want without at least informing or consulting my partner. What's worse, suppose my partner objects to what I want or has a different preference? If I give in to that, doesn't that mean I will lose part of me?"

Attributes, Themes, and Complexes

Stability	Value is placed on constancy and continuity. Focus is on the refinement and expression of all facets of their selfhood.
Differentiation of Self	Focus is on differentiation—on the refinement and expression of all facets of their selfhood.
Separateness	Accept their partners as separate, independent individuals and want that same kind of acceptance for themselves.
Autonomy	Value independence, uniqueness, and distinctness from social and cultural environments.
Negotiating	Negotiating is the natural way of resolving differences and conflicts.
Staying in Love	Place high value on faithfulness and constancy in the love relationship.

Kind of Intimacy

Temperature	Cool—minimal physical contact, nonverbal and nonphysical expressions of affection, politeness in public.
Proximity	Close—deeply affected by the other's unspoken distress.

Expression of Psychic Energy

Focus	Broad—many expressions of love.
Intensity	Mild expressions of love.

Honoring each other's individuality and independence enhances the breadth and complexity of their expression of love. Having the beloved recognize and accept their respective differences is therefore very important. If a beloved seems insensitive to a Steadfast Lover's desire for independence, the Steadfast Lover's sense of him- or herself as a self-determined individual will feel threatened.

In typical Innocent Lover–Steadfast Lover partnerships, these different complexes, in combination with each partner's assumption of "similarity of motivation," influence the way the couple deal with everyday issues. We will see that sometimes a misinterpretation of the beloved's motivation won't create any difficulty at all—the important need or desire involved can still be satisfied. At other times, misinterpretation can lead to a clash of complexes that disrupts the relationship.

Managing money is one way in which their different complexes are complementary to each other. The Steadfast Lover partner is

Different Complexes
Relatedness vs. Separateness[1]
Togetherness vs. Autonomy

likely to approach managing money as a necessary *instrumental task* for dealing with everyday responsibilities. The Innocent Lover is more likely to focus on the *meaning* that money has for present and future togetherness. Therefore, an Innocent Lover is usually pleased when the Steadfast Lover partner is willing to be responsible for money management tasks. The Innocent Lover sees this as a sign of love.

Steadfast Lovers may be puzzled by, yet tolerant of, their Innocent Lover partner's attitude toward purchases. For example, Irwin, an Innocent Lover, is frequently accused by Melissa, his

Different Complexes
Relatedness vs. Separateness

Steadfast Lover wife, of being impractical. "I wouldn't mind so much if you actually used the things you buy," she said. "But you buy stuff, put it in the garage, and then buy something else. Sometimes you don't even open the box! You collect things as if they're toys you can play with for a while and then forget."

Irwin has difficulty expressing the value and meaning the purchases have for him. He agrees that he sometimes loses his enthusiasm for the things he buys. "But I use most of what I buy, and I really enjoy those things a lot. Besides, just because I haven't used something yet doesn't mean I never will," he says.

The purchases of Innocent Lovers are little ways of actualizing the future. A tool, a figurine, some sports equipment, a lamp, a coin collection—even a pair of socks—may be endowed with meaning from the past as well as an anticipation for the future. The purchases are ways of creating a bridge from the present to the future. This is difficult for a Steadfast Lover to appreciate, as the complex of Separateness makes such a connection irrelevant.

Just as Steadfast Lovers see their Innocent Lover partners as too free in spending money, so Innocent Lovers see Steadfast Lovers' concern with economizing and planning as unnecessarily controlling, and taking the fun out of life. Their opposite points of view, however, can yield a balanced approach that avoids either extreme position. The Steadfast Lover's vigilance about money can temper an Innocent Lover's potential for excessive spending; the Innocent Lover's approach can

Different Complexes
Change (Instrumental) vs. Stability
Development of Relationship vs. Differentiation of Self

remind the Steadfast Lover that spending for pleasure and meaningfulness is fun and allowable. On occasion, the Innocent Lover might enjoy forgoing something simply as a way of pleasing the Steadfast beloved; or the Steadfast Lover may buy something frivolous just for the fun of enjoying it with the Innocent beloved.

Here is another example of the effects of the different meanings of money for Innocent and Steadfast Lovers: Anna, an Innocent Lover, told Paul, her Steadfast Lover husband, that she thought she should know where he was investing their money so in case something happened to him, she would know

Different Complexes
Relatedness vs. Separateness

what to do and how to get access to it. In response, Paul spent four or five hours making up a seven-page report giving the names of accounts, their purpose, whom to contact, how much was in each account, and so on. He then gave Anna the report.

"She never read it and now isn't even sure where she put it," he related. He went on to explain, "I think in general when it comes to money she just wants to feel like she has some kind of connection to what I'm doing, rather than to know specifically what I have done or to evaluate my decisions and have any input into them."

Paul understood and accepted his wife's different approach to money. If he hadn't, a clash of complexes could have occurred. He might have accused Anna of making him waste his time, of not taking money matters seriously, and so on. Anna would probably have been hard put to explain the motivation for her request.

Opposite approaches in acquiring a sense of self can contribute to a unique kind of balance in Innocent Lover–Steadfast Lover relationships. For example, a Steadfast Lover partner is likely to prefer a division of labor, with each partner responsible for independently accomplishing different tasks. The Innocent Lover prefers doing things together, feeling that not sharing tasks is a missed opportunity for relating. He or she is therefore unlikely to initiate working on a task alone, so the Steadfast Lover may "remind" the Innocent Lover partner about what needs to be done. Even if the Steadfast Lover doesn't wish to work on the task together with the Innocent Lover, the Innocent Lover partner is likely to view the reminders as expressions of caring, not as autocratic demands.

Different Complexes
Relatedness vs. Separateness
Cooperating vs. Negotiating

When exaggerated, such behavior can be erroneously viewed as a parent-child kind of interaction. For example, Sylvia (a Steadfast Lover) and Scott (an Innocent Lover) invited Tony and Karen (both Mercurial Lovers) to a dinner party at their home. During the evening, Sylvia reminded Scott several times to check on the roast in the oven, and later prompted him to get the coffee and dessert as well. Whenever this happened, Tony and Karen exchanged knowing glances. On the way home from the dinner, they agreed that Scott certainly was a "henpecked husband." However, Scott didn't see it that way at all. He viewed Sylvia's reminders as a loving act of togetherness. Tony and Karen "empathized" with Scott as if he, like they, was a Mercurial Lover, and his independence and autonomy were being violated by a domineering wife.

Given their different complexes of Separateness and Relatedness, the Steadfast Lover can easily interpret an Innocent Lover's "asking for help" with tasks he or she could do alone as controlling, needy, or lazy. The Innocent Lover might feel rejected and put down by the Steadfast Lover's annoyance and refusal to cooperate. Fortunately, when particular household activities legitimately require both partners to cooperate, both complexes can be accommodated: The Innocent Lover can appreciate the intimacy of a shared experience, and the Steadfast Lover can enjoy the beloved's company while accomplishing a task.

Different Complexes
Relatedness vs. Separateness

Steadfast Lover–Innocent Lover couples also report that occasionally adopting the partner's approach to household responsibilities is a way of feeling closer to each other. The Innocent Lover can understand the pleasure the beloved gets from doing things alone, while the Steadfast Lover can experience the satisfaction of cooperating with the beloved. It is important for both partners to explicitly appreciate and acknowledge each other when they're making such efforts. They are then more likely to persist when they have to do things that go against their natural inclination.

Different Complexes
Relatedness vs. Separateness
Cooperating vs. Negotiating

The difference in sympathetic versus empathetic understanding can be a major source of discord in the communication of

Innocent Lover–Steadfast Lover couples. Innocent Lovers often assume that their Steadfast Lover partners are aware of their desires and feelings without being specifically told of them—

Different Complexes
Relatedness vs. Separateness

understanding through *sympathy*. When the Steadfast Lover fails to "know without being told," the Innocent Lover may feel unimportant and unloved. The Steadfast Lover, who relates through *empathy*, has to consciously imagine him- or herself in the partner's shoes to understand the other's inner experience. He or she must therefore be told what those feelings and desires are. From the perspective of the Steadfast Lover, the Innocent Lover's expectations of "foreknowledge" or "you should know how I feel" are unreasonable and impossible to fulfill.

The content and amount of information these couples communicate to each other is also influenced by their different complexes. For Innocent Lovers, the importance of discussing everything of interest to them stems from their

Different Complexes
Relatedness vs. Separateness
Togetherness vs. Autonomy
Cooperating vs. Negotiating

complexes of cooperating and togetherness. They want to solve problems and make decisions together with the beloved. For them, the fact that they are making decisions jointly is much more important than the decisions themselves. Therefore, even when they have the knowledge and competence to make a decision, they prefer involving the partner.

Since Steadfast Lovers focus on separateness, autonomy, and individuality, they may make decisions either together with the beloved or by themselves. Which approach is taken depends on the issue, their confidence in their abilities, and the availability of the partner at the time the decision needs to be made. They are therefore likely to interpret the Innocent Lover's need for discussion and joint decision making as a lack of self-confidence as well as distrust of the Steadfast Lover partner. "He wants to discuss almost everything with me. Why does he need my permission to make every little decision?" said one Steadfast Lover about her Innocent Lover husband. "And why does he get so upset when I go ahead and take care of things by myself? I wish he'd be more sure of himself and more trusting of me," she added.

Some Innocent Lover–Steadfast Lover couples have found that recognizing their very different approaches to communication can help them accept and accommodate each other's needs. During a lengthy and stressful moving trip from one state to another, Seth, an Innocent Lover, and Tomás, his Steadfast Lover partner, spent most of their energies dealing with moving problems and very little time talking to each other. Seth told Tomás that he "felt he couldn't connect to much of anything that was going on with him, and had a hard time with that lack of connection." Tomás suggested that they set aside a time each day to talk and reconnect with each other; and this greatly eased tensions for both partners.

It is also helpful for a Steadfast Lover to remember to consult his or her Innocent Lover partner on issues of moderate importance. In turn, the Innocent Lover partner can remember that the beloved's apparent unilateral decision making is stylistic rather than heavy-handed and uncaring. The couple are also likely to relish those times when circumstances support both their approaches. This occurs when a particular decision requires careful discussion, some independent information gathering, and then further discussion that leads to a joint decision. For example, a couple who had to find a new nursery school for their four-year-old daughter used this approach. They discussed what they thought were the important considerations; each independently visited and interviewed prospects; then they discussed things again and came to a joint decision.

Different Complexes
Cooperating vs. Negotiating
Togetherness vs. Autonomy

Many aspects of work—career choice, competence, satisfaction, and the like—are largely independent of a couple's Soul Images. Profound differences are likely to occur, however, in the relative importance that people with differing Soul Images give work versus the love relationship. Innocent Lovers, who believe that selfhood occurs only within relationships, are likely to see their work lives as secondary to the love relationship. For the Steadfast Lover, on the other hand, whose selfhood occurs

Different Complexes

Development of Relationship vs. Differentiation of Self

Togetherness vs. Autonomy

Being Loved vs. Staying in Love

through differentiation and refinement of individuality, work is a natural avenue for fulfillment. However, Innocent Lovers' focus on togetherness and being loved leads them to see their Steadfast Lover partner as *choosing* and *preferring* work over the relationship. With their natural sensitivity to indifference and emotional distance, Innocent Lovers are likely to interpret such "choices" as evidence that the Steadfast Lover partner does not fully value the love relationship.

Steadfast Lovers may readily acknowledge the greater, or at least equal, importance of work relative to the relationship. However, this fact is independent of their commitment to and enduring love for their partner. With their emphasis on staying in love, the depth and persistence of the love relationship is assumed and accepted as permanent. They don't feel the need to frequently reaffirm their feelings for the beloved. Indeed, they may be quite puzzled and impatient when their partners appear to need constant reassurance in this regard. They can easily misinterpret the partner's behavior as insecurity and childishness. At the same time, they may feel hurt and misunderstood because their beloved seems to lack trust in their love and in the depth and breadth of their commitment to the love relationship.

An Innocent Lover–Steadfast Lover couple can also be affected by the Innocent Lover's preference for harmonious, cooperative environments. As mentioned in our description of two Innocent Lovers (Chapter 6), Innocent Lovers can be unhappy in highly competitive and stressful work situations. If changes in the work setting don't improve such a situation, an Innocent Lover may change careers or stop working outside the home. Some Innocent Lovers switch from the career for which they were trained to a less competitive and more satisfying one. Others may build a former hobby into a home business, while still others may choose to be a stay-at-home partner at least for a time. In such a circumstance, having a Steadfast Lover partner can be a great asset for an Innocent

> **Different Complexes**
>
> *Development of Relationship vs. Differentiation of Self*
>
> *Cooperating vs. Negotiating*
>
> *Togetherness vs. Autonomy*

Lover: The Steadfast Lover partner may be quite pleased to have the freedom to pursue his or her career avidly, while at the same time being appreciated for supporting and encouraging the Innocent Lover's choices.

For example, Robert, an Innocent Lover, was acknowledged to be an excellent anesthesiologist. At the age of forty-five, and with the encouragement of his Steadfast Lover wife, Margaret, he cut his medical practice in half so he could devote more time to his hobby, ceramics. He built a studio at home and began taking on many more of the necessary household activities. Margaret very much appreciated having more time and freedom to pursue her accounting practice. She liked it that Robert was pursuing an artistic endeavor, and he felt he was fortunate to have a spouse who loved her work so much that she didn't mind if he earned a lot less money. Five years later, Margaret became a partner in her firm, and Robert left medicine entirely. This was a very stable and satisfying arrangement for both of them. However, not all couples are able to come to such a comfortable resolution.

Perhaps more than any other combination of Soul Images, Steadfast Lover–Innocent Lover couples can be the targets of our societal gender stereotypes. Steadfast Lovers are viewed as ambitious, driven, and determined people who care more for their work than for their families. Innocent Lovers, both men and women, are viewed as weak, needy, immature, childish, and unre-

Different Complexes
Relatedness vs. Separateness
Togetherness vs. Autonomy
Cooperating vs. Negotiating

alistic. A Steadfast Lover may believe that the Innocent Lover partner lacks drive and ambition and has a low tolerance for stress, while an Innocent Lover might see the Steadfast Lover as an overly ambitious, self-centered, and controlling workaholic.

Steadfast Lovers may also be uneasy if the Innocent Lover partner has difficulty settling on a stable career path. A young Steadfast Lover wife was concerned that her Innocent Lover husband lacked direction and feared that he would drift from one thing to another. She was therefore delighted when he expressed a clear resolve to become a physician and quickly accomplished what was needed in order to apply to medical school.

Steadfast Lovers who fail to recognize and appreciate their Innocent Lover partner's different approach to life may have an unfortunate impact on the partner's work situation. One

Different Complexes
Togetherness vs. Autonomy
Cooperating vs. Negotiating

Steadfast Lover husband frequently and emphatically advised his Innocent Lover wife to stand up for herself at work because he felt that her employer took advantage of her. She didn't interpret her employer's treatment of her in that way and very much enjoyed her work and work relationships. However, the distress she experienced from her husband's persistent complaints and criticism finally led her to quit her job and stay at home. Her husband then criticized her lack of aggressiveness in handling household affairs.

Innocent Lovers may also at times seem to be *over*committed to work, in the view of their Steadfast Lover partners. For example,

Different Complexes
Development of Relationship vs.
Differentiation of Self
Change (Instrumental) vs.
Stability

an Innocent Lover lawyer for a child advocacy organization frequently worked long hours and went out of town several times a month. Though she was torn between her desire to be with her husband

and her commitment to her work, the work usually won out. Her Steadfast Lover husband appreciated her work, but found that her schedule severely strained his own schedule of work and home responsibilities.

When the man is the Innocent Lover and the woman the Steadfast Lover, societal stereotypes of masculine and feminine roles can complicate the relationship even more. For example, a Steadfast Lover wife who had always been the major breadwinner in the family described her husband to her friends as "kind and gentle, but just not cut out to be a success in the real world." Another wife complained that her husband was never around to help her out at home because he couldn't say "no" to anyone else who asked for a favor. "Whoever gets to him first gets his time and attention," she told a friend. "Then when I get annoyed about it, he tries to make it up to me by being so helpful that it annoys me!"

For both Innocent and Steadfast Lovers, the love relationship is primary, but for quite different reasons. For Innocent Lovers, selfhood occurs only within a relationship in which they are loved and cherished above all else. For Steadfast Lovers, the intimate nature of the love relationship provides the opportunity to cultivate their own and each other's individuality. This interaction of their Soul Images supports the observation that many Innocent Lover–Steadfast Lover couples treat each other as their best friends. They very much enjoy each other's company—the Steadfast Lover for the pleasure of refining the relationship, and the Innocent Lover for the pleasure of the togetherness itself.

Different Complexes
Relatedness vs. Separateness
Togetherness vs. Autonomy

One way in which this aspect of the relationship may affect the couple can be seen when an Innocent Lover–Steadfast Lover couple divorce. Regardless of the circumstances, reasons, and other factors involved, the couple's relationship to each other after the divorce can be problematic. The Steadfast Lover would prefer a formal, distant, businesslike relationship focused on civility and the benefit of children, if there are any. For the Innocent Lover,

Different Complexes
Being Loved vs. Staying in Love
Cooperating vs. Negotiating

however, it may be difficult to suppress feelings of hurt, rejection, and loss. These may emerge in angry confrontations and vindictive acts, and possibly in attempts to influence the children against the Steadfast Lover spouse.

Whether this kind of couple have common friendships or individual, independent friendships is largely independent of their Soul Images. However, friendships are usually less important to both partners than their relationship to each other. The people with whom friendships are formed may be situational, like contacts with parents of similar-aged children and those made through work or important outside interests.

Innocent Lovers may find it satisfying, however, when their Steadfast Lover partner is interested in and involved with the Innocent Lover's friendships. Steadfast Lovers may not want to be included in these friendships; they are likely to be quite supportive

Different Complexes
Relatedness vs. Separateness
Together vs. Autonomy

of their partners' independent friendships as signs of autonomy, and they wouldn't want to intrude on these relationships. Nor do they want to include their Innocent Lover partners in many of their own friendships, as they welcome having time to pursue their own interests.

Some Steadfast Lovers, however, disparage the activities in which their Innocent Lover partners engage with friends. For example, Steadfast Lover women may refer to their partners' absorption in football or other sports as "playing with the boys." Steadfast Lover men, for their part, may make fun of their partners' shopping sprees and the amount of gossiping they engage in with their female friends. The temptation to engage in this kind of belittling of Innocent Lovers of both genders is strongly influenced by negative gender stereotypes that apply to both sexes.

Both Innocent and Steadfast Lovers are typically quite accepting of any opposite-sex friendships their partners may have. As long as both are secure in the primacy of their own love relationship, each tends to trust and feel secure in the stability and permanence of their relationship. If the Steadfast Lover is convinced that the love relationship is solid and enduring, and the Innocent Lover is sure of being loved, neither is likely to feel uncomfortable or jealous.

Different Complexes
Being Loved vs. Staying in Love

Innocent and Steadfast Lovers can have quite different perspectives about their sexual relationship. For the Innocent Lover, making love provides confirmation that he or she is loved. Frequent confirmation is desired, so when lovemaking is infrequent, it is seen as a threat to the love in the relationship. If the Innocent Lover's initiation of sex is rejected by the Steadfast Lover, this may be interpreted as indifference and emotional distancing. Steadfast Lovers may be somewhat puzzled by the importance that an Innocent Lover partner places on the frequency of sex. The Steadfast Lover emphasis on staying in love makes the frequency of lovemaking largely independent of confirming the love relationship; of greater import is the depth and breadth of the couple's experience and knowledge of each other. However, because Innocent Lovers don't assume that the partner's love is permanent and enduring, frequent verification of the love relationship is needed.

Different Complexes
Togetherness vs. Autonomy
Being Loved vs. Staying in Love

If the Steadfast Lover assumes that the Innocent Lover partner also focuses on staying in love, he or she can readily interpret the Innocent Lover partner's demand for frequent sex as self-indulgent and controlling—even though the Steadfast Lover may very much enjoy the experience. If enough affirmation of love through frequent sex doesn't occur for Innocent Lovers, they may become irritable, accusatory, and uncooperative. However, they quickly return to "normal" when their sexual desires are gratified by the Steadfast Lover partner.

Some Steadfast Lovers find that initiating lovemaking is the most effective way to restore good feeling, mutuality, and serenity in the relationship. One Steadfast Lover wife was puzzled when her Innocent Lover husband had intermittent periods of being extremely critical of her, complaining, and forgetful regarding household responsibilities. She finally realized that this nearly always occurred when, for one reason or another, they hadn't made love for a while. The next time she observed such an "episode," she tested her theory by initiating lovemaking. "It worked like a charm," she said. "The next day he was back to his usual loving, cooperative self."

Just as any two individuals can do the same thing for entirely different reasons, so can people with different Soul Images have different motivations for similar preferences and behaviors. Even when people have opposite complexes, as with Innocent and Steadfast Lovers, there may be subtle similarities in the way their preferences are manifested. An example of this occurs in the way this kind of couple relate to their extended families. Innocent Lovers are influenced by their complex of Relatedness, while Stability is the important operating complex for Steadfast Lovers. Their different complexes, however, lead to essentially the same approach to interactions with family.

For Innocent Lovers, relationships with parents, siblings, and other family members are important because they embody relat-

Complementary Complexes
Relatedness and Stability[2]

edness and harmony. They enjoy the warmth, closeness, and cooperation involved in their continuing connections to the family of origin. In contrast, Steadfast Lovers value the stability, permanence, and longevity associated with the extended family. Maintaining such relationships is an expression of the Steadfast Lover's values around responsibility, stability, and constancy. The Innocent Lover member of the couple may enjoy spending much more time with family members than does the Steadfast Lover, for whom visits and phone calls may be obligatory and not especially enjoyable.

For example, Nat, a Steadfast Lover, described his approach to his family as, "If you need me, I'm always there. But if you don't need me, you will probably hear from me only sporadically." Once when his brother was going through a hard time, Nat called him twice a week until the crisis passed. Then he went back to talking to his brother every few months. In contrast, his Innocent Lover wife, Ellen, has a different attitude toward her family: "Even if you don't need help, I'll be there anyway." She keeps in touch regularly with her parents and siblings—and she has the same kind of strong connection with the members of Nat's family. "Even if you died," she told Nat, "I'd have the same relationship with your family that I have now."

Vacation visits to family may be eagerly anticipated by the Innocent Lover and approached with some resignation by the Steadfast Lover partner. Some Steadfast Lovers may interpret the Innocent Lover's frequent contacts with family as somewhat immature and dependent. He or she may resent the partner's confiding in and seeking family members' advice, judging such involvement as intrusive. Steadfast Lover partners tend to be more comfortable being asked for help and advice by family members than requesting such help from them.

Different Complexes
Relatedness vs. Separateness
Togetherness vs. Autonomy

The similarity between the Innocent Lover complex of relatedness and the Steadfast Lover complex of stability influences their recreational interests. Involvement in civic and humanitarian pursuits may appeal to the Innocent Lover's focus on harmony, cooperation, and group problem solving, while the Steadfast Lover partner may be attracted to similar civic activities

Complementary Complexes
Relatedness and Stability

as a way of maintaining important societal values and being a responsible member of the community. Both partners are likely to enjoy the opportunity to participate together in the same important activities.

In general, Innocent Lovers are more willing to choose recreation over added work, and may see Steadfast Lovers as overly serious and task-oriented. However, sometimes this perception can be reversed: Some Innocent Lovers may, from a Steadfast Lover's point of view, become overinvolved and extreme in their devotion to a social cause that isn't work-related. This can be a source of dissension between them. The Innocent Lover can interpret the Steadfast Lover's reservations as criticism and lack of support, while the Steadfast Lover may resent the Innocent Lover's single-minded devotion to one thing as causing a corresponding neglect of other important areas. The Steadfast Lover may try to be as supportive as possible, however, if he or she is sympathetic to the "cause" and recognizes the passionate devotion of the spouse.

Neither partner is likely to favor separate vacations, unless they are connected to some work activity. Being together with the beloved adds to the experience of constancy and wholeness for the Steadfast Lover and promotes a sense of harmony and caring in the relationship for the Innocent Lover. The Steadfast Lover's desire for separateness and independence isn't relevant when it comes to relaxation and recreation, and this approach fits comfortably with the Innocent Lover's focus on the relationship itself.

Complementary Complexes
Relatedness and Differentiation of Self
Togetherness and Stability

Some Steadfast Lovers may enjoy some kind of solitary recreational activity, such as backpacking alone. Even though an Innocent Lover partner may be supportive of the occasional solo outings of the Steadfast Lover partner, the Steadfast Lover may experience conflict between the

Different Complexes
Cooperating vs. Negotiating
Togetherness vs. Autonomy

desire for separateness and responsibilities to the love relationship. Such a conflict may be a source of distress for Steadfast Lovers regardless of the partner's Soul Image. But it can be particularly problematic with an Innocent Lover partner, whose desires for togetherness may be keenly apparent to the Steadfast Lover.

As described in Chapter 6, Innocent Lovers like having a warm, close, and trusting relationship with their children. They tend to be actively involved in their children's lives and want to maintain a close relationship with them for as long as possible. Innocent Lover parents often expect from and value in their children the same things as they do from and in their beloved—to love them and be warmly loved in return, and to value the relationship above other considerations. They therefore may become hurt, accusatory, and punitive when their children pull away from them or are disobedient or disrespectful. They experience this as indifference and emotional distance.

> **Different Complexes**
> Relatedness vs. Separateness
> Togetherness vs. Autonomy

Because of their sensitivity to the nuances of their relationship with their children, Innocent Lover parents may vacillate between overindulgence and dominance. Their inconsistency in this regard can call forth critical comments by the Steadfast Lover spouse. Steadfast Lover parents emphasize and encourage independence, resilience, and responsibility in their children. From this perspective, an Innocent Lover spouse seems overly involved in the children's lives. From a Steadfast Lover viewpoint, being too involved, too indulgent, or excessively directive and controlling can impede the child's development of self-confidence, independence, and good judgment. One Steadfast Lover mother said to her Innocent Lover husband, "Amy is only five years old! It's ridiculous for you to get your feelings hurt and pout because she wants to play with her friend instead of you. You're not her friend, you're her father!"

For their part, Innocent Lovers may feel that their Steadfast Lover spouses are too demanding of and distant toward the children. The Innocent Lover can interpret the spouse's desire to remain minimally involved in the child's daily life as a lack of caring and concern; the Steadfast Lover parent, however, believes that such an approach helps foster responsibility and independence in the child.

Steadfast Lover fathers may feel like "outsiders" in a situation where an Innocent Lover mother seems overinvolved with her children. For these Steadfast Lovers, the love relationship may not progress in depth and complexity if the beloved's energies are devoted primarily to her relationship with her children. In contrast, Steadfast Lover mothers can see having an Innocent Lover spouse as "like having another child to deal with." They wouldn't likely complain about his overinvolvement with the children, but rather object to his inconsistent and contradictory parenting.

One kind of "typical" marriage that was prevalent in the United States prior to the 1960s probably describes a caricature of couples with an Innocent Lover wife and a Steadfast Lover husband. In those relationships, the husband is the primary breadwinner and the responsible, mature decision maker; his wife is charmingly naive, impractical, somewhat self-centered, and lovable. Relationships with a male Innocent Lover and a female Steadfast Lover were looked upon negatively during that era. Disparaging comments might be made by some women about their husbands' lack of ambition, irresponsibility, and childishness.[3] More moderate forms of such assessments are still seen in the way both of these kinds of relationships are often viewed today.

Others tend to see Innocent Lover–Steadfast Lover relationships as comfortably stable but unequal. The Steadfast Lover partner may be seen as overly controlling and "parental," and the Innocent Lover partner as overly dependent and childlike.

Mercurial and Romantic Lovers may find it difficult to appreciate the kind of pleasure and contentment these relationships provide for the partners, as reflected in the following story:

Sylvia (a Steadfast Lover) and Scott (an Innocent Lover) were invited to a dinner party at the home of friends. They were both looking forward to going. However, on the morning of the day of the party, Scott felt ill. His symptoms worsened during the day, and he told Sylvia that he felt too sick to go to the party.

"Well then, I guess we can't go," said Sylvia. "Why don't you go lie down and get some rest. I've been wanting to cook a big pot of soup, anyway. I'll go to the store to get the vegetables. And while I'm out, I might as well check out a few appliance stores and see what kinds of refrigerators they have, since we've been talking about getting a new one."

"I thought we were going to do that together," said Scott somewhat plaintively. "I know you like looking around yourself, but couldn't you wait till I'm feeling better so I could go with you? I'd really like it if you stayed here with me while I'm feeling so rotten."

Sylvia shrugged. "Okay," she said. "I'll just go to the grocery store, and then I'll come right back. If you feel better tomorrow, we can look at refrigerators then."

The Clash of Complexes

As can be seen in the discussion and examples in this chapter, there are many occasions for a clash of complexes between Innocent Lover and Steadfast Lover partners. Because they differ on every complex and in ways that can be easily seen as gender-related, they support the saying "opposites attract."

Complexes need not be opposite for them to clash in a disruptive way. In the following scenario, the Innocent Lover's use of cooperating and the Steadfast Lover's use of negotiating to resolve disagreements set the stage for a continuing misunderstanding for Patrick, a Steadfast Lover, and his wife, Cheryl, an Innocent Lover.

Phase One: The Disagreement

- As a disagreement continues with no resolution, tension increases.
- The persistence and increase of tension cause misunderstanding.
- Sustained tension and misunderstanding cause stress.

Patrick and Cheryl had been married for eight years, and were viewed by friends and family members as having a close, comfortable, and cooperative relationship. They seemed to see eye-to-eye on just about everything and rarely argued. Cheryl planned to return to work part-time after taking off three years following the birth of their son, Justin. They agreed that Justin would go to nursery school while Cheryl worked, so she identified three possible schools based on information from friends. Patrick and Cheryl visited these schools on a Thursday when Patrick took the afternoon off from work. They planned to discuss their impressions and make a decision that night after Justin was in bed, when they had the following conversation:

Patrick: Well, what do you think? I really liked that first one where the kids were all busy doing a lot of different things and the teachers didn't interfere.

Cheryl: Yes, that place may be okay, but the adults didn't seem to be paying all that much attention to the children. I saw one boy grab a truck away from a smaller boy, and the teacher saw it and didn't do anything.

Patrick: Yeah, I guess that happens. Did you notice the really sturdy playground equipment? I wish ours was that good.

Cheryl: I really liked the last place. There weren't so many children, and the teachers seemed to be really warm and interested in the kids. I watched the head teacher patiently tie shoelaces for six little boys one after another, and she treated each child as though he was special. I really admire that.

Patrick: Yes, that place seemed good, too. What about the second one, though? Have you ever seen such disorganization? I can't understand why the Fongs said we should look at it.

Cheryl: It certainly was disorganized and messy, and probably dangerous, too! The Fongs had their youngest child there two years ago. It must have changed hands.

Patrick: Well, then we agree that the first one would be the most stimulating for Justin. It would give him good experience in working things out with other kids. That's really important for him, don't you agree?

Cheryl: I guess we can try it out and see.

Patrick: Good. I think that one costs a little more, but it'll be worth it. Can you take care of registering him?

Cheryl: Sure. I'll do it tomorrow, and he can start on Monday.

In the above exchange, Patrick and Cheryl appear to be in comfortable agreement with each other. Note, however, that Patrick doesn't actually take Cheryl's concerns and preferences seriously—he makes passing reference to them and then promotes his own criteria for choosing a school. Cheryl's focus on accommodating hinders her from being more forceful in asserting her desires.

Justin started at the first nursery school they had seen the following Monday. He seemed to like it a lot, becoming especially attached to one of the young assistant teachers. Cheryl started a part-time job in customer service, but found it a little hard to give it her full attention, as she constantly worried about Justin. She told herself that she was being silly and that she would get used to him being without her.

When she picked Justin up from school on Friday, he started to cry as soon as they got in the car. He clung to her and said, "I don't want to go to school anymore, Mommy. I want to stay home with you."

"I thought you really liked school," said Cheryl. "Did something happen today?"

"Jason pushed me and Turner grabbed my cookie and I was afraid to tell the teacher because yesterday she made fun of Cindy when she cried," said Justin.

Cheryl comforted her son as best she could, and they went home. As soon as Justin was safely playing in his room, she called Patrick at work. He could tell at once that something was wrong.

Phase Two: The Quarrel

- Persistent misunderstanding and stress consume large amounts of energy, and can be exhausting.

- Sustained fatigue and stress jeopardize the ability to integrate and respond to the issues.

- Fatigue and stress continue to consume more energy.

- Negative aspects of the participants' Soul Images are evoked.

Patrick: Are you upset about something, honey?

Cheryl: Upset doesn't even come close. I'm so mad at you I can hardly stand to hear your voice!

(She angrily relates what has transpired. Patrick listens quietly.)

Cheryl: Now we have a child who's afraid of other kids and doesn't trust adults. He'll never want to go to school! I knew we shouldn't send him to that place!

Patrick: But we agreed it was the best place for him. How could we know this would happen?

Cheryl: We *didn't* agree. *You* decided, and I went along with it because you seemed so set on it and it apparently meant so much to you for Justin to get *stimulated.* Some stimulation!

Patrick (puzzled): But I distinctly remember us agreeing. We always discuss things and listen to each other and come to a mutual agreement. That's one of the best things about us.

Cheryl: Wrong! I wind up saying I agree even when I don't just to keep the peace. You never hear me when I give my opinion—just like you didn't about the nursery school. I said they didn't pay attention to the kids at this one and that I liked the last one better. You just ignored me and pushed for what *you* wanted. You always do that!

Patrick: I had no idea you felt that way, Cheryl. You mean all this time when I thought we were agreeing, you were really just going along for my benefit?

Cheryl (softening): Well, not really all the time. But pretty often.

Patrick: I'm really sorry. I'll try to be a better listener from now on, and if I do what I've been doing again, please tell me loud and clear. It's very important to me to know what you really think.

Cheryl: Okay, I promise I'll let you know from now on.

Several important complexes were activated for Cheryl and Patrick when they had to make the important decision regarding which school to trust with their child. Both wanted to ensure that Justin would receive the kind of care and attention that they felt was necessary for his upbringing. As we can infer from the scenario, however, the couple had developed a stable, predictable, and cooperative way of reaching agreement with each other. Unfortunately, Cheryl's unconscious complex emerged when she accused Patrick of *always* making the decisions. Cheryl saw herself as *always* cooperating while her husband did the deciding. For his part, Patrick's unconscious complex emerged when he viewed their relationship as *always* one of negotiating and cooperating.

The disparity in their contributions came to light only when the stress associated with her child's unhappiness provoked Cheryl to overcome her cooperative stance. She then "let Patrick have it" in an exaggerated, complex-ridden way. Note, however, that once she knew that Patrick truly understood what had happened, she modified her *always* and *never* statements to a more conscious, accurate, and fair *sometimes* statement. She was thus once again able to willingly cooperate with him.

Cheryl and Patrick's story illustrates how the comfortable stability created by opposite but compatible complexes can be taken for granted by both members of a couple. The same kind of misunderstanding that characterized their interaction can happen with other complexes as well. It is only when something happens to disrupt the compatibility of the complexes that a clash occurs. Often, as was the case for Patrick and Cheryl, the new awareness of each other they gain in such a clash can further differentiation of self for the Steadfast Lover and development of relationship for the Innocent Lover.

The Nature of This Love Relationship

The serenity and constancy of Innocent Lover–Steadfast Lover relationships comes from the opposite but mutually satisfying nature of their central complexes. The Innocent Lover strives for change (instrumental) as the vehicle for achieving important goals, and the Steadfast Lover's focus on stability enables those goals to be achieved. There is a mutual appreciation of the different ways each pursues a sense of self—through differentiation for the Steadfast Lover and through development of relationship for the Innocent Lover. The natural proclivity of the Innocent Lover for cooperating and the Steadfast Lover's propensity for negotiating are the vehicles for compromise and mutual satisfaction in areas that might be expected to promote conflict. In addition, being loved for the Innocent Lover and staying in love for the Steadfast Lover harmonize easily with each other.

Complexes and combinations of complexes were revealed in the argument between Cheryl and Patrick. A persistent misunderstanding in their relationship came to light when external stress increased for Cheryl, which led to the triggering of unconscious complexes in the form of *nothing-but* and *always* or *never* statements. The brevity and easy resolution of their conflict illustrate the benefit that can be gained when complexes clash openly. Cheryl's distress and anger about her son caused her to temporarily give up cooperating and lash out at Patrick. This clash of complexes provided them with the opportunity to clarify an important aspect of their relationship. Had Cheryl suppressed her feelings on this occasion and behaved "cooperatively," her resentment and anger would have built up over time and likely erupted eventually in an extreme and destructive manner.

Individual histories and circumstances may vary widely among Innocent Lover–Steadfast Lover couples, but the same complexes can be seen in their daily lives and in their quarrels. We hope you now have a better and deeper understanding of, appreciation for, and ability to appraise this kind of true love.

9 | *Mercurial Lover and Romantic Lover*

You can't worship love and individuality in the same breath. . . .
You have to balance love and individuality, and actually sacrifice
a portion of each.

D. H. Lawrence, *Love Was Once a Little Boy*

In the preceding chapter, we saw that a couple composed of the opposite Soul Images of Innocent Lover and Steadfast Lover often complete and fulfill each partner's desires and expectations, and in this way provide balance in the relationship. Mercurial and Romantic Lovers also have Soul Images that are opposite in most respects, but the balance in this kind of relationship is different. Rather than completing each other, Mercurial and Romantic Lovers temper each other's opposite qualities. For example, the Romantic Lover provides a tempering stability to the Mercurial

Lover's ardent faith in change, while by introducing the beloved to the joy and excitement of change, the Mercurial Lover tempers the Romantic Lover's poignant attentiveness to the present. The exchange of energies stimulated by this activity provides both the tension and the vitality that give Mercurial Lover–Romantic Lover relationships their distinctive character. What can emerge from the interplay of energies is an understanding and acceptance of each other's complexes. Although such a state of affairs is desirable for partners in all of the ten love relationships, it is particularly challenging for Mercurial Lover–Romantic Lover couples. This is because there is little or no overlap or natural conjunction in their opposite complexes.

Others may observe and infer that there is a good deal of explicit and implicit conflict and dissatisfaction in Mercurial Lover–Romantic Lover couples. As a result, these relationships are often judged to be quite unstable. Depending on the Soul Image of an observer, the Mercurial Lover may be seen as either controlled and stifled by the partner or detached and insensitive in the relationship; the Romantic Lover may be viewed as either unappreciated and misunderstood or demanding and critical. The partners themselves may at times make these same kinds of assessments of themselves and each other. It is in struggling with and accepting the value of their differences that a satisfying harmony emerges in the relationship.

The complexes that can be observed in the relationships of Mercurial Lover–Romantic Lover couples are as follows: the importance of change (intrinsic) and transformation of self for Mercurial Lovers, as compared with stability and enhancement of the relationship for Romantic Lovers; separateness and autonomy as the vehicles for forming a personal identity for Mercurial Lovers, contrasted with relatedness and togetherness for Romantic Lovers; discussing as the preferred way to resolve disagreements for Mercurial Lovers, and accommodating as the natural mode for Romantic Lovers; and a focus on falling in love for Mercurial Lovers, as compared with being in love for Romantic Lovers.

A comparison of the characteristics of Mercurial and Romantic Lovers is provided in Chart 14 on pages 184 and 185. The next section describes how the complexes listed in the chart are expressed in the everyday lives of Mercurial Lover–Romantic Lover couples. To highlight the complexes being discussed, they are identified in the margin beside the relevant descriptions.

The Mercurial Lover–Romantic Lover Relationship

Perhaps more than in any other kind of love relationship, Mercurial Lover–Romantic Lover couples easily and inadvertently hurt each other's feelings. The Romantic Lover may feel accused of being weak, dependent, and lacking a clear sense of self; the Mercurial Lover may feel accused of being bad, mean, or insensitive. Mercurial Lovers may feel coerced and restrained and may suspect that the beloved wants both partners to be united and indistinguishable. The Romantic Lover may feel that the loving connection in the relationship is absent, and that the beloved is indifferent and wants to maintain distance and separateness in the relationship. Virtually all of their different complexes contribute to these perceptions. The accusations and hurt feelings of each partner are in response to feeling misunderstood.

An important area of misunderstanding lies in the partners' differing attitudes about the importance of work relative to the importance of the love relationship. For Mercurial Lovers, work can be an arena for exercising separateness and autonomy, as well as for experiencing transformation of self. For Romantic Lovers, work is not directly connected to the complexes of relatedness and

Chart 14

Comparison of Mercurial and Romantic Lovers

Central Relationship Question: Mercurial Lovers

"If I am a separate, changing individual, how can I merge with a beloved in an intimate, loving relationship? Change and the flux of life sustain me with vigor, further my transformation, and engage me with life's possibilities. Yet this isn't enough. I also need the exhilaration of love through merging with my beloved. As much as I desire the passion of love, however, I also fear my beloved's love. My fear is that my beloved may innocently entice me to a life of predictability, comfort, and routine that will end in a suffocating and deadly inertia. If this happens, I will indeed lose my soul and I will become like an automaton in a Kafka novel."

Attributes, Themes, and Complexes

Change	Any change is good in itself. Change has intrinsic value.
Transformation of Self	Focus on a future filled with the potential for change and transformation.
Separateness	View their identity and sense of self as unique and distinct from relationships.
Autonomy	Value independence and autonomy; resist restrictions on freedom and are sensitive to any hint of coercion from others.
Discussing	Value explorative communication and discussing the relationship and what it means.
Falling in Love	Revel in the intensity and novelty of the experience of love.

Kind of Intimacy

Temperature	Hot—passionate sexual activity; kissing and caressing in public.
Proximity	Distant—unawareness of the unspoken distress or joy of the partner.

Expression of Psychic Energy

Focus	Broad—many expressions of love.
Intensity	Mild to strong expressions of love.

Chart 14

Comparison of Mercurial and Romantic Lovers (cont.)

Central Relationship Question: Romantic Lovers

"If my sense of self and identity is constituted by my relationship with my beloved, can I have a sense of self and fulfillment when I am alone? I can only be a complete human being if I am in a loving relationship with my beloved. For only through our love can we each lose our separateness from the world and become one with the world. Only then can 'I' become a 'We,' and then another new and true 'Me.' What happens then if I am separated from my beloved? Do I still exist? Will I no longer feel joy and pleasure? Will I be devoid of any sense of who I am? That prospect truly frightens me. If it occurs, I will be truly afflicted with a lovesickness.

Attributes, Themes, and Complexes

Stability	Value constancy, permanence, and completeness in the relationship with the beloved.
Enhancement of Relationship	Believe selfhood consists of differentiation of the relationship with the beloved.
Relatedness	Sense of identity or selfhood comes from the relationship with the beloved.
Togetherness	Emphasis is on participating in and sharing all aspects of their lives as expressions of togetherness.
Accommodating	Accommodation is the natural way of resolving conflicts and preserving the state of Being in Love.
Being in Love	Focus is on all the ways the love experience can be shared and enhanced with the beloved.

Kind of Intimacy

Temperature	Hot—passionate sexual activity; kissing and caressing in public.
Proximity	Close—deeply affected by the other's unspoken distress.

Expression of Psychic Energy

Focus	Narrow—focused expressions of love.
Intensity	Strong expressions of love.

togetherness, and it does not enhance the relationship. The satisfaction Romantic Lovers obtain from their work is related to personal enhancement through enacting important values. However, they tend to dislike it when their own or their beloved's work disrupts the love relationship. For Mercurial Lovers, the value of work and relationship is more nearly equal. As a result, Mercurial Lovers may feel torn between important complexes that can best be fulfilled in their independent work lives and the desire for a fulfilling intimate relationship.

> **Different Complexes**
> Separateness vs. Relatedness
> Autonomy vs. Togetherness
> Transformation of Self vs.
> Enhancement of Relationship

One Mercurial Lover was distressed at his Romantic Lover partner's lack of understanding of the demands of his work. He often complained to her about his stress and frustration at work but felt that she did not realize how important the job was for him in spite of its stresses. "I love the excitement and challenge it gives me," he explained. "I know you love your work, but you have an easier time letting go of it at the end of the day than I do. Work is a central part of who I am." "I know," she replied. "I wouldn't want you to be dissatisfied at work. It's just that you think nothing of dropping our plans to take care of some crisis at work. You seem to choose work over our relationship."

The intrinsic value of change for Mercurial Lovers and the opposite value of stability for Romantic Lovers may also have an impact on their choices of work settings.

> **Different Complexes**
> Change (Intrinsic) vs. Stability
> Transformation of Self vs.
> Enhancement of Relationship

Mercurial Lovers are likely to be attracted to the excitement of new enterprises and work settings with rapid change and growth. Reorganizations, frequent crises, and instability often characterize such settings. Others see Mercurial Lovers as ambitious because of the energy they devote to their complex of change and its connection to transformation of self. Romantic Lovers, on the other hand, choose work that provides them with ways to express their important values. They aren't attracted to the kinds of challenges that appeal to Mercurial Lovers. However, Romantic Lovers may find a way to enhance their sense of themselves through their work.

Mercurial Lovers may mistakenly believe that if the Romantic Lover partner had to function in the same kind of environment as the Mercurial Lover, he or she would be more understanding and accepting. Experience doesn't usually bear out this hope. Excitement, challenge, and lively discussions will be appealing only if the work involved is clearly in accord with the values of the Romantic Lover. He or she is therefore likely to leave chaotic work settings where accommodating doesn't resolve difficulties. Rather than understanding the attractiveness of such environments for the Mercurial Lover partner, he or she may be even more puzzled when the partner seems to value such a work situation over the relationship.

Different Complexes
Discussing vs. Accomodating

Household tasks don't seem to have as much potential for causing tension in the relationship as does the issue of work. In dealing with household responsibilities, Mercurial Lovers generally like to accomplish what is necessary independently, while Romantic Lovers enjoy working on tasks together. Doing chores together doesn't have the special meaning for a Mercurial Lover that it does for a Romantic Lover. This is usually only a minor source of disagreement if the Romantic Lover is comfortable with the time the couple spend together and the Mercurial Lover has sufficient time for independent activities. The partners are then quite willing to work either together or separately without difficulty.

Different Complexes
Separateness vs. Togetherness
Transformation of Self vs. Enhancement of Relationship

At times, however, this difference can exacerbate a difficult situation. For example, a Mercurial Lover had been putting in extremely long weekdays and weekends at work for several months, leaving little time to spend with her Romantic Lover husband, who was unhappy but tried to be accepting of the situation. They agreed that on the first free weekend that occurred, they would tackle some overdue projects around the house. When that weekend arrived, the Romantic Lover husband was hurt, resentful, and angry when the Mercurial Lover wife suggested that it would be most efficient to divide up the chores and accomplish them separately. He accused her of "avoiding me even when you don't have work as an excuse. All your energy goes for work and none for us." His Mercurial Lover wife was equally hurt, resentful, and angry at this reaction. "I'm just trying to get these household things out of the way so we can enjoy ourselves," she exclaimed. "It has nothing to do with not wanting to be with you!" For the Romantic Lover, the household projects were an opportunity to enhance and reestablish the love in the relationship; but this effort provided no transformative opportunities for the Mercurial Lover.

The meaning of money for Mercurial Lover–Romantic Lover couples is linked most clearly to Mercurial Lover complexes of intrinsic change and autonomy and Romantic Lover complexes of stability and togetherness. Mercurial Lovers tend to prefer separate checking accounts and are uncomfortable with the idea of merging their independently earned money. Doing so might put their independence and autonomy in jeopardy and restrict their freedom of choice. For the Romantic Lover, however, jointly held money represents a commitment to the togetherness of the relationship. It affirms the stability and permanence of the couple's love for each other and verifies the complex of being in love. How money is dealt with neither enhances nor detracts from the Mercurial Lover's corresponding complex of falling in love.

How money is spent can be an area of agreement and pleasure for the couple. Mercurial Lovers are comfortable spending money

> **Different Complexes**
>
> Change (Intrinsic) vs. Stability
> Autonomy vs. Togetherness
> Falling in Love vs. Being in Love

freely and spontaneously. For Romantic Lovers, spending money is connected to the meaning the expenditure has for the relationship. Their thoughtful "gifts of love" often please the Mercurial Lover partner, especially when the romantic meaning of the gift also addresses important complexes of the Mercurial Lover. When that is not the case, however, the Mercurial Lover may appear insensitive to the meaningfulness of an experience for the beloved. For example, a Romantic Lover husband commented that when he and his Mercurial Lover wife go out to dinner, "All she's interested in is eating, and she doesn't care what kind of wine we have or even where we eat dinner much of the time. She just gobbles down her food and it's over. There is nothing relaxing and conversational about the dinner. She just wants to get it over with."

Different Complexes
Transformation of Self and Accommodating
Falling in Love vs. Being in Love

For some other couples, the Romantic Lover's tendency to demonstrate love through expensive dinners, gifts, or holiday trips can fit well with the Mercurial Lover's focus on falling in love. Disagreement may sometimes occur, however, when the couple must choose between spending money on individual pursuits versus things that enhance the relationship itself. In such circumstances, the Mercurial Lover may feel constrained and controlled, and the Romantic Lover may feel unimportant and unloved.

The complexes of discussing and accommodating are pervasive in the way Mercurial and Romantic Lovers communicate. Mercurial Lovers favor open communication and active discussion of issues in the relationship, including the acceptability of renegotiating the relationship from time to time. Such discussing and renegotiating can rekindle the feeling of falling in love for a Mercurial Lover. To a Romantic Lover, discussing and renegotiating the relationship can threaten the important complexes of stability and

Different Complexes
Discussing vs. Accommodating
Change (Intrinsic) vs. Stability
Falling in Love vs. Being in Love

being in love. Romantic Lovers assume that the power of their love can overcome disagreements and minimize anything that might disrupt the relationship. Anything wrong or hurtful can be eradicated by the experience and expression of love. This belief on the part of Romantic Lovers underlies their tendency to avoid the direct expression of anger toward the beloved. Expressing anger inhibits feelings of love, and their hope is that by suppressing feelings of anger and continuing to be loving and accommodating, harmony and the state of being in love will be restored. Mercurial Lover partners often become quite sensitive to subtle signs of the beloved's withheld anger. They may interpret a Romantic Lover partner's unusual silence or lack of enthusiasm as a passive communication that the Mercurial Lover has done something wrong. Mercurial Lovers may erroneously see such behavior as passive-aggressive attempts at control on the part of Romantic Lovers. In doing so, they misunderstand the true nature of the Romantic Lover's attempts to accommodate in order to maintain love and harmony. One Mercurial Lover was so frustrated with her husband's perceived passivity that she said, "What I feel like doing is beating on his chest so I can get some reaction!"

Mercurial and Romantic Lovers may have individual friendships as well as relationships with couples with whom they socialize. Mercurial Lovers often continue friendships that were important to them before they knew the Romantic Lover. For Romantic Lovers, however, the friendships that preceded the love relationship may diminish in importance as their energies become focused on being in love with the beloved. They may therefore spend less time with individual friends than will Mercurial Lovers. This can be a source of difficulty for the couple if the amount of time a Mercurial Lover spends with friends seems disproportionate and excessive to the Romantic Lover. Romantic Lovers may feel about

Different Complexes
Separateness vs. Relatedness
Autonomy vs. Togetherness
Falling in Love vs. Being in Love

the beloved's friendships the same way they feel about the Mercurial Lover's work—that something else is more important to the partner than the togetherness and relatedness of the relationship. In the absence of extremes with regard to friends, however, there is usually little disagreement.

In general, Mercurial Lover–Romantic Lover couples enjoy spending time together as a couple. For Mercurial Lovers, who tend to like variety and change, doing new and different things with their beloved is very appealing. For the Romantic Lover partner, the nature of an experience is generally secondary to the togetherness it permits. In experiencing things together— be they recreational activities, vacation spots, or meeting new people—Mercurial

Complementary Complexes

Autonomy and Enhancement of Relationship

Change (Intrinsic) and Togetherness

Lovers' and Romantic Lovers' complexes can be very much in accord. Some Mercurial Lovers, however, may at times become impatient with and even somewhat disdainful toward the recreational preferences of the Romantic Lover partner. This can feel hurtful to the Romantic Lover, who may accuse the Mercurial Lover partner of being negative and cynical. In turn, the Mercurial Lover may view the Romantic Lover as being unrealistic and Pollyannaish.

For example, Theresa, a Romantic Lover, and Andrew, her Mercurial Lover husband, were invited to a dinner party at the home of friends. They were both looking forward to going. However, on the morning of the day of the party, Andrew felt ill. His symptoms worsened during the day, and he told Theresa that he felt too sick to go to the party.

"I'll call and tell them we can't make it," said Theresa.

"Listen," said Andrew. "Why don't you go anyway? Diane's been your best friend for years, and you haven't seen her and Christopher and the others in a long time. I'll be fine staying here."

"I really couldn't go without you," replied Theresa. "I'll stay here with you. I wouldn't enjoy the evening if you weren't with me."

"Why not?" asked Andrew in an exasperated tone. "I'd go without you if you were sick and it was my best friend. I just don't understand why we always have to do things together!"

"Okay, I'll go without you if that will make you happy," Theresa replied.

However, early that evening Theresa told Andrew that she didn't really want to go to the party. Andrew shrugged his shoulders in resignation, and the two spent an uncomfortably silent evening together.

In this example, Theresa tried to accommodate Andrew's notion that he and Theresa were separate and autonomous individuals.

Different Complexes
Autonomy vs. Togetherness
Discussing vs. Accommodating

Her agreement to go to the party alone led Andrew to believe that he had convinced her by discussing the matter. In the end, however, her desire for togetherness in the relationship was more important to Theresa. This Mercurial Lover–Romantic Lover couple seem unaware and unaccepting of the different complexes with which they approach their relationship.

Mercurial Lovers enjoy spending vacation time with the beloved. They also like to take separate vacations either to engage in an unshared interest or to make family visits. Visiting family without the beloved can be acceptable, but

Different Complexes
Separateness vs. Relatedness
Autonomy vs. Togetherness

is not preferred by Romantic Lovers. A similar attitude applies to the work-related trips of either partner; these are necessary but not desirable ways to spend time for a Romantic Lover. If it is possible and appropriate for either partner to accompany the other on a work trip, Romantic Lovers welcome the opportunity. Mercurial Lovers may be ambivalent about this, however. Their work lives are an important avenue for expressing their complexes of separateness and autonomy. They may therefore be reluctant to have the beloved "intrude" on their independent pursuits.

For Romantic Lovers, being apart when it isn't necessary is not at all appealing. If unshared interests are an issue, a Romantic Lover may be receptive to adopting one of the Mercurial Lover's interests. If the area involved also includes some of the Mercurial Lover partner's independent friendships, this may add to its appeal for the Romantic Lover: It provides another way of sharing something with the beloved and thus enhancing the relationship. The Mercurial Lover partner may appreciate the beloved's interest and also feel uncomfortable about sharing a previously independent activity and separate friendship. For example, a Mercurial Lover was an avid sailor, and both he and his Romantic Lover wife enjoyed their trips on his sailboat. The Romantic Lover learned a lot about sailing from him, but not enough to be able to participate in his racing competitions. The Mercurial Lover had always raced with longtime friends. When the Romantic Lover wife expressed interest in improving her skills so that she, too, could race, the Mercurial Lover firmly discouraged her. "This is something I want to do on my own," he said.

Complementary Complexes
Autonomy and Enhancement of Relationship

Relationships with extended family members are unlikely to be a central issue for the couple. Both prefer to do things by themselves rather than include family members. Visits to family and holiday gettogethers are preferably brief encounters done more out of obligation than anticipation of great enjoyment. The Romantic Lover prefers togetherness with the beloved, and the Mercurial Lover values autonomy in relation to family. In this instance, their opposite Soul Images lead the partners to agree. Of the two, the Romantic Lover is more oriented toward attending to family obligations and may do so without the Mercurial Lover. Romantic Lovers' preference for accommodating to maintain harmony

Complementary Complexes
Autonomy and Togetherness
Separateness and Accommodating

contributes to their desire to meet family obligations. There is no particular complex that would present the same motivation for Mercurial Lovers. The value they place on separateness contributes to their approach to family obligations. Exceptions and modifications to the general attitudes toward family of Mercurial and Romantic Lovers are related to factors other than the couple's Soul Images.

Romantic Lovers generally have an optimistic outlook on life. This is due to their trust in the permanence of being in love, the belief that "love conquers all," and their use of accommodation to resolve disagreements. In comparison, Mercurial Lovers can appear to be negative, fault-finding, focused on problems, and therefore somewhat pessimistic. Although Romantic Lovers are likely to enjoy being called optimistic, Mercurial Lovers may well be puzzled and take offense at being regarded as pessimists. What to Romantic Lover partners may look like negativity, complaints, and pessimism are actually the Mercurial Lover's way of tempering a possibly excessive enthusiasm and natural trust in change and transformation. Ironically, such perceived "negativity" may actually be a way for Mercurial Lovers to moderate their natural complexes and thereby be in greater accord with the stability and enhancement of relationship complexes of the Romantic Lover partner.

> **Different Complexes**
> *Change (Intrinsic) vs. Stability*
> *Transformation of Self vs.*
> *Enhancement of Relationship*

For example, a Mercurial Lover was surprised and felt insulted when his Romantic Lover partner accused him of being negative and cynical in his outlook on life. He saw himself as enthusiastic, carefree, and basically optimistic. When he asked his beloved why she saw him in this way, she replied with some surprise, "Why, you're always quick to point out what could go wrong with a plan, or suggest that someone has a hidden motive, that somebody may resent you so you probably shouldn't count on his or her support, and other similar negative things. What else am I to think? You seem to expect the worst of life, and it makes me think you're unhappy with everything, including our relationship." The Mercurial Lover acknowledged that indeed he frequently said such things, but maintained that he had never viewed them as negative, merely as cautionary and a reminder to himself not to be overly optimistic. He explained this to his partner, and also took care in the future to give her a more balanced account of his beliefs.

In spite of their acknowledged optimism, Romantic Lovers often appear to be serious, intense, and uncompromising about the importance of the love relationship. By comparison, Mercurial Lovers can appear to their Romantic Lover partners as too carefree, changeable, and halfhearted in their commitment to the relationship. Romantic Lovers can interpret this apparent lack of seriousness on the part of the beloved as a negative comment on the importance of the relationship. Nowhere is this more apparent than in the couple's sexual relationship.

To Mercurial Lovers, Romantic Lovers place too much emphasis on sexuality; they see Romantic Lovers as finding meaning where there is none other than the mutual physical pleasure of lovemaking. The seriousness with which Romantic Lovers treat sex may be constraining to Mercurial Lovers, causing them to feel that they are frequently disappointing their Romantic Lover partners. The passion of lovemaking is very important to Mercurial Lovers, both for the pleasure it gives both partners and for its renewal of the feeling of falling in love. It is not, however, the central expression of love as it is for Romantic Lovers, for whom the expression of love is habitually *narrow* and *strong*. For Mercurial Lovers, sexual expression is typically broad, and it varies in intensity from *mild* to *strong*. The Romantic Lover is likely to misinter-

Different Complexes
Falling in Love vs. Being in Love
Change (Intrinsic) vs. Stability
Separateness vs. Togetherness

pret instances when there is a mild expression of love as a sign that something is wrong. As a result, Romantic Lovers can be very sensitive to any mood changes in a Mercurial Lover during sex, interpreting these as either a positive or a negative comment on the relationship.

If Mercurial Lovers are unaware or unaccepting of the centrality of sex for the beloved, they may become impatient and critical, or even make fun of the Romantic Lover's feelings. From a Mercurial Lover point of view, lovemaking is important in relation to change and transformation of self, while for the Romantic Lover, stability and enhancement of the relationship are involved. If there is a perceived demand to "perform," this may interfere with the desire for autonomy and independence. One Mercurial Lover expressed frustration because she felt that "I can never live up to his [her Romantic Lover partner's] sexual expectations." For a Romantic Lover, a Mercurial Lover's failure to appreciate the meaning of sexual passion is equally distressing. One Romantic Lover expressed dismay and confusion regarding his Mercurial Lover's behavior during lovemaking. He sheepishly admitted that he felt "used" by her. "She giggles and wants to talk when we're making love," he said. "I really don't like it when she does that. It's like talking in church. You just don't do those things. Talking breaks the spell of mixing and being together. She's making sport of it." When he expressed his concerns to his partner, she was hurt that he believed that sex wasn't important to her. Neither of them was aware that sex had a different meaning for each of them.

Mercurial and Romantic Lovers tend to have strong values about raising their children, but their emphases can be quite different. Neither is likely to neglect the love relationship because of the presence of children. For a Romantic Lover of either gender, the love relationship is central, and the arrival of children heralds

Different Complexes
Change (Intrinsic) vs. Stability
Transformation of Self vs.
Enhancement of Relationship

an additional way to enhance it. For the Mercurial Lover, children provide an opportunity for new and transformative experiences for themselves, the beloved, and the love relationship. In raising children, Mercurial Lovers try to provide the broadest opportunity for them to develop freely and make autonomous choices. As a result, Mercurial Lovers tend to be quite tolerant of their children's exploratory behavior and lapses of con-

Different Complexes

Transformation of Self vs. Enhancement of Relationship

Discussing vs. Accommodating

Autonomy vs. Togetherness

ventional "proper" behavior. They believe that their children need to learn from their own experience and trust in the power of change and transformation in promoting a positive outcome. Romantic Lovers are less sanguine in this regard. They want their children to appreciate the importance of relationships with others, the fulfillment of responsibilities, and the maintenance of harmony through accommodation and conciliation. They are less likely to be comfortable allowing their children to freely make their own mistakes. (In this they are similar to both Innocent and Steadfast Lovers, who also prefer to provide a fair amount of guidance to children.)

A couple disagreed about the college their daughter should attend. The Romantic Lover father was in favor of her going to his alma mater, a small liberal arts college. He was comfortable with the values of the institution and felt it would be a safe and inviting atmosphere for her. His Mercurial Lover wife disagreed. She felt that the small college wouldn't provide enough choices or opportunities for their daughter to experience new ideas and different kinds of people. She believed that the daughter would have a better experience at the larger state university, which was just as close as the smaller school. To the disappointment of the father, the daughter, who had a Mercurial nature, not only agreed with her mother, but chose a very large university in a distant state! Even the Mercurial Lover mother was a little uneasy about that decision.

When a Mercurial Lover–Romantic Lover couple divorce, the Romantic Lover usually prefers minimal direct contact, whereas the Mercurial Lover may wish to maintain a friendship relationship with the former partner. Contact of this kind may be painful for the Romantic Lover, however.

If there are children involved, the Romantic Lover may make the effort for their sake, so that at least occasionally, the former couple and their children might spend time together. If the Mercurial Lover should remarry, however, the Romantic Lover may experience a renewed sense of sadness and rejection. Mercurial Lovers are less likely to be distressed when a Romantic Lover former spouse remarries, as it seems easier for them to adapt to the change to a separate life without the former beloved.

Gender stereotypes can influence all of the Soul Images because of the nature of the complexes involved. However, they are particularly potent for female Mercurial Lovers and male Romantic Lovers, regardless of the Soul Images of their partners. When a couple consists of a female Mercurial Lover and a male Romantic Lover, gender stereotypes add both internal and external stress to the relationship. Male Mercurial Lovers fit the common stereotype expressed in the complaint of many women that "men just don't want a commitment." Female Mercurial Lovers appear to change more after marriage than men or women with any other Soul Image. Society doesn't value independence, autonomy, and separateness in women, whereas these qualities are not only acceptable but encouraged in men. Therefore, it may take age, experience, and maturity for female Mercurial Lovers to gain the confidence necessary to assert the complexes that are natural to their Soul Image. When they do, it can be quite disconcerting for their partners, especially if they are Romantic Lovers. A male Romantic Lover is likely to mistake his Mercurial Lover wife's desire for autonomy as a rejection of him and the love relationship. If the Mercurial Lover's newly recognized independence emerges in an exaggerated and insistent fashion, as often happens with a previously suppressed aspect of a person, the Romantic Lover's sense of rejection can be overwhelming.

Male Romantic Lovers also risk being misunderstood because of gender stereotypes. Because togetherness and relatedness are socially associated with being female, a Mercurial Lover woman may mistake a male Romantic Lover's natural complexes of relatedness and togetherness as efforts to control and restrict her freedom. In contrast, male Mercurial Lovers will likely see a female Romantic Lover not as controlling, but as possessive. Possessiveness in a woman is expected, if not entirely approved.

⎛ The Clash of Complexes

David, who is forty-nine years old, and Lori, who is forty-five years old, have been together for almost ten years. They are not married and they have no children. Both of them have been divorced, and neither has been eager to remarry. David, a Romantic Lover, is a college professor of history. Lori, a Mercurial Lover, is a producer at a television station in a neighboring city. She has a forty-five-minute commute to and from work each day. They both work long hours. Because Lori's work is project-oriented, she takes advantage of the station's "flex-time" policy in setting up her work schedule. Sometimes she arrives at work as early as 7:30 in the morning, but at other times as late as 11:00. The end of her workday is also variable. She typically leaves her office anytime between 5:00 and 8:00 P.M. David's workday is also long. However, he leaves home at the same time every day, and usually arrives home between 5:00 and 6:00 P.M. He sometimes brings some work home.

Phase One: The Disagreement

- As a disagreement continues with no resolution, tension increases.
- The persistence and increase of tension cause misunderstanding.
- Sustained tension and misunderstanding cause stress.

David and Lori's opposing complexes of change and stability are a continual source of tension between them. The tension becomes particularly strong when Lori comes home late from work. For several days in a row, Lori arrived home after 8:00 P.M. On the fourth night that this occurred, she found David working in his study. He was unusually quiet. The following conversation ensued:

Lori: Sorry I'm late again, but we had some problems getting this new show together.

(David remained silent.)

Lori: What's wrong, honey?

David: You're late again.

Lori: I said I was sorry. What's the big deal?

David: You said yesterday that it was the last night you'd be late. I cooked a special dinner for us. It's in the fridge.

Lori: Gee! I'm sorry, David. A glitch came up and we had to fix it.

David: I wish I had a dollar for every time you've said "I'm sorry." I could retire rich.

Lori: Now don't get sarcastic! I can't control my job the way you can. I don't come home late on purpose.

David: Well, sometimes I think you do. Sometimes I feel you work late to avoid being with me.

Lori: That's silly!

David: Well, have you been mad at me?

Lori: Of course not! But I'm getting mad now, damn it! My job is important to me. I sometimes feel you'd be happier if I quit my job and stayed home all the time.

David: No, no, I'd just like to spend a nice quiet evening together now and then. When you work late, you're all wired up, and it takes the whole evening for you to relax. I just like us being together, that's all.

Lori: Well, you know that I'm going to work late once in a while. Would you feel better if I called you and told you when I'll be leaving work? It'll take me about an hour to get home. Then you'll know, and if you want to, you can make dinner.

David: That would help. You know I don't want to be rigid about this. It would just be nice to be together more often, that's all.

Lori: Okay, sweetheart. I promise.

The above exchange highlights the importance David places on being together with Lori in a meaningful way. He tries to be understanding about her work demands, but he can't help resenting the persistent intrusion of her work into their intimite life—when she comes home late, she's "all wired up." Susan understands this and offers to compromise by keeping David informed of her hour-by-hour plans when she works late. Both are optimistic that this will help meet both their desires.

Phase Two: The Quarrel

- Persistent misunderstanding and stress consume large amounts of energy and can be exhausting.

- Sustained fatigue and stress jeopardize the ability to integrate and respond to the issues.

- Fatigue and stress continue to consume more energy.

- Negative aspects of the participants' Soul Images are evoked.

For the next two weeks, Lori phoned David each day and told him when she would be home. On several nights she came home early and prepared a fine dinner for them. They were becoming quite content with the new routine. One evening while David was thinking about his imminent fiftieth birthday, he casually suggested to Lori that perhaps they should get married. Somewhat surprised, she jokingly replied, "Why spoil a good thing?" David smiled and didn't respond. A few nights later, Lori called David at 6:00 to tell him that she would be leaving in about fifteen minutes. Then, for the next hour and a half, she called David at fifteen-minute intervals to say that she would be leaving shortly. When she finally arrived home, it was almost 9:00. David was quiet, and Lori knew he was angry. They had the following conversation:

Lori: Hi, honey! I'm sorry I'm late, but it was a bitch at work tonight.

David (sarcastically): It's not only the work that's a bitch.

Lori: Now what is that supposed to mean?

David (sarcastically): Whatever you think it means.

Lori (angrily): If you're going to be passive-aggressive, do it somewhere else.

David: That's what I thought! You really would like me to leave, wouldn't you?

Lori: What's gotten into you? Do you want to leave?

David: Don't put it on me. You're the one who doesn't like it here.

Lori: What in heaven's name are you talking about?

David: Well, it seems that ever since I mentioned that maybe we should get married, you've been more busy at work. It doesn't take a rocket scientist to figure that one out.

Lori: David, what are you talking about? I don't understand. I have a tough job. There are too many elements that I can't control. It has *nothing* to do with you. It just comes with the territory. We both knew that when I took the job five years ago.

David: Well, I've had it. I've tried to be understanding, but it's too much. I might as well live alone. I thought we were a couple and that we liked being together. Spring break is coming up and I know you're going to be too busy to take a few days off.

Lori: Well, I've been keeping something from you—

David (interrupting): You really like that new anchorman, don't you?

Lori: Don't be absurd. It's not that at all. I've arranged to take the week off during spring break. I was going to tell you today. I put in the request two weeks ago. I didn't want to tell you until it was approved because I knew you'd be disappointed if I didn't get it.

David: That's great, honey! Please forgive me. I get stupid sometimes.

Lori: I certainly agree with that. But I love you anyway, even though you're stupid and give me a hard time.

David: I love you, too … (smiling) even if you do make my life a living hell.

(They embrace, kiss, and then have dinner.)

All of their complexes created tension and misunderstanding for Lori and David. Lori had a job well suited to her complexes of change, transformation, and autonomy. David's teaching was in accord with his values, and it provided him with the stability and relatedness that were important to him. These differences, coupled with their different work demands, caused considerable misunderstanding and hurt feelings for them both.

David tried to be accommodating to Lori's need for change and autonomy. Lori, on the other hand, had assumed that David was agreeable with regard to her irregular schedule. Lori assumed that if he was not agreeable, then he would discuss this issue with her to arrive at a mutually acceptable solution. With tension and the ensuing stress, an unconscious complex was evoked when she accused David of being *nothing but* passive-aggressive and *always* wanting her to stay home. She perceived David's behavior as attempts to control her; this evoked the potential threat to her Autonomy and Independence complexes. This tension then placed David's complexes of stability, relatedness, and togetherness in jeopardy. The unconscious complexes that emerged from David were that Lori *always* worked late and *never* wanted to be with him, and that she was *nothing but* a bitch. If the tension had persisted and they hadn't been able to accept the important differences between them, their relationship would have continued to be unstable and contentious.

The Nature of This Love Relationship

Mercurial Lover–Romantic Lover relationships are distinct in both the vitality and the tension inherent in their particular combination of Soul Images. The balance in their relationship is achieved through the frequent dissonance of their complexes. As a couple, their opposite complexes can temper the tendency for the relationship to become one-sided. Such one-sidedness often emerges in the complexes of change, transformation, separateness, and autonomy for the Mercurial Lover, as these meet opposition from the Romantic Lover's stability, enhancement of relationship, relatedness, and togetherness. Mercurial Lover discussing and Romantic Lover accommodating can also be exaggerated when the couple attempt to resolve or avoid disagreements. Similarly, the Mercurial Lover's wish to experience the excitement of falling in love can become intensified in response to the Romantic Lover's focus on the experience of being in love.

In addition, we saw that gender-related issues, though they can influence all of the ten love relationships to some extent, are likely to have the greatest impact on Mercurial Lover–Romantic Lover couples. Of greatest importance are the opposite complexes of separateness versus relatedness and autonomy versus change.

These complexes also emerged in the disagreement and quarrel between David and Lori. Each was puzzled by the other's different perspectives about the relative values of work and their relationship in their lives. Unconscious complexes were evident in the quarrel, with each making implicit or explicit *always* or *never* and *nothing-but* statements. In the end, their strong commitment to the relationship helped them accept their differences.

Individual histories and circumstances may vary widely among Mercurial Lover–Romantic Lover couples, but the same complexes can be seen in their daily lives and in their quarrels. We hope you now have a better and deeper understanding of, appreciation for, and ability to appraise this kind of true love.

IO ⟩ *Mercurial Lover and Innocent Lover*

Let there be spaces in your togetherness.

Kahlil Gibran, *The Prophet*

The different meanings of time and change make Mercurial Lover–Innocent Lover couples distinctive. The Mercurial Lover views time as a flowing river, while the Innocent Lover regards time as a placid lake. Just as a river flows continuously and naturally toward the sea, so the placid lake is nourished and replenished by the flowing river. The partners relate through the conjunction of these contrasting images. They are eager to experience life together and are optimistic about the future, even though their views of the future are different. Both value change, but the meaning of change for themselves and for the relationship is different.

The difference between the Mercurial Lover's and the Innocent Lover's view of change is central to understanding and appreciating the different facets of their relationship. For the Mercurial Lover, change has *intrinsic* value; it is important in and of itself. For the Innocent Lover, change is *instrumental;* it is the vehicle through which explicit and implicit goals in the relationship are accomplished. The difference between an intrinsic and an instrumental view of change has implications for the partners' sense of self and their experience of their respective autonomy and togetherness. This difference is often complementary. If they have many interests and values in common, the Innocent Lover's view of instrumental change provides a goal, while the Mercurial Lover's view of change as intrinsic provides the "engine" or enthusiastic energy to arrive at the goal. Common interests and values, whether these involve their family, interest in the arts or outdoors, or other activities, provide Mercurial Lover–Innocent Lover couples with a strong sense of cohesiveness. The more common their interests, the more their different complexes of transformation of self and development of the relationship will be in harmony.

A comparison of the characteristics of Mercurial and Innocent Lovers is provided in Chart 15 on pages 210 and 211. The next section describes how the complexes listed in the chart are expressed in the everyday lives of Mercurial Lover–Innocent Lover couples. To highlight the complexes being discussed, they are identified in the margin beside the relevant descriptions.

The Mercurial Lover–Innocent Lover Relationship

Perhaps more than that of any of the other true loves, the relationship of a Mercurial Lover and an Innocent Lover can appear to change markedly over time. Of course, changes occur in all relationships as a result of life circumstances, spiritual development, deeper and more specific knowledge of self and of each other, and various other life occurrences. A Mercurial Lover–Innocent Lover couple's interests and values may be in accord at the beginning of their relationship. Over time, however, each may sense that the other has become different, while believing that their own values and desires have remained the same. An understanding of the differences in their complex of change helps explain why they are accurate as well as inaccurate in their perception of the changes that have occurred during the course of their relationship.

For the Mercurial Lover, change is the natural way to evolve and become different or transformed. For the Innocent Lover, change is a purposeful movement toward a future goal in which a desired development of the self within the relationship occurs; change for its own sake is not appealing. The purpose of change for the Innocent Lover is to achieve a state of relatedness, togetherness, and *mutual love through shared values and goals* with the beloved. The Mercurial Lover, for whom all change is potentially transformative, embraces the prospect of *changing alongside the beloved* so that each can become the unique individual he or she wishes to be. In the early phases of their love relationship, the two feel very much in tune with each other. The Mercurial Lover, who enjoys the excitement of falling in love, wants to be with the beloved as much as possible and to do everything together. The Innocent Lover, who enjoys being loved, shares in the pleasure and excitement of togetherness that accompanies being in the company of the beloved.

This level of accord with each other may lessen over time, but, when reexperienced by the partners, it can be a central unifying aspect of the relationship. When this occurs, difficulties that arise

Different Complexes

Change (Intrinsic) vs. Change (Instrumental)

Transformation of Self vs. Development of Relationship

Falling in Love vs. Being Loved

Chart 15

Comparison of Mercurial and Innocent Lovers

Central Relationship Question: Mercurial Lovers

"If I am a separate, changing individual, how can I merge with a beloved in an intimate, loving relationship? Change and the flux of life sustain me with vigor, further my transformation, and engage me with life's possibilities. Yet this isn't enough. I also need the exhilaration of love through merging with my beloved. As much as I desire the passion of love, however, I also fear my beloved's love. My fear is that my beloved may innocently entice me to a life of predictability, comfort, and routine that will end in a suffocating and deadly inertia. If this happens, I will indeed lose my soul and I will become like an automaton in a Kafka novel."

Attributes, Themes, and Complexes

Change	Any change is good in itself. Change has intrinsic value.
Transformation of Self	Focus on a future filled with the potential for change and transformation.
Separateness	View their identity and sense of self as unique and distinct from relationships.
Autonomy	Value independence and autonomy; resist restrictions on freedom and are sensitive to any hint of coercion from others.
Discussing	Value explorative communication and discussing the relationship and what it means.
Falling in Love	Revel in the intensity and novelty of the experience of love.

Kind of Intimacy

Temperature	Hot—passionate sexual activity; kissing and caressing in public.
Proximity	Distant—unawareness of the unspoken distress or joy of the partner.

Expression of Psychic Energy

Focus	Broad—many expressions of love.
Intensity	Mild to strong expressions of love.

Chart 15

Comparison of Mercurial and Innocent Lovers (cont.)

Central Relationship Question: Innocent Lovers

"If my sense of self is confirmed by my beloved in an intimate relationship, can I develop and have a sense of self when I am not being loved? It is an old adage that one only exists when one is loved. That's the way it is for me. My beloved's love for me is what sustains me and grants me the will and the energy to grow, develop, and be at one with the world. What I dread is the possibility that my beloved will no longer love me. If that happens, I will lose not only my sense of self, but also my dreams and goals for the future. It is for this reason that my beloved must confirm the love that sustains me. If not, I will truly be lost."

Attributes, Themes, and Complexes

Change	Change and growth toward a goal establish a connection to people and the world. Change has instrumental value.
Development of Relationship	Relationship results in the assurance that development toward mutual wholeness will occur.
Relatedness	A sense of selfhood comes from the relationship with the beloved.
Togetherness	Togetherness with the beloved is maintained by sharing projects, plans, and dreams for the future.
Cooperating	Cooperating is the natural way of resolving conflict and preserving the state of Being Loved.
Being Loved	The knowledge and comfort of being loved is the nourishment that will lead to change and growth.

Kind of Intimacy

Temperature	Warm—holding hands, touching, and physical closeness in private and public; use of terms of endearment.
Proximity	Close—deeply affected by the other's unspoken distress.

Expression of Psychic Energy

Focus	Broad—many expressions of love.
Intensity	Mild to strong expressions of love.

from other complexes are minimized and put into the larger perspective of the couple's love for each other. It is for this reason

Different Complexes

Falling in Love vs. Being Loved

that sexual passion as an expression of love is important for a Mercurial Lover–Innocent Lover couple. Passionate lovemaking for the Mercurial Lover ignites the excitement that accompanied the initial falling in love. The passion of lovemaking for the Innocent Lover is the quintessential expression of being loved. When there is any estrangement or discord in their relationship, lovemaking rekindles their love for each other. It has a transformative function for the Mercurial Lover that occurs in the "swirl" of their passion. For the Innocent Lover partner, it restores their togetherness. Their frequent and passionate lovemaking sustains the profound feeling of harmony between them.

Regardless of the renewal that lovemaking bestows, their different complexes can be complementary and satisfying, and at other times they can clash and result in disagreements and

Different Complexes

Separateness vs. Relatedness

Autonomy vs. Togetherness

Discussing vs. Cooperating

quarrels. For example, it is natural for Mercurial Lovers, who value their independence, to be most energized when doing things on their own. They take pride in their accomplishments and are excited and pleased when they can overcome obstacles and meet life's challenges on their own. For Innocent Lovers, however, solving problems and meeting life's challenges together with the beloved contribute to self-development and personal identity. Innocent Lovers may therefore feel excluded and deprived of selfhood when their Mercurial Lover partner makes a separate and independent decision without including the Innocent Lover. The Mercurial Lover doesn't think of his or her actions as excluding the beloved; the erroneous expectation is that the Innocent Lover also desires autonomy and independence in decision making. If the Innocent Lover isn't available, the Mercurial Lover is quite comfortable taking action and informing the partner later. The expectation is that the Innocent Lover will take the same approach, especially in areas where she or he has more knowledge. Mercurial Lovers are likely to be just as puzzled by the Innocent Lover's desire for joint problem solving as Innocent Lovers are by the Mercurial Lover's forgoing the opportunity to develop the relationship further through shared problem solving.

In addition, the Mercurial Lover's emphasis on discussing and the Innocent Lover's focus on cooperating to resolve problems seem to produce some subtle differences in communication styles. Both value discussions, but the Innocent Lover prefers to continue the discussion until a cooperative and mutually accept-

Different Complexes
Discussing vs. Cooperating

able solution is reached. For the Mercurial Lover, a cooperative resolution isn't necessary and may not be desirable. The Mercurial Lover may be comfortable simply with an "agreement to disagree." Also, the Mercurial Lover may wish to think about the issue alone or solicit other views on the matter. A Mercurial Lover may be puzzled by the intensity of the beloved's desire to come to a conclusion before a matter can be left. For Innocent Lovers, a disagreement left unresolved can be experienced as a rift in the relationship; consequently they feel uncomfortably separate and detached from the beloved.

One Mercurial Lover learned that she and her Innocent Lover husband handled disagreements more productively if she stayed with the discussion until at least a partial resolution was reached. It was then less likely that her husband would continue to dwell on the problem. Later, they could both come back to it refreshed and more able to reach agreement. The Mercurial Lover had enough time to ponder the matter on her own, and it was less likely that her husband would be distracted from the issue by feeling a loss of love in the relationship. In another couple, the Innocent Lover wife observed that early in their marriage, her Mercurial Lover husband would refuse to continue a discussion and would sometimes actually leave the house when they reached an impasse in a discussion. "That was really hard for me," she said. "I felt quite rejected and unloved. But now he's willing to continue to talk to me, even when we each think the other one is being unreasonable. The fact that he stays with it seems to be more important than whether we actually wind up agreeing."

Their complexes and the different emphases placed on mutuality and closeness have implications in the way the partners relate to their extended families. A close relationship with parents and other family members is more important for Innocent Lovers than for Mercurial Lovers. How much time is spent on phone calls, visiting, holiday events, and vacations may be viewed differently by the partners.

Different Complexes
Separateness vs. Relatedness
Autonomy vs. Togetherness
Transformation of Self vs.
Development of Relationship

Whether it is their own or the beloved's family, Mercurial Lovers may find the sameness of the people, conversation, and family dynamics to be uninteresting and unstimulating. If the family involved is close-knit and very active in each other's lives, a Mercurial Lover may resent family expectations of involvement and obligation. Unsolicited advice by family members can also be a source of irritation and encourage the Mercurial Lover to withdraw further from family relationships.

The Innocent Lover values a continuing close association with family as important for a sense of togetherness and personal development. Advice offered by family members is taken as a sign of love and concern, even if it is unsolicited and not followed. The Mercurial Lover partner's outlook can therefore be distressing. Often, the Mercurial Lover, acknowledging the importance of family to the beloved, will encourage the Innocent Lover to relate to family alone while the Mercurial Lover does something enjoyable

Different Complexes
Autonomy vs. Togetherness
Transformation of Self vs.
Development of Relationship

independently. This solution may be unsatisfying for the Innocent Lover, for whom participating together with the beloved is important. The Innocent Lover's dissatisfaction may be puzzling to Mercurial Lovers; from their perspective of separateness and autonomy, they are respecting and encouraging the beloved's independent selfhood.

One Innocent Lover was very close to his younger brother, who lived in another state. They had lengthy phone conversations at least once a week and spent a week together at the family vacation cabin every summer. Even though the Mercurial Lover wife liked her brother-in-law, after a few years she objected to the annual vacation. The couple compromised by having the Mercurial Lover wife spend only a weekend at the cabin and then go off with a friend on a different trip each year. The Innocent Lover husband and the couple's two children spent the remainder of the vacation week with the brother and his family. Another Mercurial Lover did his best to be enthusiastic about a big family reunion his mother was planning, though it meant he would have to skip a fishing trip with his best friend. He reported that his Innocent Lover wife was "enthusiastic and excited enough for both of us, even though it's my family. She thinks it's really important for our daughters to get to know their cousins and aunts and uncles who live far away. I hope I'll enjoy talking to some relatives I haven't seen for a long time, but there are other things I'd rather be doing."

Relating to family is just one of the areas in which the couple disagree. They also differ in their views on the amount of time they want to spend together, what they will do during that time, and with whom they will do it. This can be seen in their recreational preferences and their values concerning friendships. In these and other areas, the Mercurial Lover's desire for separateness and autonomy may be at odds with the Innocent Lover's desire for relatedness and togetherness. These differences are evident in the Mercurial Lover's desire to have independent friendships with a variety of people. Engaging in recreational activities that exclude the beloved is also desirable. Such friendships and activities are in addition to what the couple do together and their common friendships. The couple are likely to have close relationships and to socialize with other couples as well as with their separate friends.

The issue of independent friendships and activities arose for Donna, a Mercurial Lover, and Greg, her Innocent Lover husband, when they were invited to a dinner party at the home of friends. They were both looking forward to going. However, on the morning of the day of the party, Greg felt ill. His symptoms worsened during the day, and he told Donna that he felt too sick to go to the party.

"You don't mind if I go by myself then, do you?" asked Donna. "They're more my friends, anyway. Lisa and Brett will be there, and I was especially wanting to talk to Lisa about our plans for a weekend together."

"I really wish you'd stay here with me," said Greg somewhat plaintively. "I wouldn't go without you if you were sick."

"But I'd want you to go by yourself," said Donna. "I wouldn't see the sense in you missing out on something because of me. Why can't you be as considerate of me?"

"It seems to me you're the one being inconsiderate," replied Greg. "But I don't want you to stay if you really don't want to. I'll be all right alone."

"Good, I'm glad you agree," said Donna. "I won't stay late."

A Mercurial Lover–Innocent Lover couple are likely to disagree about the acceptability of opposite-sex friendships. The Mercurial Lover is quite comfortable with them, whereas the Innocent Lover regards such relationships as jeopardizing his or her partner's commitment and desire for togetherness. When an Innocent Lover expresses this concern to a Mercurial Lover partner, his or her response can range from disbelief to anger. Such friendship relationships are separate and distinct from the relationship with the beloved for the Mercurial Lover. For the Innocent Lover, however, everything is related; the energy the Mercurial Lover partner devotes to

Different Complexes
Separateness vs. Relatedness
Autonomy vs. Togetherness

another person is a reduction in energy devoted to the Innocent Lover. With the Innocent Lover's assumption that both partners find identity through relatedness, the Mercurial Lover's opposite-sex relationships can only mean a deficiency in satisfaction with the love relationship. For the Mercurial Lover, however, relatedness has little to do with it. Outside friendships and activities address her or his search for identity through separateness and autonomy. "There are a lot of men in my field," said one Mercurial Lover woman, "so of course I work closely with them, and we like getting together and talking about things other than work. I need the freedom to be with the people I like, and I don't think I should have to pay attention to their gender. Kerry [her Innocent Lover partner] gets all bent out of shape about it. I could lie to him about who I've been with, but that would be really bad for our relationship. He just needs to trust me."

From the point of view of the Mercurial Lover, "too much" togetherness with the beloved is restrictive and puts limits on the transformative potential of change. For the Innocent Lover partner, who focuses on the common values and goals that accompany being together with the beloved, time away from the relationship can be experienced as diminishing the unity of the relationship. As a result of these differences, an Innocent Lover partner may encourage the Mercurial Lover beloved to reduce some activities or time with friends so that they can have more time together alone or as a family. The fact that the Mercurial Lover wants to spend time apart may be seen as a flaw in the relationship. The Mercurial Lover, from the perspective of finding identity through separateness and independence, will in turn urge the Innocent Lover partner to develop more independent interests and friendships, in order to achieve the requisite identity.

One Mercurial Lover described feeling that her freedom as an individual was at risk because her Innocent Lover husband reacted so negatively to her outside activities. She found herself feeling guilty and dreading having to tell him her plans. He felt that most of her nonworking time should be spent with him and their family. She would automatically try to build in ways to make up for the time away from him by proposing some joint outing. She couldn't understand why he saw the time they spent away from each other as a threat to their relationship. For her, having separate interests and sources of satisfaction enhanced the relationship. She was unaware that her beloved's sense of self was connected to the unity of being at one with her, and therefore saw him as needy and lacking initiative.

Different Complexes
Separateness vs. Relatedness

In light of their differences, it isn't surprising that a Mercurial Lover–Innocent Lover couple have different attitudes about taking separate vacations. The idea can be quite appealing for the Mercurial Lover, as a way of pursuing interests that aren't shared with the beloved. Innocent Lovers find separate vacations difficult or simply unacceptable. As mentioned earlier, however, a couple may compromise in this area in order to respect their different approaches to spending time with extended family.

You may recall that understanding through *sympathy* comes naturally to Innocent Lovers, whereas *empathy* is the vehicle for understanding for Mercurial Lovers. This difference can lead Innocent Lovers to expect the Mercurial Lover partner to anticipate needs and desires without being explicitly told of them. The Mercurial Lover is likely to be frustrated, annoyed, and unable to fulfill the beloved's perceived unreasonable expectation. For the Innocent Lover, who assumes a sympathetic capability in the beloved, its absence is interpreted as insensitivity and a lack of closeness and caring in the relationship.

The couple's attitudes toward work and career can be influenced by their openness to change and faith in the future. Both partners may be willing to accept even major life changes in pursuit of interesting challenges for the Mercurial Lover, or important goals for the Innocent Lover. In other respects, they differ about the relative importance of work in their relationship. Work and individual accomplishment are central for a Mercurial Lover's identity through separateness and autonomy. Working hard, being successful in the work world, and enjoying one's job can be just as important to an Innocent Lover as they are to a Mercurial Lover. However, selfhood for an Innocent Lover comes most significantly from the love relationship itself. As a result, an Innocent Lover can view both partners' time and energy spent on work as diminishing the relationship.

Different Complexes

Change (Intrinsic) vs. Change (Instrumental)

Separateness vs. Relatedness

Autonomy vs. Togetherness

For one couple, the Mercurial Lover husband's time at work and in work-related social activities was a continuing source of distress for the Innocent Lover wife. She accused her husband of loving his work more than her. "The more you work, the farther apart we become." Her Mercurial Lover husband attributed her complaints to her own lack of fulfillment in her career. He therefore tried to be supportive by encouraging her to change jobs or go back to school to find something more satisfying; he didn't appreciate the difference in their identity complexes. His Innocent Lover spouse interpreted his encouragement to "find herself" as dismissive and as further evidence of his alienation from the relationship.

As mentioned in earlier chapters, Innocent Lovers prefer working on household tasks together with the beloved: The opportunity to do things together contributes to their development of self. This approach isn't likely to be transformative for Mercurial Lovers, however. Therefore, a Mercurial Lover may

prefer to get through chores more quickly by having each partner be responsible for specific tasks. Some Mercurial Lovers may want the freedom to decide how and when to take care of necessary chores; others may be reasonably comfortable with a set routine. One Mercurial Lover found it burdensome to have a rigid schedule at home, even though at work he was known for being well organized, methodical, and task-oriented. His Innocent Lover partner complained that she ended up taking on more of the household responsibilities than he did because of his inconsistency. "We both have full-time jobs," she said. "And I don't like having to be in charge of the house and kids all the time. I wish he could notice when things need doing without my telling him."

The Mercurial Lover husband doesn't understand why "she makes such a big deal about household stuff. It all gets done. When she does more than I do, I make it up to her by doing something else for her or doing more the next week."

For the Innocent Lover wife, however, that isn't the issue. "He says he's always willing to help out, but he doesn't like working side by side like I do. Sometimes I think he's resentful and would rather be away from home with someone else." It may not occur to the Mercurial Lover partner that the issue for the beloved is *sharing* an experience that adds to her sense of unity and being loved.

Innocent Lovers may be more attentive to establishing a strict budget for household expenditures because of its contribution to future goals. They are more likely to take on the responsibility of managing a budget. An Innocent Lover may object to an expenditure by the Mercurial Lover partner if there is no clear purpose in mind. The Mercurial Lover may want to use money to promote change and transformation. In response, an Innocent Lover partner may want to know what goal spending the money will accomplish. If the Mercurial Lover cannot specify one, the Innocent Lover partner is likely to propose alternative uses to which the money can be put. On the other hand,

> **Different Complexes**
> *Transformation of Self vs. Development of Relationship*

an Innocent Lover may be quite supportive of expenditures that could contribute to the Mercurial Lover's development toward goals shared by both of them.

As a result of their different complexes, Innocent Lovers tend to devote more time and energy to childrearing than do Mercurial Lovers. As is true in other areas, it doesn't matter much whether the mother or the father is the Innocent Lover. When circumstances permit, an Innocent Lover father may choose to be the primary caregiver to the children, perhaps working at home. A Mercurial Lover mother may welcome the freedom

> **Different Complexes**
> *Transformation of Self vs. Development of Relationship*
> *Autonomy vs. Togetherness*
> *Discussing vs. Cooperating*

this affords her to pursue career and other interests. In other couples, each parent may provide for different aspects of the children's well-being, and the time contributed by both may be equal.

The disagreements about childrearing that occur in a Mercurial Lover–Innocent Lover marriage are characteristic of their different complexes. The Mercurial Lover may feel that the Innocent Lover is overly involved with the children when they're young and too intrusive and perhaps controlling when they're older. The Innocent Lover parent, on the other hand, may find the Mercurial Lover parent too uninvolved with the children when they're younger and too lenient and willing to permit them independence when they're older. Contributing to these perceptions is the Mercurial Lover's value of independence and self-sufficiency; there is a faith that the freedom to experiment with and process experiences will be transformative for a child. Similarly, the Innocent Lover's value of developing oneself through cooperation and union with others encourages closer scrutiny and involvement in children's lives.

One couple strongly disagreed about whether their fourteen-year-old son should watch an R-rated film at the home of a friend. The Mercurial Lover parent was confident that the experience would not be harmful and would add to the son's ability to make choices. The Innocent Lover parent focused on the parental role of guidance, upholding prevailing values, and protecting the son from harmful influences.

The Clash of Complexes

As we have seen, Mercurial and Innocent Lovers may find that their differences complement each other. However, if their communication styles lead to frequent and persistent misunderstandings, internal tension may ensue. The subtle and important differences in the meaning of change for them can also result in much misunderstanding and unhappiness. This is illustrated in the example of Tom, an Innocent Lover, and Elisse, a Mercurial Lover.

When they first met, Tom almost literally swept Elisse off her feet. He was charming and attentive and was a sensitive and passionate lover. Tom and Elisse have been married for fifteen years and have three children, one in middle school and the others in elementary school.

For several years, Elisse was a stay-at-home mom while her husband, an engineer, devoted most of his energies to work. She had complete charge of the household, arranging for maintenance, housekeeping, and child-care needs whenever necessary.

The challenge and variety of being a full-time mother and home-maker were rewarding. She had many friends, and was a volunteer at the local hospital. Tom had confidence in Elisse's managerial skills. Every evening when he came home from work, they engaged in what they lovingly called their "ritual." Elisse would relate the day's events to Tom, who listened attentively. They were very much in love.

After their youngest child entered school, Elisse became increasingly restless and bored. When she expressed her restlessness and boredom to Tom, he reassured her by saying that when the children were grown and he retired, there would be plenty of time to do exciting things together. Several times during their marriage, Elisse voiced interest in obtaining a graduate degree. Tom said she could pursue her interests after he retired. One evening, however, an ostensibly minor incident set in motion a course of events that would change both their lives.

Tom and Elisse were invited to a New Year's Eve party at the home of Tom's boss. It would be a large open-house party with about fifty or sixty guests. Elisse was looking forward to the party as a chance to meet new people and perhaps acquire some new friends. At the party, she met Nicole, the wife of one of Tom's colleagues. Elisse liked Nicole very much. She was an attorney and had just started working at a law firm. They chatted amiably for a while until Nicole asked Elisse what kind of work she did. Elisse said, "I'm a homemaker and mother." Nicole replied, "Oh," and abruptly excused herself. Elisse was devastated and felt like a non-person. Holding back her tears, she told Tom that she wanted to go home. For the remainder of the week, she was depressed and in a bad mood. She snapped at Tom and the children. Tom feared that she was angry at him, especially when she said that she was not in the mood for sex.

Phase One: The Disagreement

- As a disagreement continues with no resolution, tension increases.

- The persistence and increase of tension cause misunderstanding.

- Sustained tension and misunderstanding cause stress.

Several weeks passed. One evening after the children had gone to bed, Elisse went into Tom's study, and this exchange occurred:

Elisse: Tom, we have to talk.

Tom: Sure, honey. What's wrong?

Elisse: There's plenty wrong. That's what I want to talk about.

Tom: Is it me? Are you mad at me?

Elisse: Why do you have to be so arrogant? Can't something be bothering me without it being about you?

Tom: You're always mad at me.

Elisse (ignoring his comment): Just listen, I want to talk to you about my plans. I would like to go back to school and get an MBA.

Tom: What? What about the children? What about me?

Elisse: Don't get all bent out of shape. They have a weekend and evening program at the university. It'll take two to three years.

Tom: Have you already decided? Aren't we going to talk about it?

Elisse: I've tried to talk to you in the past, but you tell me that it will change our plans and postpone your retirement.

Tom: Well, it will. You'll have to get a housekeeper, and that will cost money. And if you have classes at night, the children and I will have to eat out. That will cost more money. And what about the tuition? We're on a tight budget now. You aren't considering us.

Elisse (getting angry): Look! I've been considering all of you for the past fifteen years! It's time I considered myself, too. Don't lay that guilt trip on me.

Tom: I'm not laying any guilt trip on you. I'm just concerned about how this will affect our plans to retire. You know I'm not that happy with my work.

Elisse: Yes, I know that Tom, but they're really *your* plans, not *mine*. I feel I'm being suffocated with boredom.

Tom: Are things that bad?

Elisse: Yes, they really are.

Tom: Okay. We'll try it and see how it goes. Just don't get mad.

(That night they make passionate love.)

Two years later, Elisse was nearing the completion of her studies. She had been attending to the household chores as well as her studies. Tom, in order to allay his fears about postponing his retirement, micromanaged their budget. Elisse was tired, and looked forward to the end of her studies. It was taking longer than she had hoped to complete the program; because of the demands at home, she limited her enrollment to two classes each semester. Chauffeuring the children and attending to their needs was time-consuming. Tom tried to help, but he complained that the children didn't listen to him and that she was really the disciplinarian.

Phase Two: The Quarrel

- Persistent misunderstanding and stress consume large amounts of energy and can be exhausting.
- Sustained fatigue and stress jeopardize the ability to integrate and respond to the issues.
- Fatigue and stress continue to consume more energy.
- Negative aspects of the participants' Soul Images are evoked.

Toward the end of her fourth semester of study, Elisse phoned Tom one night to tell him that she needed to stay at the library until closing time and wouldn't be home until 11:00. She asked if he would take care of dinner and put the children to bed, and he agreed that he would. When she arrived home shortly after 11:00, however, the children were still up watching a movie and Tom was working on the computer. There were dirty dishes in the sink. Elisse was hurt, angry, and despairing. She sent the children to bed, then had the following conversation with Tom:

Elisse: You know, you're a lazy goddamn son of a bitch!

Tom: What's gotten into you?

Elisse: Why couldn't you have cleaned up after dinner? I told you I had to study at the library. Can't I depend on you once in a while? And why did you let the kids watch an R-rated video?

Tom: Look, I work hard all day at a job I don't like, and then you take off and are busy all the time doing your thing. You don't care about the kids and me, and they don't listen to me. I've had it up to here!

Elisse: You just don't listen. I've told you that I feel like a nonperson. I'm only a wife and nothing else.

Tom: What's wrong with being a wife and a mother? I don't know what you're complaining about. I'm a good provider, aren't I? Have I refused you anything?

Elisse: You never listen to me! I'm tired, and I want a life of my own! I don't want to be only a wife and a mother! There's more to life than that. I can be something else, too!

Tom: You know, I think the strain is too much for you.

Elisse (shouting): Now you think I'm crazy!

Tom: Well, look at you. You're screaming and you're irrational.

Elisse (trying to contain herself): I am not irrational! What am I doing that's irrational?

Tom: Well, besides screaming, you claim that you love me and the children and then you claim that being a mother and a wife isn't meaningful for you. To me you're contradicting yourself. All you're saying is that you don't want to be with me and the children. To me, that's irrational. I just don't understand.

(At this point Elisse throws her arms up in despair and leaves the room. Tom remains and begins to tremble and sob.)

The persistent tension and the clash of complexes resulted in despair, anger, and fear for both Tom and Elisse. Elisse's life lacked the change necessary for her to feel fulfilled. A life apart from her marriage was necessary to achieve this. Tom's unhappiness at work contributed to his tension so that he couldn't comprehend his wife's need for separation and change. For him, fulfillment was found in the development of their marriage and relationship; it was the complex of relatedness that was important for him. He viewed his retirement as benefiting both of them in that they would be able to have more time with each other. Each of them regarded the other as rejecting and dismissing what was important. Both were unhappy, and the stage was set for the eruption of their unconscious complexes. Elisse accused Tom of being *nothing but* arrogant, a "lazy son of a bitch" who *never* listened and did *nothing but* plan for his retirement, and who *always* treated her as *nothing but* a wife. Tom's unconscious complexes erupted in his accusing Elisse of *always* being mad at him, and being *nothing but* selfish and uncaring.

For Elisse, falling in love with Tom when they first met had been transformative. Everything in her life took on a different order and value. However, she began feeling bored when the excitement of falling in love was subordinated to everyday chores in raising a family. Tom, for his part, had felt for the first time that he was truly loved. Elisse was caring and attentive to his needs. She was also a passionate lover. He anticipated that they would do everything together and was disappointed by her growing restlessness, which he saw as distancing and indifference. His attempts to manage the finances were a way of demonstrating his caring and concern for their developing togetherness. She viewed it, however, as his attempt to control and restrict her. Their different complexes, coupled with their respective unhappiness, caused misinterpretations of each other's behavior and motives, resulting in severe misunderstanding and arguments.

The Nature of This Love Relationship

Even though Mercurial and Innocent Lovers experience their common change complex in subtly different ways, they both have a shared optimism and eagerness to experience the future together. Change for these couples can be unifying as well as a potential source of misunderstanding. Mercurial Lovers appreciate change for its own sake, while for Innocent Lovers, change is directed toward achieving mutual goals. This subtle difference in their shared complex cuts across many aspects of their relationship, distinguishing this kind of love relationship. For the Mercurial Lover, the complexes of transformation of self, separateness, and autonomy are the most apparent areas of misunderstanding in relation to the Innocent Lover's complexes of development of relationship, relatedness, and togetherness. The Mercurial Lover's comfort with discussing to deal with disagreements works well with the cooperating of the Innocent Lover, as long as a resolution to the disagreement occurs at the end of the discussion. Finally, the central focus of the Innocent Lover on being loved works well with the Mercurial Lover's desire to experience falling in love. Both enjoy the passion, excitement, and renewal that accompany fulfillment of these desires.

These same complexes and combinations of complexes were revealed in the disagreement between and quarrel of Elisse and

Tom. We saw the emergence of unconscious complexes in both phases of their encounter. Each partner made implicit and explicit *always* or *never* and *nothing-but* statements in their stressed state. In the account of their relationship, we saw that each assumed that the other valued the same things. Tom, whose sense of himself came from the love relationship with Elisse, believed that Elisse should also feel fulfilled by it. But Elisse, who was only vaguely aware that she required separateness and autonomy in order to feel like "a person," viewed Tom's reaction as selfish and controlling.

Individual histories and circumstances may vary widely among Mercurial Lover–Innocent Lover couples, but the same complexes and issues we saw here are likely to emerge in their daily lives and in their quarrels. We hope you now have a better and deeper understanding of, appreciation for, and ability to appraise this kind of true love.

II $\Big\rangle$ Innocent Lover and Romantic Lover

We are shaped and fashioned by what we love.

Johann Wolfgang von Goethe, *Elective Affinities*

A sense of self for Innocent and Romantic Lovers comes from their relationships. As a result, they place great emphasis on their intimate love relationship as the source and vehicle of their satisfaction and well-being. The distinctive aspect of their love relationship lies in the different meanings attached to the renewal of being loved for the Innocent Lover and the constancy of being in love for the Romantic Lover. Both partners desire togetherness, but they may have somewhat different notions of how and when such togetherness should occur. For Romantic Lovers, togetherness exists in the ongoing shared love with the beloved. By ensuring the stability and constancy of their relationship, Romantic

Lovers sustain the complete experience of their love. For the Innocent Lover, ideal togetherness is achieved through continual movement, change, and development toward the future; it is not a state that is to be completed. Innocent Lovers may see stability and constancy as inhibiting the growth of the relationship toward the ideal state that is to come. If the beloved appears to be indifferent to the future, an Innocent Lover may see this as detrimental to the relationship. Innocent Lovers are likely to express some dissatisfaction with the present and instead focus on how things should be and will be in the future. A Romantic Lover partner may be somewhat puzzled and hurt by the Innocent Lover partner's "complaints," and in turn criticize her or his lack of appreciation for the pleasures of ongoing romantic intimacies in the present. Romantic Lovers can interpret an Innocent Lover's indifference to the nuances of the love relationship as shallowness and a lack of ardor.

Innocent and Romantic Lovers share a cooperative approach toward each other and the world at large. Their central concern is what happens in their relationship, not what is happening in the world. As a result, the couple may relate primarily to close friends and family members, with little interest in widening their circle of outside relationships. People who are in relationships with other Soul Image combinations can misjudge the true nature of Innocent Lover–Romantic Lover couples in a variety of ways. From a Mercurial or Steadfast Lover perspective, for example, Innocent Lover–Romantic Lover couples seem too dependent on each other and lacking in individual initiative. Two Innocent Lovers may judge an Innocent Lover–Romantic Lover relationship as full of conflict about goals for the future; they may see the Romantic Lover partner as too demanding, hypersensitive, and unrealistic.

Some of the complexes of Innocent and Romantic Lovers are similar and others are quite different. The complexes that can be observed in their day-to-day relationships are as follows: relatedness and togetherness as the vehicles for forming a sense of self for both partners; cooperating as the natural way of resolving disagreements for the Innocent Lover, and accommodating as the natural mode for the Romantic Lover; a focus on being loved for the Innocent Lover, as compared with the importance of being in love for the Romantic Lover. The couple differ markedly in that for the Innocent Lover, change (instrumental) and development of relationship are important, while stability and enhancement of relationship are the focus for Romantic Lovers.

A comparison of the characteristics of Innocent and Romantic Lovers is provided in Chart 16 on pages 234 and 235. The next section describes how the complexes listed in the chart are expressed in the everyday lives of Innocent Lover–Romantic Lover couples. To highlight the complexes being discussed, they are identified in the margin beside the relevant descriptions.

The Innocent Lover–Romantic Lover Relationship

There are many complementary ways in which Innocent Lover–Romantic Lover partners can fulfill each other's desires. For example, the Romantic Lover partner may enjoy planning and spending money on romantic experiences with the beloved—a weekend in a country inn, a

Shared Complexes
Relatedness
Togetherness

candlelit dinner on a riverboat, or a helicopter trip over the Grand Canyon. Thoughtful gifts to commemorate anniversaries and other special occasions may also be bestowed by the Romantic Lover partner as a way to enhance his or her own sense of self as well as the breadth, depth, and perpetuation of the love relationship. Of great importance to many Romantic Lovers is imagining

Chart 16
Comparison of Innocent and Romantic Lovers

Central Relationship Question: Innocent Lovers

"If my sense of self is confirmed by my beloved in an intimate relationship, can I develop and have a sense of self when I am not being loved? It is an old adage that one only exists when one is loved. That's the way it is for me. My beloved's love for me is what sustains me and grants me the will and the energy to grow, develop, and be at one with the world. What I dread is the possibility that my beloved will no longer love me. If that happens, I will lose not only my sense of self, but also my dreams and goals for the future. It is for this reason that my beloved must confirm the love that sustains me. If not, I will truly be lost."

Attributes, Themes, and Complexes

Change	Change and growth toward a goal establish a connection to people and the world. Change has instrumental value.
Development of Relationship	Relationship results in the assurance that development toward mutual wholeness will occur.
Relatedness	A sense of selfhood comes from the relationship with the beloved.
Togetherness	Togetherness with the beloved is maintained by sharing projects, plans, and dreams for the future.
Cooperating	Cooperating is the natural way of resolving conflict and preserving the state of Being Loved.
Being Loved	The knowledge and comfort of being loved is the nourishment that will lead to change and growth.

Kind of Intimacy

Temperature	Warm—holding hands, touching, and physical closeness in private and public; use of terms of endearment.
Proximity	Close—deeply affected by the other's unspoken distress.

Expression of Psychic Energy

Focus	Broad—many expressions of love.
Intensity	Mild to strong expressions of love.

Chart 16

Comparison of Innocent and Romantic Lovers (cont.)

Central Relationship Question: Romantic Lovers

"If my sense of self and identity is constituted by my relationship with my beloved, can I have a sense of self and fulfillment when I am alone? I can only be a complete human being if I am in a loving relationship with my beloved. For only through our love can we each lose our separateness from the world and become one with the world. Only then can 'I' become a 'We,' and then another new and true 'Me.' What happens then if I am separated from my beloved? Do I still exist? Will I no longer feel joy and pleasure? Will I be devoid of any sense of who I am? That prospect truly frightens me. If it occurs, I will be truly afflicted with a lovesickness.

Attributes, Themes, and Complexes

Stability	Value constancy, permanence, and completeness in the relationship with the beloved.
Enhancement of Relationship	Believe selfhood consists of differentiation of the relationship with the beloved.
Relatedness	Sense of identity or selfhood comes from the relationship with the beloved.
Togetherness	Emphasis is on participating in and sharing all aspects of their lives as expressions of togetherness.
Accommodating	Accommodation is the natural way of resolving conflicts and preserving the state of Being in Love.
Being in Love	Focus is on all the ways the love experience can be shared and enhanced with the beloved.

Kind of Intimacy

Temperature	Hot—passionate sexual activity; kissing and caressing in public.
Proximity	Close—deeply affected by the other's unspoken distress.

Expression of Psychic Energy

Focus	Narrow—focused expressions of love.
Intensity	Strong expressions of love.

what an experience with the beloved will be like. Then, if it actually turns out as planned, complete with the fantasied reaction of the beloved, perfect harmony has been achieved.

Innocent Lover partners are likely to fulfill a Romantic Lover's hopes and expectations—they interpret the caring and thoughtfulness of the Romantic Lover as confirmation that they are loved and cherished. However, for Innocent Lovers, the romantic ambience surrounding an experience, a gift, or a celebration is of secondary importance.

Different Complexes
Being Loved vs. Being in Love
Cooperating vs. Accommodating

What is primary for Innocent Lovers is simply being together with and connected to the beloved. As a result, there may be times when the Romantic Lover experiences hurt, disappointment, and loss of love if the Innocent Lover partner doesn't seem to fully participate in the meaningfulness of an experience. One Romantic Lover created an elaborate, intimate birthday experience for her Innocent Lover husband and took great pains to recreate the same romantic atmosphere there had been when they first became engaged. She was quite hurt when he said, "It's wonderful that you did all this for me, but you didn't have to go to the trouble and expense. I would have been just as happy being alone with you." For the Romantic Lover wife, however, "just being together" wasn't the same; for her, it was important that their togetherness be romantically expressed and experienced.

Much of the time, though, the couple's togetherness and relatedness complexes meet both their needs. For example, Carol, a Romantic Lover, and her Innocent Lover partner, Deborah, were invited to dinner at the home of a couple who were good friends. Both were looking forward to going. On the morning of the day of the dinner, however, Carol felt ill. Her symptoms worsened during the day, and she told Deborah that she felt too sick to go to the party.

"Oh, that's really upsetting. I was so excited about spending time with all those people," said Deborah.

"I know," replied Carol. "I wish I felt up to going. Maybe I'll feel better later. Or, you know, I'd be okay if you went alone, as long as it wasn't for the whole evening. Do you want to do that?"

"Nonsense!" said Deborah. "It wouldn't be the same without you, and I'd feel bad knowing you were here all alone. If we can't go together, I'll read to you from your new book of poetry, and we'll have a nice fire in the fireplace. We'll be fine just being together."

For Deborah, showing care and concern for Carol and spending the evening with her made up for the disappointment of missing the dinner. Carol appreciated the commitment to their relationship as well as Deborah's attention to creating an inviting experience in a meaningful setting.

Because the romantic, expressive meaning of their interactions isn't very important for the Innocent Lover, he or she may hurt and disappoint the Romantic Lover partner. Sentimental occasions may be forgotten, and insufficient attention may be given to the way the couple spend their time together. Innocent Lovers may feel that their Romantic Lover partner's negative reaction is excessive when the Innocent Lover's handling of such experiences doesn't meet the Romantic Lover's expectations. After several such incidents, however, most Innocent Lovers accept the importance of romantic expressions and take pains to provide them. The experience of togetherness is then enhanced for both of them.

Different Complexes
Being Loved vs. Being in Love

Disagreements about spending money can also be affected by their different desires around togetherness. For the Romantic Lover partner, spending money to enhance the relationship can at times take precedence over other financial needs. Innocent Lovers' focus on goals in the future makes them more concerned with and attentive to long-term needs. They are likely to pay attention to plans for how

Different Complexes
Change (Instrumental) vs. Stability

Development of Relationship vs. Enhancement of Relationship

money will be used. In stressful circumstances, a Romantic Lover may perceive an Innocent Lover partner as stingy, withholding, and controlling. If the Innocent Lover derides or fails to appreciate a romantic expenditure, the Romantic Lover may also wonder whether the Innocent Lover partner is truly committed to the relationship.

This important area of difference between partners with these two Soul Images can affect their choices of recreation, vacations, household purchases, and gifts. Any situation or activity that opposes "just being together" and "being together romantically" can create a potential clash of their subtly different relatedness and togetherness complexes.

The couple are likely to find mutual satisfaction, however, in the way they approach household responsibilities. Both enjoy working together, the Innocent Lover for the closeness and cooperative spirit, the Romantic Lover for the special meaning any chore can take on when done in the company of the beloved. The Romantic Lover can experience a profound sense of harmony quite similar to that achieved when a fantasied plan has come to fruition. Both partners like to work together cooperatively and harmoniously. For the Innocent Lover, important goals are addressed; for the Romantic Lover, the immediacy of the common activity enhances feelings of love. For both, however, should the demands of the household prove too disruptive of other ways they enjoy being together, hiring help when circumstances permit is quite acceptable.

Shared Complex
Togetherness
Different Complexes
Change (Instrumental) vs. Stability
Cooperating vs. Accommodating

Their harmonious and cooperative styles may also encourage them to prefer work environments that emphasize fellowship, collegiality, and cooperation. Neither is likely to feel comfortable in impersonal and competitive environments. In this respect, they are quite similar to two Innocent or two Romantic Lovers.

Sometimes, however, one or both of the partners work in a highly stressful situation with long hours that limit their time together. When this happens, it takes its toll on both of them. If the Innocent Lover is the overworked one, he or she may feel disconnected from and out of balance with the relationship. Innocent Lovers may fear that the partner will lose passion and interest, and that the relationship won't develop toward their goals.

Shared Complex
Relatedness
Different Complexes
Change (Instrumental) vs. Stability
Cooperating vs. Accommodating
Being Loved vs. Being in Love

When the Romantic Lover's energy is consumed by work, he or she may feel estranged and without a firm anchor in the world. There will be a concern that without attending to the relationship, the beloved will also experience discontent. When either one must deal with a partner who is overworked when they themselves are not, resentment and dissatisfaction are likely; both may see the partner as "choosing" work over the relationship, in spite of protestations to the contrary.

Sympathy is a natural aspect of the Innocent Lover–Romantic Lover relationship, so the partners share an expectation of sensitivity to each other's emotional state. In communicating, therefore, they may use their "reading" of the beloved as a barometer of the partner's satisfaction with the relationship. However, such sensitivity doesn't ensure an accurate reading of the other person's feelings and motivations.

Shared Complex
Relatedness
Different Complexes
Cooperating vs. Accommodating
Being Loved vs. Being in Love

Misjudgments in this area can be a source of misunderstandings and misperceptions. For example, a Romantic Lover–Innocent Lover couple eagerly anticipated walking along the beach in the moonlight on a holiday trip to Bermuda. On the evening they arrived, they had dinner and then went out to the beach to fulfill their dream. After a short while, however, the

Romantic Lover husband noticed that his Innocent Lover wife was being unusually quiet.

"Is anything wrong?" he asked anxiously. "Yes, there is," answered his wife with some annoyance. "It's really selfish and inconsiderate of you to make me come out on this walk when I'm tired and wanted to stay in. I didn't know you could be so insensitive!" The Romantic Lover was crushed by her comment. In his zeal to enact what he believed was their *shared* romantic fantasy, he had failed to notice and respond to his wife's state of mind.

Communication about problem solving reveals some subtle differences for couples in this kind of relationship. Innocent Lovers assume that when they have a problem, especially in their relationship, it can be solved through a discussion that leads to a collaborative solution. They greatly value the sense of togetherness and closeness achieved through such a cooperative effort.

> **Shared Complex**
> *Togetherness*
> **Different Complexes**
> *Change (Instrumental) vs.*
> *Stability*
> *Cooperating vs. Accommodating*

Romantic Lovers, on the other hand, prefer a minimum of discussion around problems, especially problems in the relationship. Once the Romantic Lover becomes aware that something is wrong or causing difficulty for the beloved, she or he resolves to change things to accommodate the beloved. For the Romantic Lover, togetherness is diminished by attending to what is wrong. It seems best to resolve problems through a change in behavior and thus restore stability to the relationship. If the Innocent Lover wants to continue discussing the issue, the Romantic Lover may interpret this as a failure to trust the intentions of the Romantic Lover. The Innocent Lover, who is looking for cooperation from the beloved, may view the refusal or reluctance to engage in discussion as controlling or placating. It's natural for Innocent Lovers to want to arrive at a joint decision and plan through discussion. However, Romantic Lovers may criticize Innocent Lovers' insistence on talking things out as "just talk" that isn't backed up by action.

Sometimes the Innocent Lover's togetherness complex clashes with the Romantic Lover's enhancement of relationship complex. For example, an Innocent Lover habitually sought his Romantic Lover wife's input on everything from what restaurant they should eat at to what kind of car they should buy. Each time he would

Different Complexes
Togetherness vs. Enhancement of Relationship
Being Loved vs. Being in Love

ask "What should we do?" she responded, often with irritation, "Can't you just decide yourself? Do you need me to make the decision about everything?" She viewed his questioning as an unwillingness to do his part in the relationship. As a Romantic Lover, she was particularly distressed when he asked her such questions as, "What would you like for our anniversary?" or "Tell me where you want to eat on your birthday." For her, being required to make such decisions seriously diminished the romance involved. "Shouldn't he know what will please me by now?" she asked, misinterpreting his behavior as a lack of love and understanding.

For this Romantic Lover, her husband's attempt to be considerate and cooperative and to decide things "together" failed to fulfill her Romantic Lover expectations for enhancement of the relationship and the harmony of being truly understood by the beloved. An added irritant for the Romantic Lover was the contrast between her husband's "neediness and indecisiveness" at home, and his competence and decisiveness in his job. For their part, Romantic Lovers may make a presumption about what a partner would like and be hurt and disappointed when the Innocent Lover responds to a gift or gesture with indifference or even annoyance.

The complexes of being loved and being in love often converge for this couple in their sexual relationship. Making love fulfills the expectations of both, and couples characterized by these two Soul Images usually report frequent

Shared Complex
Relatedness
Togetherness

Different Complexes
Being Loved vs. Being in Love
Cooperating vs. Accommodating

and passionate sex, often regardless of any serious problems in other areas of their life together. In fact, couples who report great dissatisfaction with many aspects of their relationship may "stay together for the great sex."

Innocent Lovers enjoy knowing that they are loved and cherished and will be forever. Any deviation from this threatens their comfort and security. Sustaining and developing the state of being in love is also important for the contentment and serenity of the Romantic Lover. However, whereas the Romantic Lover is generally concerned with whether the Innocent Lover enjoys the sexual experience, the Innocent Lover may be inattentive to the partner's satisfaction or lack of it. This isn't selfishness and lack of caring on the part of the Innocent Lover—which at times may be how the Romantic Lover interprets it. Rather, the Innocent Lover assumes that the beloved will experience the joy of being loved through a sexual encounter; the partner's desire for and satisfaction with this result of lovemaking is presumed. Even when the Romantic Lover suspects self-centeredness on the part of the partner, however, the pleasure of lovemaking is a sufficient motivation to participate fully.

Romantic Lovers who understand and accept the loving nature of their Innocent Lover partner's experience of sexuality won't judge their partner as shallow or as using sex to avoid dealing with problems in the relationship. Making love at the (often frequent) request of the Innocent Lover then becomes a satisfying shared experience of cooperative and harmonious loving and being loved. One Romantic Lover who was genuinely dissatisfied with many aspects of his marriage continued to enjoy the sexual relationship because it "kept the romance alive in the marriage."

Different Complexes
Cooperating vs. Accommodating
Development of Relationship vs.
Enhancement of Relationship

When for one reason or another an Innocent Lover has a temporary loss of interest in sex, the Romantic Lover's care and attention to this will be much appreciated. This occurred when an

Innocent Lover became temporarily impotent as a side effect of some medication he was taking. He was quite appreciative of his Romantic Lover partner's devoted attention and concern with his welfare during this difficult time.

As mentioned in Chapter 6, Innocent Lovers may withhold sex as a way of expressing anger and dissatisfaction with their partner. Any such withholding that is either lengthy or frequent is likely to prove intolerable to a Romantic Lover. The energy of the Romantic Lover's *strong* and *narrow* expression of love will have no outlet if sex is withheld, and this might provoke the Romantic Lover to seek release in a sexual affair.

Relationships with extended family members can be a cause of friction in Innocent Lover–Romantic Lover couples. Innocent Lovers typically enjoy and value ongoing and frequent contacts with parents and other members of their own and the beloved's family. These relationships are central aspects of change and development toward a sense of connection and continuity with the world. Innocent Lovers who become estranged from their family can be quite unhappy, blaming either themselves or others for the estrangement. For the Romantic Lover, time spent with family is time that could have been spent relating to the beloved; being with the beloved when family members are also there is not nearly as satisfying or enhancing. Romantic Lovers' relative lack of interest in participating in family events and using vacation time for family visits can be interpreted by the Innocent Lover partner as rejection, indifference, and a wish to be separated from the beloved. If the Innocent Lover insists that "being together" at family events is important, the Romantic Lover may accommodate the request. However, lengthy interactions with family may feel to the Romantic Lover like a loss of a meaningful connection with the

Shared Complexes
Relatedness
Togetherness
Different Complexes
Change (Instrumental) vs. Stability
Development of Relationship vs. Enhancement of Relationship

beloved; he or she is then likely to feel isolated and alone—even though the couple may be physically together most of the time. For the Innocent Lover, being with the beloved in the cooperative and accepting atmosphere of extended family can be a source of great satisfaction.

Romantic Lovers may feel diminished when the Innocent Lover partner spends a lot of time with family members. One Romantic Lover was troubled when her Innocent Lover fiancé seemed to be "at the beck and call" of his widowed mother. She objected to the time he spent doing things with his mother because it was time away from their relationship. She viewed her beloved as too obliging, and his mother as demanding and dominating. It seemed to her that "he was choosing to spend time with his mother rather than me too much of the time." This led her to question the permanence and stability of the love relationship and his commitment to it. As a Romantic Lover, she viewed "time" as something that can be measured and allotted to different activities and people. For her Innocent Lover partner, the amount of time spent doing something was irrelevant; "time" for him represented change, growth, and progression toward a goal. The time he spent with his mother was integrally woven into the meaning and fulfillment of his values and goals. His Romantic Lover partner, however, viewed the amount of time he spent with his mother as time subtracted from the articulation and expression of their love relationship.

Different Complexes

Change (Instrumental) vs. Stability

Development of Relationship vs. Enhancement of Relationship

These same issues are often involved in the way the couple view friendships. Innocent Lovers often have close friends, usually of the same sex. Such friendships enhance their feelings of being loved and connected with others through shared plans and goals. Friends are less important for Romantic Lovers, whose primary focus is on being in love with one person, the beloved. Sharing him or her with others represents time and energy taken away from the relationship. For the Innocent Lover, community events or activities with the parents of their children's friends are more pleasurable when the Romantic Lover partner participates. If the Romantic Lover is reluctant to cooperate

Shared Complexes
Togetherness
Relatedness
Different Complexes
Cooperating and Being in Love

in this, the Innocent Lover's enjoyment is diminished. The Romantic Lover's participation enhances the Innocent Lover's sense of community and fellowship.

Neither partner is likely to feel comfortable with the partner having significant opposite-sex friendships. For the Innocent Lover, there is the potential for a withdrawal of love; for the Romantic Lover, energy used by the partner in any other relationship is a threat to the stability and permanence of the love relationship. Both may be sensitive to hints of flirtation from other people

Different Complexes
Being Loved vs. Being in Love
Change (Instrumental) vs. Stability

toward the partner, and may not appreciate people joking about intimacies or commenting about the sexual affairs of others. One Innocent Lover wife took her Romantic Lover husband to task because she felt he should have more aggressively rebuffed or avoided the flirtatious advances of an intoxicated woman at a party.

Recreational preferences are also affected by the couple's ideas about togetherness. The Romantic Lover looks forward to trips and vacations alone with the beloved or in the company of a few like-minded couples. Visiting family during vacation time can be intrusive and burdensome. When

Shared Complexes
Togetherness
Relatedness

Romantic Lovers agree to family-style vacations, they try to build in sufficient time alone with the beloved—for example, by staying in a hotel rather than within the homes of family members. At times, and depending on the quality of family relationships, the Romantic Lover may reluctantly encourage the Innocent Lover to visit family alone or with their children. In general, however, neither member of the couple favors separate vacations, and both enjoy being together when possible, even on business trips.

Similar issues can be involved in the couple's approach to their children. A Romantic Lover husband in particular may feel discounted if the Innocent Lover wife becomes absorbed in caring for the children. Alternatively, an Innocent Lover father may eagerly take the lead in caring for a new baby and in its continuing nurturance. In this case, the Romantic Lover mother may feel like an outsider intruding on the father-child relationship, in addition to feeling unloved, disconnected, and out of harmony with her Innocent Lover spouse. For example, a pregnant Romantic Lover wife and her Innocent Lover husband both agreed that he was by nature more nurturing and "maternal" than she was. She welcomed his offer to do much of the childcare when their baby was born. However, she did not anticipate his total absorption in and dedication to his new role as father of a helpless infant. When he enthusiastically attempted to include her in the joys of parenthood, she felt resentful and inadequate; for her, the primary relationship with her beloved was jeopardized by the energy he devoted to the child. Eventually, they had a major argument that resulted in some helpful changes in their division of responsibilities for their child.

A similar situation occurred when a Romantic Lover woman married an Innocent Lover man who had two children from his previous marriage. The Romantic Lover felt that she was always "in second place" relative to her husband's children because his devotion to them left him with little time for or interest in her. As a

> **Different Complexes**
>
> *Change (Instrumental) vs. Stability*
> *Development of Relationship vs. Enhancement of Relationship*
> *Cooperating vs. Accommodating*

Romantic Lover, she wanted and needed her love relationship with her husband to be primary.

When issues of attention to children are balanced or have been resolved, Innocent and Romantic Lovers often share great attentiveness and warmth toward their young and adolescent children. Both enjoy encouraging a child's spontaneity, imagination, and capacity for wonder and fun. The playfulness and freshness of children appeal to the Innocent Lover parent, and both enjoy developing a close and trusting relationship with the child. They convey to their children an optimism about both the present and the future, as well as a capacity to appreciate the value of a cooperative and accommodating approach to others.

Different Complexes
Change (Instrumental) vs. Stability
Cooperating vs. Accomodating

Divorce in an Innocent Lover–Romantic Lover couple can be quite difficult for both. Feelings of anger and a sense of despair may occur for the Innocent Lover. Depending on the circumstances causing the divorce, she or he may make attempts to win back the beloved with alternating pleading, verbal attacks, and references to the Romantic Lover abandoning the Innocent Lover and the children, if there are any. Romantic Lovers may alternate between feeling responsible for their part in the divorce and being angry at the partner's failure to fulfill whatever their expectations were of the marriage. Both during and after the divorce, there may be intermittent attempts at reconciliation, sometimes stimulated by the couple making love and reexperiencing the joys of being in love and being loved. Many such couples find that they are least distressed after a divorce if they can maintain minimal contact with each other.

Shared Complexes
Relatedness
Togetherness
Different Complexes
Development of Relationship vs. Enhancement of Relationship
Being Loved vs. Being in Love

The Clash of Complexes

Rick and Andrea have been married for almost two years. This is a second marriage for both of them. Their children from their previous marriages are attending college, and none of them lives with the couple. Rick is a stockbroker, and Andrea is a part-time real estate agent. They live at the outskirts of a large city because they prefer a countrylike environment.

They had met at a party and were immediately attracted to each other. They made love shortly after their first meeting. Andrea found Rick to be a tender, ardent, and passionate lover. She said that she felt loved for the first time in her life. Lovemaking with her previous husband had been mechanical and infrequent (once or twice a week). However, she and Rick made love every night and several times on the weekend when they could sleep in. Andrea was as passionate a lover as Rick. He said that making love with her was like losing himself in her ardor; he had never been with a more fervent lover than Andrea.

Rick, a Romantic Lover, is a gourmet cook. During their courtship he frequently made lavish dinners for Andrea, an Innocent Lover. Evenings were spent embracing each other while watching television. They would even hold hands while reading. Andrea felt very much loved, and Rick felt at one with Andrea.

Phase One: The Disagreement

- As a disagreement continues with no resolution, tension increases.

- The persistence and increase of tension cause misunderstanding.

- Sustained tension and misunderstanding cause stress.

One morning Rick was at work when the plumbing backed up. Andrea became frantic and left a message at Rick's office that there was an emergency and she needed him to call home. She waited impatiently until noon and again called his office. His secretary told her that he was out of the office and had not picked up his messages. Andrea was furious. At 3:00, Rick finally called her, and they had the following conversation:

Rick: Honey, I got your message that there's an emergency. What's wrong? Are you all right?

Andrea: Where the hell were you?

Rick: I know you're upset. What's wrong?

Andrea (loudly and emphatically): Where were you? Don't you pick up your messages? You're certainly prompt when they're from someone else!

Rick: I had lunch with a new client, that's all.

Andrea (suspiciously): Is your new client a woman?

Rick: No, no. He's just a hotshot guy in his forties. I'm sorry. Tell me what's the emergency.

Andrea: The toilets are backed up. There's something wrong with the septic tank. The place is a smelly mess. You know you take care of these things.

Rick: Did you call the service company? Were you able to clean the place up?

Andrea: Of course I cleaned up. There you go accusing me of being messy. Do you think I like shit all over the floor?

Rick: Please, honey. I didn't mean anything. I'm sorry. Did the service man come by?

Andrea: No! They can't come until tomorrow. They told me they were short-handed. A couple of their workers are sick with the flu.

Rick: Did you try another service company?

Andrea: Of course I did. Do you think I'm stupid?

(Andrea slams the phone down and starts to cry. The phone rings. She lets it ring five times before she picks it up.)

Rick: Sweetie, I'm really sorry. I didn't mean anything by that. I was just concerned about you being in the house alone with that mess. I should be home in an hour, okay?

Andrea (soothed): Well, are you sure it's okay? It would be nice if you could come home.

Rick: See you soon. I love you.

Andrea: I love you, too.

Rick arrives home within the hour and helps Andrea with the cleaning. The remainder of the day is pleasant for both of them. She feels loved, and Rick has a sense of togetherness and being in love. The repairs that need to be made are incidental to their shared complexes of Relatedness and Togetherness.

Phase Two: The Quarrel

- Persistent misunderstanding and stress consume large amounts of energy and can be exhausting.

- Sustained fatigue and stress jeopardize the ability to integrate and respond to the issues.

- Fatigue and stress continue to consume more energy.

- Negative aspects of the participants' Soul Images are evoked.

Occasionally, Rick erroneously presumes what Andrea wants or likes. For example, one weekend he decided to give her a little "gift of love." While she was out shopping, he rearranged the contents of her bedroom closet so that the space could be used more efficiently. When she came home, however, the following exchange occurred:

Rick: I have a surprise for you.

Andrea: What is it, sweetie? Will I like it?

Rick: I think so. Go to the bedroom and see.

(Andrea quickly goes into the bedroom. Rick hears the exclamation, "Oh, my God!")

Andrea (shouting): How dare you go into *my* closet and change things! How dare you!

Rick: But, but, but, I thought you'd like it!

Andrea: If you loved me, you'd know what pleases me.

Rick: You know you don't like cleaning. Your closet was such a mess.

Andrea: You always say I'm messy. What else is wrong with me besides being messy? Maybe you think I'm a lousy cook. That's why you do all the cooking.

Rick: You just don't like cooking and I like to cook. But you like clutter and I don't.

Andrea: So you think you're better than me.

Rick (getting angry): Well, you clutter the place up with your shit.

Andrea: That's right! Be crude! You're just foul and coarse.

(Andrea runs back into the bedroom, throws herself on the bed, and cries. Rick is angry and doesn't understand why she' so upset. He thought he was being caring. He comes into the bedroom, rubs her back, and says he's sorry. She resists and shouts at him to leave. He promises he will be more considerate and leaves. The rest of the day they are silent and cold to each other.)

Rick's complexes of enhancement of the relationship and accommodating combined with his complex of relatedness caused him to presume that what he likes, Andrea will like as well. However, this presumption of oneness and shared identity conflicted with Andrea's complexes of being loved and development of the relationship. It didn't occur to Rick to ask Andrea about her preferences; he was unaware that asking her would be a sign that he loved her. From Rick's point of view, such a question would indicate that he didn't know her likes and preferences and therefore didn't truly love her. Such questions would be a sign that he and she were not "at one" with each other. Andrea's hurt and anger were truly a surprise to him, especially when her unconscious complexes erupted and she accused him of *never* loving her, *always* saying she's messy, and being *nothing but* stupid.

Their severe tension persisted for several days and then dissipated gradually. Eventually the hurt feelings and anger receded into the background of their lives, and the two renewed their experiences of love for each other. This sequence of angry encounter, silent hurt, and eventual reconciliation is typical for Rick and Andrea. Even though it doesn't occur frequently, the pattern is basically the same in style and duration.

The Nature of This Love Relationship

Both Innocent and Romantic Lovers give a central place to their intimate love relationship as the avenue for experiencing satisfaction and well-being. The distinctive aspect of their relationship is connected to the renewal of being loved for the Innocent Lover and the constancy of being in love for the Romantic Lover. This difference influences their somewhat different perspective on togetherness, even though they share this complex. The Romantic Lover wants the meaningful togetherness that comes with stability and enhancement of the relationship, while the Innocent Lover desires the cooperative togetherness that results from development of the relationship toward future goals. In this kind of couple, the Innocent Lover's focus on cooperating and the Romantic Lover's use of accommodating make both partners value harmony in the relationship, so both are sensitive to each other's desires. Similarly, the central aspects of their love relationship—for the Innocent Lover, being loved, and for the Romantic Lover, being in love—converge effectively to satisfy both their desires.

These same complexes emerged in the disagreement and quarrel between Rick and Andrea. Andrea's Innocent Lover complex of togetherness quickly emerged as a result of the plumbing crisis. When Rick wasn't there to help with the problem, this made her hypersensitive to her other complexes about cooperating and being loved. In the telephone exchange that occurred, Andrea's stress led her to make several *always* or *never* and *nothing-but* statements that revealed unconscious complexes. Rick responded with his own complexes, but because he was not experiencing undue stress, none of his statements reflected unconscious complexes. However, this wasn't the case in the quarrel that resulted from his erroneous presumption about what would please her. Both partners made several *always* or *never* and *nothing-but* statements in the heat of their altercation.

Individual histories and circumstances may vary widely among Innocent Lover–Romantic Lover couples, but the same complexes and issues we saw here are likely to emerge in their daily lives and in their quarrels. We hope you now have a better and deeper understanding of, appreciation for, and ability to appraise this kind of true love.

12 | *Mercurial Lover and Steadfast Lover*

*Love consists in this, that two solitudes protect
and touch and greet each other.*

Rainer Maria Rilke, *Letters to a Young Poet*

The distinctive character of the Mercurial Lover–Steadfast Lover
relationship is due to the partner's opposite complexes of change
(intrinsic) versus stability. Although change versus stability is also
an aspect of the Innocent Lover–Steadfast Lover relationship, the
goal-directedness of *instrumental* change for Innocent Lovers is in
accord with the constancy associated with the Steadfast Lover complex of stability. Change for Mercurial Lovers has *intrinsic* value, so
that goals and purposes are relatively unimportant. This does not
mean that Steadfast Lovers avoid change; rather, they believe that
change should be planned, gradual, and in accord with one's

255

values. For a Mercurial Lover, in contrast, abrupt and radical change is acceptable and often preferred.

The shared complexes of separateness and autonomy add to the mutuality in this kind of relationship. This conjunction is the basis for the respect and admiration that Mercurial Lover–Steadfast Lover couples often show each other. While recognizing the very different paths each may take toward independence and self-fulfillment, they tend to be interested in and supportive of each other's endeavors. The Mercurial Lover's preference for discussing to resolve disagreements and the Steadfast Lover's use of negotiating can lead to some lively and productive interchanges, as well as misunderstandings. The two also differ about what is central in their love relationship, with the Mercurial Lover emphasizing falling in love and the Steadfast Lover focusing on staying in love.

A comparison of the characteristics of Mercurial and Steadfast Lovers is provided in Chart 17 on pages 258 and 259. The next section describes how the complexes listed in the chart are expressed in the everyday lives of Mercurial Lover–Steadfast Lover couples. To highlight the complexes being discussed, they are identified in the margin beside the relevant descriptions.

The Mercurial Lover–Steadfast Lover Relationship

Shared Complexes
Separateness
Autonomy
Different Complexes
Change (Intrinsic) vs Stability
Transformation of Self vs. Differentiation of Self

The Mercurial and Steadfast Lover complexes of change versus stability, in conjunction with their shared complexes of separateness and autonomy, lead to some interesting points of agreement and disagreement. For example, work is connected to autonomy and fulfills both partners' desires for independent accomplishment. However, for the Mercurial Lover, work has transformational value, while for the Steadfast Lover, work promotes differentiation of the self. In line with its importance of transformation is the Mercurial Lover's desire to be free to change the kind of work he or she does or the work situation if it becomes stagnant and unsatisfying.

"I am most comfortable when I feel that I'm choosing to do my work every day, not that I have to do it; otherwise, I feel trapped," said one Mercurial Lover. "I want to feel free to change my work, stop doing it, or even do something else entirely." His Steadfast Lover wife was somewhat uneasy with her beloved's attitude toward work, at times worrying that her husband lacked perseverance and maturity in the face of adversity.

For Steadfast Lovers, even if work is somewhat unsatisfying, it may be instrumental to something that is important to them. One Steadfast Lover developed a very successful real estate business so that he could have enough money to retire early and devote himself full-time to his true passion, photography. Other Steadfast Lovers may tolerate a somewhat dissatisfying work situation if it permits them the autonomy to address other important interests.

For example, a Steadfast Lover professor of English tolerated the political aspects of academia, which he disliked intensely, because his job provided him with the opportunity to encourage and influence young writers. His Mercurial Lover wife often became impatient listening to his complaints about work and would encourage him to "teach somewhere else, or find another career. I don't understand why you put up with that stuff!" The Steadfast Lover professor, however, had made a "negotiated decision" based on what was important to him. His frequent complaints to his wife were his way of diffusing and minimizing the negative aspects of his career. His Mercurial Lover wife, who valued change in response to dissatisfaction, wasn't supportive of his choice to differentiate himself through his love of teaching.

Chart 17

Comparison of Mercurial and Steadfast Lovers

Central Relationship Question: Mercurial Lovers

"If I am a separate, changing individual, how can I merge with a beloved in an intimate, loving relationship? Change and the flux of life sustain me with vigor, further my transformation, and engage me with life's possibilities. Yet this isn't enough. I also need the exhilaration of love through merging with my beloved. As much as I desire the passion of love, however, I also fear my beloved's love. My fear is that my beloved may innocently entice me to a life of predictability, comfort, and routine that will end in a suffocating and deadly inertia. If this happens, I will indeed lose my soul and I will become like an automaton in a Kafka novel."

Attributes, Themes, and Complexes

Change	Any change is good in itself. Change has intrinsic value.
Transformation of Self	Focus on a future filled with the potential for change and transformation.
Separateness	View their identity and sense of self as unique and distinct from relationships.
Autonomy	Value independence and autonomy; resist restrictions on freedom and are sensitive to any hint of coercion from others.
Discussing	Value explorative communication and discussing the relationship and what it means.
Falling in Love	Revel in the intensity and novelty of the experience of love.

Kind of Intimacy

Temperature	Hot—passionate sexual activity; kissing and caressing in public.
Proximity	Distant—unawareness of the unspoken distress or joy of the partner.

Expression of Psychic Energy

Focus	Broad—many expressions of love.
Intensity	Mild to strong expressions of love.

Chart 17

Comparison of Mercurial and Steadfast Lovers (cont.)

Central Relationship Question: Steadfast Lovers

"How can I maintain my individuality and still be in a loving relationship? If I am a separate individual and I have a distinct identity, will I have to surrender or lose part of my identity and individuality to be in a loving relationship? After all, to be in a loving relationship means that I will have to take into consideration what my partner wishes and desires. I can't just do what I want without at least informing or consulting my partner. What's worse, suppose my partner objects to what I want or has a different preference? If I give in to that, doesn't that mean I will lose part of me?"

Attributes, Themes, and Complexes

Stability	Value is placed on constancy and continuity.
Differentiation of Self	Focus is on differentiation—on the refinement and expression of all facets of their selfhood.
Separateness	Accept their partners as separate, independent individuals and want that same kind of acceptance for themselves.
Autonomy	Value independence, uniqueness, and distinctness from social and cultural environments.
Negotiating	Negotiating is the natural way of resolving differences and conflicts.
Staying in Love	Place high value on faithfulness and constancy in the love relationship.

Kind of Intimacy

Temperature	Cool—minimal physical contact, nonverbal and nonphysical expressions of affection, politeness in public.
Proximity	Close—deeply affected by the other's unspoken distress.

Expression of Psychic Energy

Focus	Broad—many expressions of love.
Intensity	Mild expressions of love.

It is natural for Mercurial Lover–Steadfast Lover partners to be interested in each other's work lives. Many avoid offering advice, however, in order to honor the separateness and autonomy of the beloved. However, as occurred for the English professor and his wife, Mercurial Lover values about change may overcome good intentions not to interfere. Similarly, a Steadfast Lover may become impatient when her Mercurial Lover beloved seems to lack direction and purpose in his work; and a Mercurial Lover may become frustrated and critical watching his Steadfast Lover wife persist in a situation she dislikes. At times, such differences in perspective can create hurt feelings and resentments in the relationship.

> **Shared Complexes**
> *Separateness*
> *Autonomy*
> **Different Complexes**
> *Change (Intrinsic) vs. Stability*

For example, one evening a Mercurial Lover excitedly told her Steadfast Lover husband what a wonderful day she had had at the art gallery where she worked. "You must have made a lot in commissions," he said. "Commissions? I wasn't keeping track," she replied with some annoyance. "And that has nothing to do with it, anyway. My day was wonderful because I had great discussions with patrons and I made a really good connection with the director of the art museum in Phoenix." Knowing his wife worked on commission, this Steadfast Lover husband erroneously assumed that what gave her a sense of accomplishment was her skill at selling artwork. For the Mercurial Lover wife, however, the new ideas and experiences and the opportunities she cultivated gave her a sense of competence and gratification.

> **Different Complexes**
> *Transformation of Self vs. Differentiation of Self*

This same combination of complexes influences the partners' attitudes toward money. In general, the Mercurial Lover focus on change encourages an unplanned and spontaneous approach to both making and spending money: Spending money to promote personal transformation is not only acceptable but desirable. A Steadfast Lover partner is likely to be most comfortable with such an approach when he or she knows the Mercurial Lover has a definite purpose or goal in mind. For example, a Steadfast Lover was concerned when her Mercurial Lover fiancé decided to quit work and live

Different Complexes

Change (Intrinsic) vs. Stability

Transformation of Self vs. Differentiation of Self

for six months on an inheritance he had just received. He was unhappy with his work and wanted to be free to travel. He thought he might discover something else he would like to work at if there was no pressure to earn money. "Won't that just be wasting your money?" she asked. "You won't find something else unless you have some plan." The Mercurial Lover had noted before that his beloved was uncomfortable with uncertainty. He described to her what he had in mind and some contacts he had already made. This relieved the Steadfast Lover fiancée, who both admired and was puzzled by her beloved's spirited attitude toward life.

A Mercurial Lover–Steadfast Lover couple may disagree about whether their money should be combined or kept separate. One Mercurial Lover said, "I need to have my independence, so a separate checking account is important for me." A Steadfast Lover partner might easily appreciate the partner's desire for autonomy, but question the beloved's commitment to the

Contrasting Complexes

Autonomy and Stability

Transformation of Self and Staying in Love

Change (Intrinsic) and Negotiating

permanence and stability of the relationship. Steadfast Lovers prefer that money be pooled and that the couple arrive at a consensus about spending it through discussion and negotiation. Keeping finances separate appears to have a very different meaning for the partners in this relationship.

Their different views are attributable to a major source of misunderstanding in this kind of relationship—the pairing of autonomy and intrinsic change for Mercurial Lovers, versus the pairing of autonomy and stability for Steadfast Lovers. Autonomy and intrinsic change lead to unpredictability in Mercurial Lovers, while the Steadfast Lover pairing of autonomy and stability promotes predictability and coherence. Predictability and coherence give meaning to the love relationship for Steadfast Lovers; meaning for Mercurial Lovers comes from change, difference, and flexibility. This difference in outlook lies at the heart of the observation that Mercurial Lovers are optimists while Steadfast Lovers are realists.

Different Complexes

Autonomy and Change (Intrinsic) vs. Autonomy and Stability

Negotiation and reaching consensus about spending money can feel restrictive to Mercurial Lovers. If each partner is separately in charge of specific money, there's no need to discuss and make joint decisions. The Mercurial Lover is then free to respond independently to any change that occurs, especially a change that can contribute to transformation of the self. The Steadfast Lover's preference for negotiation, consultation, and joint decision making can feel coercive and controlling to a Mercurial Lover partner. For Steadfast Lovers, however, the Mercurial way of doing things is fraught with instability and unpredictability. A Steadfast Lover may react with hurt and anger if a Mercurial Lover is adamant and inflexible about keeping money separate. The Steadfast Lover may question the viability of the relationship due to a lack of constancy and permanence. Lack of consistency and predictability inhibits differentiation of the self and the complexities of the relationship. This also places the complex of staying in love in jeopardy.

Different Complexes

Transformation of Self vs. Differentiation of Self

Change (Intrinsic) vs. Staying in Love

Although issues about the meaning of work and the appropriate use of money may create some disagreements in a Mercurial Lover–Steadfast Lover couple, many other areas of daily life go very smoothly. This is primarily a result of the shared complexes of Separateness and Autonomy. Doing household chores independently is assumed to be the best way to accomplish them, and since both partners value equity and fairness, there is little difficulty in arriving at a mutually satisfactory division of labor. If the couple criticize each other's efforts, this will be more likely due to factors other than their Soul Images.

Shared Complexes

Separateness

Autonomy

For example, one Mercurial Lover preferred an organized and systematic method of cleaning the house, completing all of the tasks in one room before starting on another. Her Steadfast Lover husband, however, liked to spread out the housecleaning over several weeks. He liked flexibility and variety in accomplishing tasks. Compromising about their different styles was at times difficult, especially when both were anxious to be free to do other things.

Another typical area of agreement for Mercurial Lover–Steadfast Lover couples is the relative importance of their extended families. Both are likely to value their own and each other's independence and separation from family, and neither will feel any strong desire to be involved in the lives of parents, siblings, or other relatives. Therefore, the amount of contact, closeness, or distance in those relationships will be largely dependent on factors other than the part-

Shared Complexes

Separateness

Autonomy

ners' Soul Images and associated complexes. An exception to this can occur, however, if a Steadfast Lover feels obligated to help family members in need. A Mercurial Lover partner may at times find it difficult to understand and support the beloved's attitude. One Steadfast Lover, who maintained little contact with his rather shiftless and irresponsible brother, nonetheless felt obligated to lend him several thousand dollars to help pay for the medical care of an ailing child. "It's not the fact that we'll never see the money again that bothers me," his Mercurial Lover wife said. "It's that your brother is interfering in our lives because of his own bad judgment. I just resent that."

Recreational pursuits and independent friendships also pose little stress for a Mercurial Lover–Steadfast Lover couple. Whether their leisure activities are done together or separately is a function of the nature of the recreation, and has little inherent meaning for the relationship itself. If both partners enjoy the same activities, they will do them together or separately, depending on circumstances and availability. Deciding how to use their free time can be easily accomplished through discussion and negotiation. Neither partner is likely to want to accompany a beloved on a business trip unless there is a compelling interest in the activity or the geographic area involved. (This contrasts with Romantic and Innocent Lovers, who are more likely to want to accompany a partner whenever possible.) For Mercurial and Steadfast Lovers, simply accompanying the beloved with no individual purpose or pleasure in mind wouldn't be meaningful. Both partners tend to be accepting of each other's separate activities.

Different Complexes
Discussing vs. Negotiating

For example, Matt, a Steadfast Lover, and his partner, Sam, a Mercurial Lover, were invited to a dinner party at the home of friends. Both were looking forward to going. However, on the morning of the day of the dinner, Matt felt ill. His symptoms worsened during the day, and he told Sam that he felt too sick to go to the party.

"Do you want to go anyway?" Matt asked Sam.

"Sure, I might as well. Want me to bring you back some food?"

"Okay. I probably won't feel like eating anything tonight, but I can have it tomorrow. You can tell me all about the party when you get back, if I'm still up."

Sam went to the party by himself. When he got home, Matt was asleep, and had left a note saying he hoped Sam had had a good time and that he'd talk to him in the morning.

Just as two Mercurial or two Steadfast Lovers risk becoming alienated by overemphasizing separateness and autonomy, so does a Mercurial Lover–Steadfast Lover couple. Shared recreational interests can be helpful in avoiding this, as can planned

Different Complexes
Falling in Love vs. Staying in Love

vacations where the focus is on enjoying the excitement or relaxation of doing something different together. For example, a Mercurial Lover flight attendant and his Steadfast Lover wife took advantage of his free flights to go abroad at least once a year. They enjoyed traveling together, especially since it reminded them of their initial courtship when they first met on a plane trip. Taking trips together rekindled the Mercurial Lover's feeling of falling in love, and for the Steadfast Lover it validated the permanence and stability of their love.

A Mercurial Lover–Steadfast Lover couple will have shared friendships with other couples as well as individual friendships formed in relation to work and special interests. Both partners are unlikely to be concerned with the amount of time the other spends with friends or in pursuing individual interests. In general, opposite-sex friendships pose no difficulty for

Shared Complex
Autonomy
Different Complexes
Change (Intrinsic) vs. Stability
Falling in Love vs. Staying in Love

either one. Should a Mercurial Lover's attraction to change and transformation lead to flirtations, the Steadfast Lover could be relatively tolerant of this. As is the case for Steadfast Lovers and their Romantic Lover partners, this tends to be more true for Steadfast Lover wives than husbands, which may be due to societal tolerances and stereotypes. With Mercurial Lover partners, Steadfast Lovers may see flirtations as harmless ways for them to have fun. The Steadfast Lover's acceptance is based on confidence that staying in love will ultimately be more important to the beloved than temporary fun. However, if the Mercurial Lover oversteps the bounds of the Steadfast Lover's tolerance, he or she may meet firm resistance and clear demands for change. If the Steadfast Lover discovers that staying in love is not a shared value, hurt and anger may result. In response, the Mercurial Lover may see the Steadfast Lover partner as controlling, parental, unloving, and intolerant.

Mercurial Lover–Steadfast Lover couples can have quite divergent views on childrearing. Their differing complexes of change and transformation of self versus stability and differentiation of self are the basis for their disagreements. Both readily agree about the importance of encouraging their children to become independent, competent, and successful in their lives. They have very different notions, however, as to how to ensure that this happens. Mercurial Lover parents believe it is important to provide a child with wide latitude to explore the world and discover what is possible. In contrast, Steadfast Lover parents encourage a child's autonomy by guiding him or her toward responsibility, goals, and individual values. The Mercurial Lover may view the Steadfast Lover's "guidance" as interference and control, while the Steadfast Lover may see the Mercurial Lover's value about freedom of choice as indifference to the child's welfare. Their disagreement in this regard reflects the optimism of the Mercurial Lover and the realism of the Steadfast Lover: The Mercurial Lover trusts that positive outcomes will occur for the child; the Steadfast Lover believes that positive outcomes will be more likely if potential problems and obstacles are anticipated and avoided. One Mercurial Lover mother described childrearing as "watching a little flower bloom." She contrasted this with her Steadfast Lover husband's belief that, "As the twig is bent, so grows the tree."

Steadfast Lovers in this type of relationship may at times feel that their partners aren't involved enough in childrearing because of the Mercurial Lover's tendency to be relaxed about giving the

Shared Complex
Autonomy
Different Complexes
Change (Intrinsic) vs. Stability
Transformation of Self vs.
Differentiation of Self

children direction and rules. This occurs regardless of the sex of the Mercurial Lover. Steadfast Lovers may also believe that the children lack respect for their Mercurial Lover parent because that parent may make fewer demands on them. One Steadfast Lover wife saw her husband's willingness to discuss issues at length with the children as a sign of his indecisiveness. She believed that any discussion with one of the children should be brief and end in a clear message regarding the child's behavior. For his part, the Mercurial Lover father accused his Steadfast Lover wife of being too hard on the children and of having too many expectations of them.

> **Different Complexes**
> *Transformation of Self vs. Differentiation of Self*
> *Discussing vs. Negotiating*

This same kind of misunderstanding regarding discussing versus negotiating to resolve disagreements strongly influences the general way Mercurial Lover–Steadfast Lover partners communicate with each other. Misunderstandings can easily occur because of the Mercurial Lover's focus on the intrinsic worth of change and the Steadfast Lover's contrasting emphasis on stability. For Mercurial Lovers, discussing is an open-ended, continuing process of exploring alternatives and being attentive to changing circumstances, thoughts, and feelings. Steadfast Lovers, in contrast, see a discussion as goal-oriented and as culminating in a negotiated conclusion. As a result, when a Mercurial Lover and a Steadfast Lover end a discussion in agreement, the Steadfast Lover believes that the matter is settled. However, as one Mercurial Lover put it, "Nothing is forever. Things might be different tomorrow, or next week. One of us might feel differently. We need to be free to respond to change." From a Steadfast Lover point of view, such an approach is uncomfortably indecisive and unstable.

> **Different Complexes**
> *Change (Intrinsic) vs. Stability*
> *Discussing vs. Negotiating*

With regard to their sexual relationship, Steadfast Lover–Mercurial Lover couples are surprisingly similar to

Romantic Lover–Mercurial Lover couples. The similarity of Romantic and Steadfast Lovers lies in their shared complex of stability rather than change. In addition, the Romantic Lover focus

on being in love and the Steadfast Lover focus on staying in love both contrast markedly with the Mercurial Lover focus on falling in love. This makes Romantic and Steadfast Lovers believe that they take sexuality "more seriously" than do Mercurial Lovers. Just as making love contributes to stability and enhancement of the relationship for Romantic Lovers, so does it contribute to stability and differentiation of self for the Steadfast Lover. However, for the Mercurial Lover, lovemaking appears more lighthearted and focused on the experience itself rather than on its meaning for the relationship.[1] Making love is an opportunity for change and transformation of self for the Mercurial Lover, and promotes the experience of falling in love.

To Steadfast Lovers, their Mercurial Lover partners may seem self-absorbed and too hedonistic with regard to sex and insufficiently involved with the meaning of sex for the partner and

the relationship. From the Mercurial Lover point of view, on the other hand, Steadfast Lovers may not be hedonistic enough because they may not appear to be enjoying sex very much. For Mercurial Lovers, sex is a party. In contrast, Steadfast Lovers view sex as a conversation. (To complete this summary, Romantic Lovers consider sex to be the meeting of mind and body, while Innocent Lovers see sex as a merger of two into one.)

The postdivorce relationship of a Mercurial Lover–Steadfast Lover couple tends to be comfortably cooperative. Confident with regard to their own and each other's separateness and autonomy, they can adjust to being apart with relative ease. When children are involved, the couple's very different ideas about childrearing can actually be less of an issue than they were during the marriage: Both partners can be appropriately attentive to agreeing regarding some common guidelines for rearing the children, while at the same time, each is free to promote his or her own style when alone with the child. One divorced couple easily adapted

Same Complexes
Separateness
Autonomy
Different Complexes
Discussing vs. Negotiating

to a cordial and collaborative relationship that extended beyond the need to consult each other about their children. They occasionally got together and spent a holiday with their children. However, neither made any demands on the other for either time or attention. Many months could go by comfortably with no contact between them.

The Clash of Complexes

Adam, a Steadfast Lover, and Stephanie, a Mercurial Lover, met in high school. They married shortly after they graduated, and Stephanie became pregnant within the first year of the marriage. Adam worked for an insurance company and attended a local college part-time. He didn't want Stephanie to work because he felt it was important for her to remain home with their child or children. They were very frugal and looked forward to Adam graduating from college and acquiring a better job. Adam worked very hard. In order to do her share, Stephanie was entirely in charge of the household and the children.

Many years passed. Adam graduated from college with a business degree, and through his hard work acquired his own insurance agency. They now had three children, the youngest of whom was in middle school. Stephanie continued to be in charge of the household and the needs of the children.

Phase One: The Disagreement

- As a disagreement continues with no resolution, tension increases.
- The persistence and increase of tension cause misunderstanding.
- Sustained tension and misunderstanding cause stress.

One evening, after the children had gone to bed, Stephanie went into the living room, where Adam was reading a business journal, and started the following conversation:

Stephanie: Adam, I want to talk to you about something.

Adam: Sure. What is it?

Stephanie: I'm thinking of getting a job.

Adam (somewhat agitated): Why?

Stephanie: Well, I'm kind of bored. The children are needing me less. I feel a little restless.

Adam: I don't understand. I'm making good money. You don't have to work.

Stephanie: It has nothing to do with that. I'm just a little bored.

Adam: Are you getting bored with me?

Stephanie: That has nothing to do with it. I would just like to have something to do that isn't related to you or the children.

Adam (getting more agitated): Do you see me as controlling you?

Stephanie: Adam, please! It has nothing to do with you or the children.

Adam: Well, you may not think so, but I do. Here you want a life separate from the children and me. Of course it has something to do with us! I thought we had a good life. We've accomplished a lot in the past ten years. Now you say you're unhappy.

Stephanie: Adam, please listen to me. I didn't say I was unhappy. It's just that I want something more. You've accomplished a lot, but I haven't.

Adam: You mean being a good mother and raising decent kids is no accomplishment. Shame on you!

Stephanie (angry and hurt): You really don't understand me.

Adam (somewhat sarcastically): Well, educate me.

Stephanie: Adam, we have accomplished a lot. We have a good marriage and good children. You have achieved a lot. You're a good father and you have a good career. I believe that I'm a good mother and wife. But I have no career. Your career is important for you. Why can't doing something for myself be important for me, too? Who knows, I may not even like working. That's a possibility.

Adam (thoughtfully): You're right. If it's important to me, why can't it be important to you? I'm sorry I didn't understand. I guess I sounded a bit like a male chauvinist.

Stephanie: You certainly did! ... And Adam, there's something else I would like.

Adam: What, there's more? What do you have, a list?

Stephanie: No, No! Nothing like that. I would just like to have the money I earn be my own money.

Adam: What do you mean, "your own money"? Do we have a marriage, or are we business partners?

Stephanie: As a matter of fact, we're both. We have a marriage *and* we're business partners. What's wrong with that?

Adam: Plenty! We put everything in the same pot and divvy it up as needed. That's what a marriage is for me.

Stephanie: Don't be sarcastic! I just want my own checking account. Keeping money I make separate is important to me.

Adam (shouting): That's too much! Isn't a job enough? The next thing you'll want is your own apartment, and that will mean the end of our marriage! This independence thing of yours is getting out of control.

Stephanie: You're the one who's getting out of control! You don't listen to me, you jump to conclusions. Just let me finish what I was going to say and then you can shout. Okay?

Adam: Okay! Okay!

Stephanie: Now, listen. I would like my money to be in my own checking account. The account will be in both our names, but it will be mine. I will be the only one to use it. I'll have my own checks. It will be like found money. Doesn't that make sense?

Adam: Actually, it is reasonable. Okay. But if you get a job, what about the kids?

Stephanie: That's what we need to discuss.

Adam: I agree, we do. Okay. Let's do it.

A few weeks later, Stephanie obtained a part-time job as an office worker at a pharmaceutical company. She soon discovered that she had a natural flair for management. She made several suggestions at work that saved time and cut costs. Her suggestions were so well regarded that she was asked to work full-time. Several months later she was given a promotion. Furthermore, she anticipated that she would be promoted again within the year to a managerial position. Adam became accustomed to and pleased with Stephanie's working. Her salary enabled them to indulge in small luxuries. They managed to negotiate child-care responsibilities, and each helped the other as needed.

Phase Two: The Quarrel

- Persistent misunderstanding and stress consume large amounts of energy and can be exhausting.
- Sustained fatigue and stress jeopardize the ability to integrate and respond to the issues.
- Fatigue and stress continue to consume more energy.
- Negative aspects of the participants' Soul Images are evoked.

One evening after the children had gone to bed, Stephanie asked Adam to come into their bedroom. Adam sensed some tension in her voice. The following exchange occurred:

Adam (anxiously): What's wrong? Is there something you want to talk about?

Stephanie: Now, don't get upset, there's nothing wrong. I just want to show you what I bought today.

Adam (relieved): Oh, did you buy a new dress?

Stephanie: More than that. Look at these.

(Stephanie opened her closet and displayed several elegant and expensive-looking outfits.)

Adam: Those look really expensive. Was there a sale? How much did this cost?

Stephanie (matter-of-factly): About two thousand dollars.

Adam (exclaiming): What? How could you spend that kind of money without our talking about it first? That's not the way we do things!

Stephanie: Well, it's my money and I can do what I want with it. I don't have to ask you. Don't be so controlling.

Adam (ignoring her comment): Why do you need all these clothes, anyway? Are you dressing up for someone?

Stephanie: You're like all the men in my office. You all think the only reason women dress up is for men.

Adam: Well, that's what other women do, isn't it?

Stephanie: I'm not "other women"—I'm me. I'm going to get a promotion, and I want to dress professionally. You really are a male chauvinist.

Adam: I knew this job thing was a bad idea. The next thing that'll happen is you'll be on the road for your company, and then what? You'll probably screw around on me.

Stephanie (shouting): You're impossible! You don't listen to me. There's no point in my talking to you.

(Stephanie angrily leaves the room. Adam remains in the bedroom, pacing back and forth. He is angry, hurt, and frustrated.)

The cause of the misunderstanding and ultimately the severe quarrel was the clash of Stephanie's complex of transformation of self through change and autonomy with Adam's complexes of stability, negotiation, and staying in love. The intrinsic value that change and autonomy had for Stephanie was interpreted by Adam as disrupting the value he placed on stability in their relationship. His unconscious complexes were evoked when he accused Stephanie of being *nothing but* independent and uncaring. Stephanie interpreted Adam's need for constancy and predictability as restricting and limiting her access to autonomy, change, and transformation. Her unconscious complexes emerged when she censured him for being *nothing but* controlling, a male chauvinist, and out of control, and for *never* listening to her. These differences resulted in a severe clash of their complexes.

⎰ *The Nature of This Love Relationship*

The Mercurial Lover complex of intrinsic change and the Steadfast Lover complex of stability give this relationship its distinctive character and identify many of the sources of agreement and disagreement for these two lovers. Central to their appreciation and respect for each other are their shared values about individual independence, autonomy, and separateness. These similar perspectives enable them to accept each other's different views about change and stability as well as their alternative notions of how to achieve selfhood—transformation for the Mercurial Lover, and differentiation for the Steadfast Lover. Discussing for

Mercurial Lovers and negotiating for Steadfast Lovers can work well or poorly, depending on the couple's ability to define the point at which a disagreement has been resolved. However, accommodating the different perspectives of falling in love for Mercurial Lovers and staying in love for Steadfast Lovers requires some effort and compromise for this kind of couple.

Many of these same complexes were evident in the disagreement and quarrel between Adam and Stephanie. The context for their clash of complexes is similar in many ways to that of the Mercurial Lover–Innocent Lover couple, Tom and Elisse. You will recall that Elisse, the Mercurial Lover, was also a homemaker whose life circumstances did not permit her satisfying outlets for separateness, autonomy, and transformation of self through intrinsic change. The scenarios depicted for these two couples have different characters, however. These differences are due to the fact that Elisse's partner is an Innocent Lover and Stephanie's partner is a Steadfast Lover. The Innocent Lover Tom focused on the impact the Mercurial Lover partner's desires were having on his Innocent Lover complexes of relatedness, togetherness, cooperating, and being loved. In the present case, Steadfast Lover Adam was more concerned with what Stephanie's behavior meant for his complexes of stability, negotiating, and staying in love.

Unconscious complexes emerged for both Adam and Stephanie. Both partners made explicit and implicit *always* or *never* and *nothing-but* statements in the heat of their disagreement and quarrel. In some ways, we might have expected that Adam's Steadfast Lover complexes of separateness and autonomy would make him more understanding and accepting of Stephanie's attempts to fulfill these same complexes in her life. However, he saw her newfound independence as a threat to the relationship's stability and as possibly interfering with his complex of Staying in Love. Perhaps some gender stereotypes implicit in Adam's attitude toward his wife's working were also at work here.

Individual histories and circumstances may vary widely among Mercurial Lover–Steadfast Lover couples, but the same complexes and issues we saw here are likely to emerge in their daily lives and in their quarrels. We hope you now have a better and deeper understanding of, appreciation for, and ability to appraise this kind of true love.

13 ⟨ Romantic Lover and Steadfast Lover

How do I love thee? Let me count the ways.
I love thee to the depth and breadth and height
My soul can reach . . . .

Elizabeth Barrett Browning, *Sonnets from the Portuguese*

A distinctive aspect of a Romantic Lover–Steadfast Lover relationship is how it begins. With two Mercurial Lovers, two Innocent Lovers, and a Mercurial Lover–Innocent Lover couple, there is typically an immediate attraction. They fall in love and become caught up in the "swirl" of their passion. In contrast, for two Steadfast Lovers or two Romantic Lovers, the relationship begins with fondness that gradually develops into a romantic love affair. The love of a Romantic Lover–Steadfast Lover couple has a similar beginning. First there are reciprocal warm feelings, a growing comfort and openness, then a yearning, and finally the passionate consummation of their love.

For both Romantic and Steadfast Lovers, the complex of stability permits a gradual and tranquil unfolding of the many facets of a love relationship. It is for this reason that they begin their love relationship with warmth and fondness. The distinctive expression of the Romantic Lover–Steadfast Lover relationship is the result of the conjunction of the partners' different complexes: enhancement of the relationship for Romantic Lovers versus differentiation of self for Steadfast Lovers; relatedness and togetherness for Romantic Lovers versus separateness and autonomy for Steadfast Lovers; accommodating to resolve disagreements for Romantic Lovers as compared with negotiating for Steadfast Lovers; and a central focus on being in love for Romantic Lovers in contrast to staying in love for Steadfast Lovers.

The Steadfast Lover's proclivity for responsibility and efficiency and the Romantic Lover's fondness for romantic enchantment can complement each other. In concert, these different complexes moderate the Romantic Lover partner's fanciful excesses and lighten the Steadfast Lover's ponderous responsibilities. However, in times of internal or external stress, these opposing complexes can cause considerable discord in the relationship.

A comparison of the characteristics of Steadfast and Romantic Lovers is provided in Chart 18 on pages 280 and 281. The next section describes how the complexes listed in the chart are expressed in the everyday lives of Romantic Lover–Steadfast Lover couples. To highlight the complexes being discussed, they are identified in the margin beside the relevant descriptions.

The Romantic Lover–Steadfast Lover Relationship

Steadfast Lovers are most concerned with the everyday aspects of their love relationship, while Romantic Lovers are more interested in the small romantic interludes that enhance their sense of being in love. At times, Romantic Lovers may feel estranged from their Steadfast Lover partners, even though they know that the partner loves and cherishes them. The Romantic Lover partner may feel that something is missing in the relationship, not that there is something wrong with it.

Lack of time for romantic interludes or a partner's failure to appreciate romance increases the internal stress for the Romantic Lover partner. For example, as a result of fatigue or the pressures of work, the Steadfast Lover may become indifferent to or impatient with the Romantic Lover partner's romantic niceties. Such romantic gestures are important expressions of love for the Romantic Lover but of minimal importance to the Steadfast Lover. If indifference on the part of the beloved persists, Romantic Lovers may become emotionally vulnerable and receptive to someone else who can fulfill their romantic yearnings. The complexes that create this kind of estrangement are separateness for the Steadfast Lover versus relatedness for the Romantic Lover.

These same complexes influence the couple's sexual relationship. Sex has different meanings for Romantic and Steadfast Lovers. It is the most important expression of love for Romantic Lovers, and its expression is *narrow* and *strong*. Romantic Lovers can tolerate harshness and even

anger from their beloved as long as sex is frequent and lovemaking is passionate. Steadfast Lovers, however, express their love in a *broad* and *mild* manner, which contributes to their less frequent and intense lovemaking. This may be unsatisfying for a Romantic Lover partner and can contribute to a lack of sexual attraction. One Romantic Lover said this about his Steadfast Lover partner: "I really love her. She's my best friend; I enjoy being with her. She's interesting and intelligent. We can talk about anything.

Chart 18

Comparison of Romantic and Steadfast Lovers

Central Relationship Question: Romantic Lovers

"If my sense of self and identity is constituted by my relationship with my beloved, can I have a sense of self and fulfillment when I am alone? I can only be a complete human being if I am in a loving relationship with my beloved. For only through our love can we each lose our separateness from the world and become one with the world. Only then can 'I' become a 'We,' and then another new and true 'Me.' What happens then if I am separated from my beloved? Do I still exist? Will I no longer feel joy and pleasure? Will I be devoid of any sense of who I am? That prospect truly frightens me. If it occurs, I will be truly afflicted with a lovesickness.

Attributes, Themes, and Complexes

Stability	Value constancy, permanence, and completeness in the relationship with the beloved.
Enhancement of Relationship	Believe selfhood consists of differentiation of the relationship with the beloved.
Relatedness	Sense of identity or selfhood comes from the relationship with the beloved.
Togetherness	Emphasis is on participating in and sharing all aspects of their lives as expressions of togetherness.
Accommodating	Accommodation is the natural way of resolving conflicts and preserving the state of Being in Love.
Being in Love	Focus is on all the ways the love experience can be shared and enhanced with the beloved.

Kind of Intimacy

Temperature	Hot—passionate sexual activity; kissing and caressing in public.
Proximity	Close—deeply affected by the other's unspoken distress.

Expression of Psychic Energy

Focus	Narrow—focused expressions of love.
Intensity	Strong expressions of love.

Chart 18

Comparison of Romantic and Steadfast Lovers (cont.)

Central Relationship Question: Steadfast Lovers

"How can I maintain my individuality and still be in a loving relationship? If I am a separate individual and I have a distinct identity, will I have to surrender or lose part of my identity and individuality to be in a loving relationship? After all, to be in a loving relationship means that I will have to take into consideration what my partner wishes and desires. I can't just do what I want without at least informing or consulting my partner. What's worse, suppose my partner objects to what I want or has a different preference? If I give in to that, doesn't that mean I will lose part of me?"

Attributes, Themes, and Complexes

Stability	Value is placed on constancy and continuity. Focus is on the refinement and expression of all facets of their selfhood.
Differentiation of Self	Focus is on differentiation—on the refinement and expression of all facets of their selfhood.
Separateness	Accept their partners as separate, independent individuals and want that same kind of acceptance for themselves.
Autonomy	Value independence, uniqueness, and distinctness from social and cultural environments.
Negotiating	Negotiating is the natural way of resolving differences and conflicts.
Staying in Love	Place high value on faithfulness and constancy in the love relationship.

Kind of Intimacy

Temperature	Cool—minimal physical contact, nonverbal and non-physical expressions of affection, politeness in public.
Proximity	Close—deeply affected by the other's unspoken distress.

Expression of Psychic Energy

Focus	Broad—many expressions of love.
Intensity	Mild expressions of love.

She's good-looking. But I'm not especially attracted to her. That bothers me." This was the most disappointing aspect of the relationship for him. From a Steadfast Lover point of view, however, such an attitude reflects an overemphasis on lovemaking to the exclusion of other expressions of love.

Another potential source of misunderstanding is the difference in the couple's perspectives about gifts. More than any other Soul Image, Romantic Lovers enjoy giving *gifts of love* rather than *gifts of power*. A gift of power is meant to give pleasure to the recipient. For example, a wife may ask her husband what he would like for his birthday; he mentions several items, and she gives him one of them. The gift pleases him. This is a gift of power—it has *instrumental* value in that it pleases the beloved. A gift of love, on the other hand, has no instrumental value; its value is *intrinsic*. The joy in a gift of love is in the joy of giving. Whether the gift will please the beloved is not a Romantic Lover's primary concern.

> **Different Complexes**
> Relatedness vs. Separateness
> Being in Love vs. Staying in Love

Some Steadfast Lovers experience ambivalence when a Romantic Lover partner continues to give these gifts of love after the initial courtship period. From a Steadfast Lover's instrumental point of view, continuing to give intrinsic gifts of love makes little sense. A Steadfast Lover may therefore be concerned about the partner's lack of a mature, responsible attitude toward the relationship. At the same time, a Romantic Lover partner may feel hurt and misunderstood when gifts of love are criticized or not appreciated. Some Steadfast Lovers, however, recognize the meaning of the beloved's gifts and may be tenderly touched by them. Such gifts can be especially welcome to a Steadfast Lover who is burdened with day-to-day responsibilities.

Steadfast Lovers' gifts are more likely to be gifts of power that are instrumental to pleasing their Romantic Lover partners. Finding out what pleases the Romantic Lover partner is therefore important. The gifts given by Steadfast Lovers often take the form of attending to the minutiae of everyday living. It is through taking care of everyday details that Steadfast Lovers express their love. Their Romantic Lover partners may welcome these mundane expressions of love, seeing them as an aspect of the complex of togetherness.

Steadfast Lovers communicate caring and concern by focusing on things that will contribute to the stability and constancy of the relationship. This focus is consistent with their emphasis on staying in love as the central aspect of the love relationship. Romantic Lovers communicate caring by offering meaningful mementos, comfort-

Shared Complex
Stability
Different Complexes
Being in Love vs. Staying in Love

ing foods, and loving attention when the beloved is ill or tired. These very personal attentions also contribute to stability, as well as reflecting the Romantic Lover's emphasis on being in love. Neither one may fully appreciate what is proffered, though both will likely recognize it for what it is. At times, a Romantic Lover may misinterpret the actions of the Steadfast Lover as controlling or as criticism of the way the Romantic Lover does things. And a Steadfast Lover may sometimes see the actions of a Romantic Lover as foolish and overly sentimental.

One Steadfast Lover was aware that she often felt she was disappointing her Romantic Lover partner, in spite of being kind, supportive, attentive, and loving. She knew that her efforts were recognized and appreciated; nevertheless, she felt that she failed to live up to her beloved's expectations of romantic fun and lightheartedness. At infrequent times, however, in the absence of stress and in the presence of tender feelings, the Steadfast Lover was able to be fanciful and romantic, to the great delight of her Romantic Lover partner.

The Romantic Lover's focus on being in love, together with a natural tendency to accommodate as a way to resolve disagreements, can create other areas of misunderstanding. When the need for a mutual decision arises, the Romantic Lover may go

Different Complexes
Accommodating vs. Negotiating

along with the Steadfast Lover's wishes in spite of not being entirely comfortable with them. The Steadfast Lover might easily believe that they have come to a mutually agreeable decision through negotiating—the Steadfast Lover's natural way of resolving disagreements. For example, a Steadfast Lover husband was dismayed when his Romantic Lover wife informed him that she had been unhappy in their marriage for several years. She said that she disliked the way they lived their lives and the decisions they made. She saw herself as going along with his way of doing things in order to keep the relationship smooth and harmonious. The Steadfast Lover husband had believed all along that everything was just fine between them and that they had a mutually satisfying relationship. He thought their decisions were made jointly through a back-and-forth discussion and negotiation. He was shocked and upset when she revealed his misperception.

Romantic Lover–Steadfast Lover couples respond to each other's distress in ways that reflect their opposing complexes of

Different Complexes
Relatedness vs. Separateness
Togetherness vs. Autonomy

relatedness versus separateness. When a Romantic Lover sees that the Steadfast Lover partner is distressed, she or he may offer suggestions to try to eliminate the source of the distress. For example, if the distress is caused by a work relationship or situation, a Romantic Lover will encourage the Steadfast Lover to fire the difficult person or complain to someone. However, the Steadfast Lover isn't likely to find this advice helpful; suggestions can be seen as unwelcome intrusions that cast doubt on the Steadfast Lover's ability to solve a problem. Steadfast Lovers want Romantic Lover partners to listen to their problems and appreciate the distress such problems are causing; however, they expect to resolve their difficulties separately and independently. Romantic Lovers are actually offering the kind of help they themselves would appreciate when they experience distress—sympathy, concern, and problem-solving suggestions from their partner. Similarly, Steadfast Lovers, when dealing with the beloved's distress, are likely to respond in the way they wish their partner would respond to their own distress—by listening, offering no suggestions, and respecting the beloved's independence and autonomy in solving his or her own problems.

Relatedness and separateness are also evident in the couple's approach to household responsibilities. For Romantic Lovers, working on chores together is an opportunity for shared love, while efficiency in task completion is the central concern for Steadfast Lovers. Sometimes when the two agree on a task that needs to be done, the Steadfast Lover will perform his or her part of it alone in order to be free to do other, more important things. A Romantic Lover partner will likely appreciate this effort but be disappointed at missing an opportunity to do the task together with the beloved.

Different Complexes
Relatedness vs. Separateness
Being in Love vs. Staying in Love

Romantic Lovers focus on creating a pleasant living space in which to enjoy the intimacy of their love relationship. A Steadfast Lover may appreciate the partner's effort as well as enjoying the agreeable atmosphere in the home. However, he or she may become impatient if the beloved wants a lot of participation in this from the Steadfast Lover. Steadfast Lovers want to spend their time in the effective completion of their minimum responsibilities so that there will be as little interference as possible with other aspects of life. When there are routine chores that are especially time-consuming and onerous for the Steadfast Lover and that hold little relationship meaning for the Romantic Lover, a couple will often hire others to take care of them.

Both mutual and individual friendships occur for Romantic Lover–Steadfast Lover partners. A Romantic Lover might object if a Steadfast Lover's independent friendships seem to take energy away from the love relationship. However, both the Romantic and the Steadfast Lover enhance and differentiate their relationship by being each other's "best friend." The Stability complex, which the

couple share, in combination with their different complexes of Being in Love versus Staying in Love, influences their attitudes toward opposite-sex friendships. Steadfast Lovers view their own and the beloved's opposite-sex friendships as separate from the love relationship. Even when a beloved is romantically attracted to someone else, a Steadfast Lover partner is likely to believe that the stability, constancy, and solidity of the love relationship will inevitably persevere over casual affairs. For this reason, Steadfast Lovers can be patient, understanding, and tolerant of a Romantic Lover partner who admits interest in someone else or even has an extramarital affair. This is particularly true for female Steadfast Lovers, and may vary considerably among male Steadfast Lovers. Steadfast Lovers of either gender, however, are tolerant and patient only up to a point. If the beloved's attraction or affair is not quickly ended and stability restored to the love relationship, the Steadfast Lover may become adamant in setting limits and conditions to deal with the situation.

For example, a young Romantic Lover–Steadfast Lover couple had been living together for over two years. One night after work, the Romantic Lover went to a bar with a woman co-worker for a drink. He came home three hours late, having spent the time in deep and intense conversation with her. He told his Steadfast Lover partner all about his encounter and that he found himself very much attracted to this woman. "What if she and I are the star-crossed lovers rather than you and I?" he asked. His Steadfast Lover girlfriend replied, "If you feel you need to explore this fling, that's fine. I'm okay with it. Our relationship is solid, and I know you're committed to me." The Romantic Lover partner saw his new love for several weeks and then abruptly stopped seeing her. He declared his love for his Steadfast Lover partner anew. She was understanding and accepting. However, when the same kind of thing happened again six months later, the Steadfast Lover told her Romantic Lover partner to move out. "Our relationship is no longer solid and reliable," she said. "I can't count on your love."

Romantic Lovers can be comfortable with the opposite-sex friendships of Steadfast Lover partners as long as their love relationship is secure and there are frequent demonstrations of love by the beloved. However, if the Steadfast Lover appears

Different Complexes
Being in Love vs. Staying in Love

distant and uninvolved, a Romantic Lover may see opposite-sex friendships as negative comments on the adequacy of the love relationship. Such friendships will therefore be seen as potentially threatening. Steadfast Lovers' complexes of Separation and Staying in Love make them unlikely to appear to have romantic attractions outside their primary love relationship. (Mercurial Lovers, in contrast, with their emphasis on falling in love, can cause much more anxiety in this regard for a beloved with any Soul Image.)

Steadfast Lovers and Romantic Lovers may be very hardworking and committed to their careers, working long hours with great concentration. Romantic Lovers find that too much time spent at work creates dissatisfaction and disconnection. They therefore seek occasional respites from

Different Complexes
Togetherness vs. Autonomy
Being in Love vs. Staying in Love

work to reconnect with and renew their love for the partner through meaningful experiences. For Steadfast Lovers, the amount of time spent working doesn't affect the relationship. Reconnecting isn't an issue since the lasting nature of their love is assumed. They may be more inclined to take breaks from work either alone, with other people, or with the beloved. At times, a Steadfast Lover partner may feel torn between using free time for independent pursuits and being with the Romantic Lover partner, who clearly prefers such togetherness.

The need for connection versus the desire for independence can also have an impact on relationships with extended family members. For a Romantic Lover, sharing responsibility for relatives with the Steadfast Lover beloved is connected to the complexes of togetherness, relatedness, and accommodating. The Steadfast Lover's complexes of stability, differentiation of self, and negotiating complement the Romantic Lover complexes in this regard. One Romantic Lover–Steadfast Lover couple shared a strong and deep commitment to both of their families, though they were at times somewhat resentful at having to give up time from other interests and their own relationship. For the Romantic Lover, jointly caring for elderly parents contributed to feelings of harmony, togetherness, and relatedness with the Steadfast Lover partner. For the Steadfast Lover, these same activities satisfied concerns for responsibility, constancy, and problem solving through negotiating. However, the added burden left even less time and energy for participating in the romantic and relatedness-focused activities that were rejuvenating for the Romantic Lover. Requests and plans for such interludes were met with such statements as, "I can't take the time. I'm spread too thin already."

The importance of shared experience for Romantic Lovers and separate endeavors for Steadfast Lovers is also evident in the way the couple approaches recreation. A Romantic Lover may adopt a Steadfast Lover's recreational pursuit for the pleasure of enjoying it with the beloved. However, this may not be appreciated by the Steadfast Lover partner, who values the independent activity and accomplishment involved. For example, prior to her marriage, a Steadfast Lover was

Different Complexes
Togetherness vs. Autonomy
Enhancement of Relationship vs.
Differentiation of Self

an amateur competitive skier. Her Romantic Lover partner skied well, but was well below her level of expertise. After the marriage, he avidly pursued skiing, devoting much of his free time to it, and insisted on trying to keep up with his wife on the slopes, which she found inhibiting. She felt she had to pay more attention to his attempts at excellence than to increasing the skills she needed for continuing competition. From her point of view, her Romantic Lover husband was intruding on this separate aspect of her life and complicating an area that would otherwise be an unambiguous source of satisfaction and differentiation for her.

Similar complexes emerge regarding vacations. For a Romantic Lover, being with the beloved in a vacation setting is in itself romantic. The Steadfast Lover is also likely to feel relaxed and open to enjoying being with the beloved. However, Romantic Lovers have a tendency to imagine romantic interludes that rarely live up to their expectations. If the vacation spot isn't quite right, or if the

> **Different Complexes**
> Relatedness vs. Separateness
> Enhancement of Relationship vs. Differentiation of Self

Steadfast Lover doesn't seem very enthusiastic about it, the Romantic Lover may have difficulty setting this aside to enjoy the experience. The Steadfast Lover may be puzzled and hurt, feeling that somehow the partner is blaming the Steadfast Lover for the imperfection of the vacation experience.

Neither Romantic nor Steadfast Lovers are likely to find separate vacations appealing. For Romantic Lovers, vacations increase the likelihood of having the Steadfast Lover's complete attention; for Steadfast Lovers, focusing on being together encourages constancy and differentiation of themselves and the beloved. Including friends and family in their vacations might not be highly desirable for either one, as this might interfere with the singular focus each wants to devote to the other.

Another way in which Romantic Lovers attend to the intrinsic meaning of being with the beloved is through private rituals and romantic celebrations. Though a Steadfast Lover might find such things excessive, embarrassing, or pretentious, he or she may willingly participate for the pleasure it gives the beloved. Such acts may also express the Steadfast Lover focus on staying in love.

Different Complexes
Being in Love vs. Staying in Love

On every birthday of his Steadfast Lover, a Romantic Lover placed a single red rose on her pillow. This was to commemorate the rose he gave her the first time he declared his love. For the Romantic Lover, the rose was an expression of the intensity of his love; for the Steadfast Lover, it validated the continuity and permanence of the relationship.

A similar complementarity of complexes occurred for another Romantic Lover–Steadfast Lover couple who were invited to a dinner party at the home of friends. Both Jennifer, the Steadfast Lover, and Charles, the Romantic Lover, were looking forward to the dinner party. However, on the morning of the day of the party, Jennifer felt ill. Her symptoms worsened during the day, and she told Charles that she felt too sick to go to the party.

"That's really too bad," he said. "We would have enjoyed the evening together so much. But it's much more important for you to feel better. Do you feel like eating something? I'll just run to the store and get some of your favorite 'comfort foods.'"

"I'd really like that," said Jennifer. "But you know I won't mind if you go to the party by yourself. I'll be perfectly fine here."

"Oh, no," said Charles. "I couldn't do that." He went to the store and then prepared an inviting array of food, which they ate together.

"I know you must be really tired and wanting to sleep," he said when they had finished eating, "so I'll put on some soft music for you and leave you alone."

"That's just what I would like," replied Jennifer. "Maybe I'll be okay tomorrow, and we can make up for missing the dinner by dropping in on Shirley and Don for a short visit."

In this brief interchange, Charles was able to fulfill his Romantic Lover values by providing meaningful and loving comforts to his ailing wife. Moveover, his understanding of and respect for her needs affirmed Jennifer's Steadfast Lover focus on staying in love.

Different attitudes toward money are affected by the value Romantic Lovers place on intrinsic gifts of love versus the Steadfast Lover's instrumental gifts of power, which we explained earlier. Romantic Lovers enjoy using money to enhance the relationship with their beloved. They tend to earmark money for specific purposes. For example, the yearly dividends on an annuity will be used only

> **Different Complexes**
> Relatedness vs. Separateness
> Enhancement of Relationship vs.
> Differentiation of Self

for vacations or birthday gifts. For the Steadfast Lover all incoming money is of equal value and should therefore be applied to whatever needs are greatest. It all goes "in the same pot." A specific, even generous amount from the pot may be budgeted for vacations or presents, but it may make little sense to the Steadfast Lover to apply funds to such things based on their source. When money is scarce, a Steadfast Lover might want to cut back on expenses and stick to a budget in order to conserve what is available. However, the Romantic Lover may be reluctant to give up the meaningful acts money permits in the relationship, and may therefore try to make more money rather than save money. In stressful times, Steadfast Lovers may believe that their Romantic Lover partners are careless and even irresponsible with money in their insistence on spending on unimportant things. For their part, Romantic Lovers may believe their Steadfast Lover partners to be withholding, controlling, and not fully valuing the relationship.

As with other love relationships, the birth of children can have a major impact on the way a couple relate to each other. For Romantic Lover–Steadfast Lover couples, the arrival of a child may modify the strong and narrow expression of love for the

Romantic Lover, who may therefore be more in tune with the Steadfast Lover partner's milder and broader expression of love.

Different Complexes
Togetherness vs. Autonomy
Accommodating vs. Negotiating

In raising children, some Romantic Lovers may leave more of the day-to-day childcare to the Steadfast Lover spouse. A Steadfast Lover mother, in particular, may resent this, especially if she has to forgo her own independent career and interests while the Romantic Lover father has freedom to pursue his own interests. This perceived inequity may lead to discussions and compromises to address the desires of both partners. A Romantic Lover may not appreciate the Steadfast Lover's desire for autonomy and independence. She or he may be more concerned with the loss of intimacy associated with the presence of children, and this issue may surface during their discussions about child-care responsibilities. The amount of intimacy will be less important for a Steadfast Lover partner, for whom childrearing is one of many expressions of love and intimacy.

A Romantic Lover is likely to find contacts with an ex-spouse after a divorce quite painful. With the passage of time, however, he or she might romanticize the marital relationship and forget the

Different Complexes
Relatedness vs. Separateness
Being in Love vs. Staying in Love

unpleasant parts. Reconciliation might even seem appealing. The Steadfast Lover, in contrast, is likely to settle into a distant but responsible role with regard to both the former spouse and any children involved. Once having settled the matter and accepted that permanence, stability, and staying in love are no longer an option, the Steadfast Lover is unlikely to be interested in reconciliation. The required investment of energy doesn't seem worthwhile. Even without a reconciliation, the Romantic Lover may wish to maintain some level of intimate friendship, which would validate the meaningfulness of the previously intimate marital relationship. Being cut off from this entirely would be a hardship and very unsatisfying. The Steadfast

Lover, however, is likely to be most satisfied in not going beyond taking a cordial interest in each other's lives.

⎧ The Clash of Complexes

Sarah and Kyle have been married for seven years. They have postponed having children as they both wanted to wait to become parents until their careers were secure. Sarah, a Steadfast Lover, is an attorney and works in a firm that deals with family law. Kyle, a Romantic Lover, is an accountant with one of the largest accounting firms in the city. They enjoy their careers very much. Kyle's workday is regular and more predictable than Sarah's. Kyle does much of the cooking, which he enjoys. Usually Sarah arrives home when Kyle is in the middle of his dinner preparations. Their custom is to talk to each other about the events of the workday while dinner preparations are completed. This is a way for Sarah to refresh herself after the day's stresses. For Kyle, the conversation is a renewal of their closeness.

Sarah often sits at the kitchen table while Kyle is cooking. She's quite willing to help him when asked. After dinner, they both clean the kitchen. This is Sarah's way of doing her share, while Kyle enjoys the togetherness of shared effort. After that they generally engage in individual activities, though often staying in the same room; Sarah might read a law article while Kyle installs some software on the computer.

Sarah has always been diligent in respecting Kyle's work and the demands it puts on his time. She expects that for the several months preceding tax time, Kyle's workdays will be very long. During this busy period for Kyle, she prepares their dinner or stops at their favorite Chinese restaurant for take-out food. However, Kyle is not as understanding about Sarah's long working days. Her heavy work schedule is somewhat irregular and unpredictable, but she has noticed that during the spring she seems to be most regularly busy. Indeed, they have jokingly noted that while April 15 is the end of long workdays for Kyle, for Sarah the beginning of April seems to herald a particularly hectic time. Spring seems to be the time when there are increasing problems with divorces, custody suits, and the settlement of community properties associated with the income tax deadline.

Phase One: The Disagreement

- As a disagreement continues with no resolution, tension increases.

- The persistence and increase of tension cause misunderstanding.

- Sustained tension and misunderstanding cause stress.

On New Year's Day one year, Kyle approached Sarah and said he wanted to talk about the coming year. They then had the following conversation:

Kyle: Could we make a joint New Year's resolution?

Sarah: Sure, Kyle, what kind of resolution? That we'll exercise at least three times a week?

Kyle: That would be nice, but I'm serious.

Sarah (smiling): For me exercise is very serious. What could be so serious on New Year's Day? We've had a good year. My practice has flourished. We'll have many more good years.

Kyle: Well, I don't think that it has been all that good for us.

Sarah: What's wrong? It's been very good. You received a raise and a generous bonus.

Kyle: You always talk about work. You never think about us.

Sarah: Kyle, I don't always think about work. You know that my career is important to me. You've known that from the day we were married. I just don't understand you.

Kyle: That's right! You don't understand me, and you don't care!

Sarah: Kyle, what's wrong?

Kyle: Well, I wish we could make a New Year's resolution that we will not work on weekends. At least when we're busy we'll have our weekends together.

Sarah: You really mean that you wish "I" would resolve not to work on weekends, right?

Kyle: No, I really mean us. You don't understand. Our weekends together are important to me. And if I may say, you've known that since the day we met.

Sarah (smiling): That's right, hon. I'm sorry I haven't made more of an effort to be here. Okay. Let's make that resolution together.

(They kiss and then have a very pleasant day together.)

Notice the different complexes emerging here. Kyle was referring to their relationship when he said, "I don't think that it has been all that good for us." But Sarah responded as if he were referring to his work. This hurts Kyle.

Phase Two: The Quarrel

- Persistent misunderstanding and stress consume large amounts of energy and can be exhausting.
- Sustained fatigue and stress jeopardize the ability to integrate and respond to the issues.
- Fatigue and stress continue to consume more energy.
- Negative aspects of the participants' Soul Images are evoked.

Five and a half months have passed; it is now the middle of May. During the past six weeks, Sarah has had to work at her office four Saturdays. She has also gotten home late from work at least three days a week. Kyle is hurt and angry. Summer is approaching, and he is fearful that Sarah will continue to be busy into the summer. He feels betrayed because she has not lived up to their resolution. On a Saturday when Sarah returns home from her office, Kyle is unusually silent and morose. They have the following conversation:

Sarah (trying to be cheerful): Well, I got a lot of work done. The property settlement should be decided this week. Then I can take a long weekend off.

Kyle: Oh, yeah. What do you plan to do?

Sarah: Well, I thought we could go to Colorado, maybe Telluride or Ouray and do some sightseeing and maybe some hiking.

Kyle: I'll believe that when it happens.

Sarah: What's wrong? I've been working my butt off and I thought you'd want to spend a weekend together!

Kyle (sulking): Don't do me any favors.

Sarah: What's wrong?

Kyle: You broke a promise.

Sarah: What promise?

Kyle: See, you don't even remember! We made a New Year's resolution not to work on weekends. I've lived up to it. Remember, for several weeks I worked until 10:00 and sometimes 11:00 at night so we could have our weekends free!

Sarah: Well, I tried! I just don't have your stamina to work those long hours.

Kyle: Don't give me that crap! You've worked at home until almost midnight. You're just making excuses.

Sarah (raising her voice): You're being unreasonable!

Kyle (shouting): If I'm unreasonable, then you're just selfish. All you care about is your ambition and your work. You just think about yourself! Good thing we don't have any children. You wouldn't know how take care of them.

Sarah (hurt and angry): Well, you'd be a lousy father. You'd whimper and cry all the time in front of them.

Kyle: At least I'd keep my promises. I wouldn't betray them.

Sarah: Well, you'd just embarrass them because you're so needy. You ought to be ashamed of yourself!

(At this point, crying and angry, Sarah leaves the room. Kyle is also crying and feels bewildered, betrayed, and isolated. Later that day, they apologize to each other. However, considerable tension remains between them.)

As noted above, Sarah and Kyle's different complexes caused the misunderstanding between them. Kyle viewed Sarah's commitment to work as a sign of unloving behavior rather than an indication of her need for autonomy and differentiation of self. Meanwhile, Sarah, from the perspective of her autonomy complex, regarded Kyle's need for relatedness and togetherness as signs of his lack of forthright masculinity. Sarah's unconscious complexes were evident when she rebuked Kyle for being *always* needy, *nothing but* a simpering wimp, and a lousy potential father; and Kyle's when he accused Sarah of being *nothing but* selfish, *always* at work, and *never* caring about him and the children they may have in the future.

The Nature of This Love Relationship

The distinctive leisurely development of love in the Romantic Lover–Steadfast Lover relationship comes from their shared comfort with stability and their acceptance of each other's different emphases regarding selfhood—enhancement of relationship for the Romantic Lover, and differentiation of self for the Steadfast Lover. These qualities create a solid foundation within which differences in their perspectives can complement and strengthen the love relationship. Romantic Lovers' desire for relatedness and togetherness and Steadfast Lovers' commitment to separateness and autonomy can both be fulfilled through mutual awareness and compromise. To accomplish such compromise, Romantic Lovers try to accommodate the desires of their Steadfast Lover partners, while Steadfast Lovers prefer to negotiate to achieve mutual equitable results. Accommodating and negotiating can also be helpful in satisfying the Romantic Lover's focus on being in love and the Steadfast Lover's primary goal of staying in love. Understanding and compromise are needed to accommodate both the Romantic Lover's intensity in the expression of love in the present and the Steadfast Lover's interest in the breadth and variety of expressions of love over time.

These same complexes and combinations of complexes were revealed in the disagreement and quarrel between Kyle and Sarah. The pressure of their busy work lives led to each partner's insensitivity to the other's important complexes. We also saw the emergence of unconscious complexes in both the disagreement and quarrel phases of their encounter. Each partner made implicit and explicit *always* or *never* and *nothing-but* statements in their stressed state.

Individual histories and circumstances may vary widely among Romantic Lover–Steadfast Lover couples, but the same complexes and issues we saw here are likely to emerge in their daily lives and in their quarrels. We hope you now have a better and deeper understanding of, appreciation for, and ability to appraise this kind of true love.

Part 3 \ *Enduring Love Relationships*

Part 3 explores facets of relating that are necessary for a lasting love relationship. Chapter
14 looks at the Soul Images with regard to the
issues of acceptance and compatibility, which
are necessary for a lasting relationship. Examples illustrate the nuances of these concepts
and how they contribute to relationships,
regardless of the Soul Images of the partners.

In the Epilogue, we acknowledge the
importance of particular personality characteristics that, in combination with a Soul
Image, may further distinguish and differentiate the nature of intimate relationships. In
addition, we also recognize the effects of
severe and/or persistent stress on the ten love

relationships. Such stress may be either *external,* such as illness, loss of employment, or divorce, or *internal,* such as disruptive unconscious complexes that are evoked in a relationship. An example of such increased external and internal stress was described in the "fight" stage of the disagreement and quarrel of Gina and Carlos in Chapter 3, "Stress in Relationships." You will recall that discussion of this stage was purposely not included in the ten relationship chapters.

14 | *Love, Acceptance, and Compatibility*

> *In the pluralist attitude one doesn't assume there is a single correct answer to human problems. One doesn't assume that the human condition is unitary, or similar to questions in mathematics, for instance, for which you have to find the one and only right solution. . . . There is only a series of explorations . . . to encourage people . . . to form new, enriched, more creative ways of making sense out of our need to love.*
>
> Irving Singer, "A Reply to My Critics and Friendly Commentators," in *The Nature and Pursuit of Love*

It is evident that the four Soul Images embody unique patterns of relating in love relationships. In addition, each Soul Image interacts with the other Soul Images in a consistent manner. As a result, the different combinations of Soul Images in love relationships have clearly defined strengths, weaknesses, stresses, and satisfactions. It is not unusual for tension, misunderstanding, and conflict to result from these distinct aspects of a love relationship. Understanding the profound differences among the Soul Images is an excellent avenue toward minimizing such tension, misunderstanding, and conflict, enabling a couple to have a lasting relationship.

Acceptance and Compatibility

Probably the question asked most frequently by couples in marital therapy is, "Are we compatible?" This question disguises another question that is of fundamental concern to every couple: "Can our relationship last?" Given the perspective described in the preceding thirteen chapters, we might frame this question as follows: In light of the four different Soul Images and their combination into ten true loves, what factors nourish and sustain a love relationship? The answer to this question is inherent in the intricate interaction between the concepts of *acceptance* and *compatibility*. In order for a relationship to last, both are necessary.

Acceptance

The difference between acceptance and compatibility is similar to the difference between loving someone and liking someone. We can love people and not necessarily like them; we can also like people and not love them. However, if we both love and like someone, that is a good indication that the relationship will last. As Singer has stated, "For love to exist, bestowal of value upon the other person is a necessary condition" (1987, p. 391). This bestowal of value is what we call *acceptance*. Implicit in the notion of acceptance is a valuing of the similarities, the differences, the virtues, and the faults of the beloved.

For example, the importance of acceptance is evident in the quarrel between Carlos and Gina that we presented in Chapter 3. In the incident described, Carlos, a Mercurial Lover, frequently visited his brother and sister-in-law. Gina, Carlos's Innocent Lover wife, objected to his visits. She was especially hurt and angry when he lied to her about them. Quarrels ensued because of the different ways in which the partners viewed their own and each other's behavior and perspective. In the end, however, their disagreement and quarrel revealed an underlying acceptance of each other. In the absence of such acceptance of Carlos by Gina—that is, if she did *not* value him—her objections would result in persistent and increasingly destructive quarrels, and such a state of affairs would jeopardize the continuation of their relationship.

Another example of the importance of acceptance is the relationship between Lori and David, the Mercurial Lover–Romantic Lover couple whose disagreement and quarrel we presented in Chapter 9. Lori's work schedule was very busy, unpredictable, and hectic. David's work life was also quite demanding, but considerably more within his control. The differences in the couple's Soul Images resulted in many disappointments and quarrels that resulted from the meaning work had for each partner. Had there been no acceptance between them, their differences could have resulted in persistent quarrels and hurt feelings. And over time, the lack of acceptance of each other might have placed their love relationship in jeopardy.

In contrast, at the end of the disagreement and quarrel between Elisse and Tom, the Mercurial Lover–Innocent Lover couple we presented in Chapter 10, there is some doubt as to their acceptance of each other. Tom, the Innocent Lover, seemed unwilling to give value to Elisse's desire for autonomy and separateness from the family, while Elisse did not seem to accept Tom's Innocent Lover perspective on instrumental change, relatedness, and togetherness. Rick and Andrea, the Innocent

Lover–Romantic Lover couple we presented in Chapter II, seemed to fare somewhat better. Their complexes emerged in extreme fashion only occasionally, and followed a pattern that ended in a renewal of their love. We can infer that a basic acceptance of each other prevailed. Had it not, their quarrels would likely have been much more frequent—and their intensity would have been magnified over time.

Compatibility

The other necessary condition for a lasting love relationship is compatibility. Compatibility is implicit when we like someone. Typically, we specify what it is we like about a person by focusing on whether he or she is *similar* to us in important ways and/or whether the person satisfies important needs we have. *Similarity* and *satisfaction* are thus the two aspects of *compatibility*. A relationship can be described as compatible if either or both of these aspects exists.

On meeting someone, we explicitly or implicitly appraise their interests, values, and outlook on the world. If the results are in accord with our interests, values, and outlook, we can say that we are *similar*. The more similar the interests, values, and outlook, the more we like the person—and the greater the compatibility. These appraisals can also be made with regard to the extent to which a person can satisfy our needs—whether these needs are for wealth, social status, sexual pleasure, or other desires. When these needs are fulfilled by the other person and we likewise fulfill the other person's needs, there is a *mutuality of need satisfactions*. The relationship can then be regarded as compatible.

Similarity Similarity of interests is not in itself a sufficient condition to ensure a lasting relationship. For example, Kristen found Nicholas to be an interesting, intelligent person. She admired his unconventionality and found him sexually attractive as well. The two shared similar interests in art, hiking, and backpacking. They enjoyed their sexual relationship. However, Nicholas had one characteristic that Kristen could not abide—his ultraconservative political beliefs. Even though Nicholas shared Kristen's ecological concerns, they differed markedly in their views on how these concerns should be addressed. Their arguments became so vitriolic and acrimonious that on one occasion Kristen slapped Nicholas when he accused her of being an "ignorant tree hugger." After this incident they did not see or speak to each other for several weeks. Eventually they got back together, but they remained unable to discuss their different political views without anger and disruptions of the relationship.

Kristen and Nicholas had many similar interests and thus were compatible in one important way. However, since neither was willing to accept and value the other's differences, their relationship—compatible up to a point—is unlikely to last. (And from the authors' perspective, it is not a true love.)

Satisfaction A couple may be compatible when important desires are satisfied for both partners. For example, James, an executive in a large manufacturing firm, attended a management conference in a distant city. While there, he met Magda, who was working at one of the product displays at the conference. There was an immediate attraction between them, and they had an intense and passionate love affair. After the conference, James and Magda arranged their business trips so that they could be together. Intermittently they spoke on the phone as well. Their relationship persisted in this fashion for several years. Occasionally, they discussed the subject of marriage, but never seriously. There was an implicit agreement between them that they would keep their relationship both circumscribed and circumspect. James was socially prominent in his home city, whereas Magda was an immigrant with relatively little formal education. They accepted that they had little in common. They loved each other in spite of this, and their relationship was satisfying to them. However, they could not give each other the kind of acceptance that would have permitted them to have an open and complete love relationship. Instead, their relationship remained limited to being together for a few days twice a year.

Another couple found that their mutual satisfaction had painful consequences. Jake met Leslie at a party and they, like James and Magda, were immediately attracted to each other. Later that night they made love. Jake described the lovemaking as the best sex he had ever had. He actively pursued Leslie, and in a few weeks they moved in together. Much to his dismay they bickered and argued loudly every day. He sadly recognized that he found Leslie to be dull and uninteresting; for her part, Leslie regarded Jake as a boorish lout. Their bickering was punctuated by lusty and lengthy lovemaking encounters. This chaotic state of affairs lasted for several months, then they finally separated. They both longed for each other and made several impassioned but unsuccessful attempts at reconciliation. They were able to satisfy each other's need for sexual pleasure, and in this regard were compatible. However, there was no acceptance between them. Jake wanted Leslie to be more interesting, and she wanted him to be more refined. This led to a failure of the relationship. Without reciprocal acceptance, it is unlikely that any relationship will be sustained—even when a couple is compatible in having their sexual desires gratified.

Even if both aspects of compatibility (similarity and satisfaction) are present, the absence of acceptance makes an enduring relationship problematical. For example, Vanessa and Elliot have been married for ten years. She is beautiful, charming, and an excellent hostess. Being married to her satisfies Elliot's desire to maintain and enhance his prominence as an important politician. Vanessa likes and admires Elliot and is particularly satisfied with their social and political prominence as a couple. The two have an amiable relationship, with sufficient interests in common to keep their relationship enjoyable. However, Vanessa is becoming uneasy about eventually losing her looks; she knows how important this is for Elliot and is wary of his increasing flirtatiousness with other women. She is correct in her assessment: Elliot is quite aware that in spite of his liking Vanessa, she might eventually become a liability to him. For her part, Vanessa is concerned about Elliot's tendency to make speculative financial investments and to take other risks that could create political enemies for him. She knows she would not stay with him if his fortunes reversed.

Elliot and Vanessa have interests in common and also satisfy important needs for each other. However, neither bestows value on the other, and thus neither accepts the other. This is evident in their acknowledgment that these two aspects of compatibility are necessary conditions for them to stay with each other.

Acceptance, Compatibility, and the Soul Images

As is evident from these examples, acceptance and compatibility can be affected by a variety of individual differences within love relationships. The importance of the Soul Images is that they determine how we perceive, acknowledge, understand, and evaluate our own as well as our beloved's behavior. Soul Images therefore have a subtle and profound effect on our acceptance and lack of acceptance of our beloved. We are often only dimly aware of the existence of these archetypes because they operate at an unconscious level. However, by understanding the extremely different approaches of people with different Soul Images, we can work to cultivate the acceptance that is necessary for a lasting love relationship.

Jacobi (1959) describes the importance of this awareness and understanding in her statement that:

> Only when the archetypes come into contact with the conscious mind, that is, when the light of consciousness falls on them and their contours begin to emerge from the darkness and to fill with individual content, can the conscious mind differentiate them. Only then can consciousness apprehend, understand, elaborate, and assimilate them. (p. 29)

In order to make the archetypal Soul Images intelligible and a source of enrichment in a love relationship, they must be divested of their mysteriousness and understood as they influence everyday occurrences. If this happens, then acceptance is cultivated between the lover and the beloved.

It is for this reason that when the essential features of the different Soul Images are described to couples, there is an immediate recognition. Such direct recognition often occurs when people are introduced to the important archetypes that profoundly influence their lives. Couples can usually identify their Soul Images and recognize the implications of both their similarities to and differences from each other. A frequent effect is that previously intractable and distressing areas of contention are viewed through a new frame of understanding. As a result, positive energy becomes available for a renewed acceptance of each other and a renewal of love.

For example, a Mercurial Lover–Innocent Lover couple were seriously contemplating divorce after a twenty-five-year marriage. The Mercurial Lover husband saw his Innocent Lover wife as intrusive and controlling in her "constant need" to be with him, as lacking in individual initiative, and as overly involved and dominating in relation to their children. For her part, the Innocent Lover wife felt undervalued, unloved, and "constantly criticized and demeaned" by her husband. She felt hurt, isolated, and despairing when she discovered that he often confided in his women friends things he did not discuss with her.

The characteristics of Mercurial and Innocent Lovers were explained and their perceptions of each other were redefined as expressions of their important complexes. This enabled them to see each other in a very different and quite positive light. The Mercurial Lover husband understood his wife's "dependency needs" as an expression of her complexes of togetherness and instrumental change rather than a desire to control him and limit his freedom. The Innocent Lover wife was able to see her husband's many outside interests and friendships as expressions of his complexes of separateness and autonomy. Their new understanding of each other resulted in a corresponding new enjoyment of each other's company and renewed acknowledgment of all of the satisfying aspects of their marriage.

For another couple, an awareness of the differences inherent in their Romantic Lover–Steadfast Lover relationship enabled them to deal with previously hurtful and distressing behaviors with lightheartedness and humor. For example, the two had been apart much of the time during a two-week period, each attending to necessary business that took them out of town. When at last they both came home late one evening, they agreed to spend much of the next day together. As she was drifting off to sleep, the Romantic Lover imagined the leisurely, intimate breakfast they would have the next morning. To her chagrin, when she awoke the next morning her beloved was busy paying the bills because, he said, "They've been neglected far too long." The Romantic Lover sighed in resignation. "I guess this is another great example of your Steadfast Lover approach and my Romantic Lover approach," she said, after describing her fantasized romantic breakfast. They both laughed, the Steadfast Lover put aside the bills, and they went out to breakfast together.

One woman changed her negative judgment about her cousin's behavior when she learned about the different perspectives of people with different Soul Images. In a conversation with a friend who was knowledgeable about the Soul Images, she related that she had been invited to her cousin's house for Thanksgiving dinner and that among the other guests would be the ex-wife and daughter of her cousin's lover of many years. "Don't you think that's weird?" she inquired of her friend. "My cousin says she really likes Kevin's ex-wife and that they have a lot of interests in common, but don't you think there must be something peculiar about these kinds of relationships?"

"As a matter of fact," her friend replied, "it may not be weird or peculiar at all, but may have something to do with the way your cousin, her lover, and his ex-wife look at relationships." She went on to describe the Soul Images and hypothesized that perhaps the people her friend was describing were Mercurial Lovers, for whom such marital and postdivorce relationships are acceptable and desirable. Although there was no opportunity to verify this hypothesis at the time, it did permit this woman to see her cousin and the relationships described from a more accepting and less judgmental vantage point.

Conclusion

We have attempted to demonstrate that there are different kinds of love, different meanings to love, and different expressions of love. The archetypes of love that we call Soul Images determine how love is expressed and experienced in a relationship. These Soul Images:

- Determine how we love and what love means to us
- Account for the many different expressions of love
- Make the different kinds of love relationships understandable

It is thus the Soul Images of love that give each relationship its distinct character. The ten true loves that result from their different combinations have their own sources of pleasure and satisfaction, their own difficulties and deficiencies. Maintaining an awareness of the Soul Images and their role in determining the character of love relationships enables us to recognize the similarities and differences between lovers. If the partners in a love relationship can accept their differences and recognize their compatibilities, perhaps they will not only love each other, but like each other as well. It is only then that their love relationship can endure.

Epilogue

In the ten chapters in Part 2, we discussed all the combinations of the Soul Images occurring in love relationships. We tried to show the influence of the Soul Images on commonly occurring aspects of relationships, ranging from relatively benign concerns, such as the way household chores are accomplished, through more stressful situations, such as relating after a divorce. Relatively little attention was paid to the impact of significant individual personality differences that may modify the manner in which the Soul Images of a particular couple are expressed. In addition, we presented scenarios of the couples when they were dealing with relatively moderate stress, rather than in some of the more intensely stressful situations that can occur with relationships. Both individual differences in personality as well as severe stress, however, have multiple coherent, predictable, and conflicting effects on the expression of the Soul Images in love relationships.

Personality Differences

It should be noted that people who share the same Soul Image may be quite different in their other personal characteristics. Brief mention was made in Chapter I of the likely different expression of the Soul Images that might occur for extraverts rather than introverts, or people who have a spontaneous rather than a methodical approach to life. These particular personality characteristics are aspects of Jung's theory of Psychological Types. This theory, which describes and identifies normal personality differences as expressed in a broad spectrum of life endeavors, can be fruitfully combined with the Jungian archetypal approach described in *True Loves*. Together, these two ways of looking at human variation are a useful and powerful way of describing and explaining love relationships. The details of the interactions involved await further exploration and development.

The Impact of Severe Stress

When a person experiences severe stress in life, equally forceful and extreme attempt to deal with it are inevitably called forth. Two sources of stress may be evident, whether singly or in interaction. Persistent and severe *external* stress can result from serious assaults on a couple's life circumstances, such as illness, career and job loss, or natural disasters.

A second source of stress is *internal*. Internal stress refers to any thoughts or feelings about a partner or oneself that disrupt the relationship. If hurtful and angry thoughts and feelings are not resolved, disruptive and even permanent damage may be done to the love and acceptance in the relationship. This was the case in the example of Gina and Carlos that was presented in Chapter 3. There was an accumulation of small hurts and slights for Gina, who felt ignored and lonely when Carlos was absent. For his part, Carlos tried to suppress his feelings of resentment at Gina's frequent irritability and her "need to be in control." The disagreement, argument, and quarrel of Gina and Carlos revealed an underlying acceptance of each other. If there had been no acceptance of each other, persistent and destructive quarrels would have resulted, which would have placed the relationship in jeopardy.

The manner in which individuals with different Soul Images respond to extreme stress is not likely to be merely an exaggeration of their typical response to mild and moderate stress, as one might expect. Rather, people tend to react to extreme stress in a fashion that may appear to be quite opposite to their usual mode. A description and analysis of these dynamics would be quite complex and lengthy, making it beyond the scope of this book.

⟩ Notes

Chapter 1

1. The subsequent points are an elaboration of a description by Adolf Guggenbuhl-Craig in *Marriage Dead or Alive* (1977).

2. Such an erroneous conclusion is most likely to be made for either the Romantic Lover or the Innocent Lover. This is due to the emphasis people with these Soul Images place on the relationship itself as central to their sense of self and capacity for fulfillment. Some views of relationships see such a characteristic as signifying a lack of individual development. In addition, readers who are familiar with the psychological concept of the "relational self" should be cognizant of the differences between that perspective and the conceptions of *Relating* and *Togetherness* we are applying in this book.

3. We are indebted to Joel Wheeler for suggesting this example.

4. The distinctions we make between *Falling in Love, Being in Love,* and *Staying in Love* are based on the discussion of these concepts by Irving Singer in *The Pursuit of Love* (1988).

Chapter 2

1. It is also the ideal yearned for by some present-day politicians and social critics, as embodied in their idea of "family values."

Chapter 3

1. The fight stage for some couples can emerge in hostile and destructive ways and often involves dysfunctional individual and/or couple dynamics that are outside the scope of this book. Our main intent here is to demonstrate the ways in which disagreements and quarrels are influenced by the Soul Images in everyday normal occurrences. The fight stage is described in this chapter as an illustration of how the Soul Images emerge in extreme states. However, in the ten chapters describing the different love relationships, the fight stage is *not* presented.

2. In Jung's notion of the dynamics of the psyche, any extreme or one-sided point of view is likely to eventually lead a person to express the *opposite* point of view, but in an equally exaggerated, primitive, and ineffective way. Such opposite and extreme expressions can be observed when, for example, a Steadfast Lover reacts to extreme stress by behaving in an exaggerated, ineffectual Innocent Lover manner, becoming demanding, petulant, and hypersensitive. Similarly, a Mercurial Lover under extreme stress may become so totally absorbed in the life of the beloved that all the former focus on independence and individuality is absent. This would be a distortion of the normal expression of the opposite Romantic Lover Soul Image.

3. This statement is a basic principle of Jungian psychology and is expressed in his notion that the psyche works via expressions of opposite conscious and unconscious energies. It follows physicist Isaac Newton's third law of motion, which states that every action force has a reaction force equal in magnitude and opposite in direction.

4. We are indebted to our friend and colleague Dr. Ted Scharf, who related this story to us and explained its meaning.

Chapter 4

1. People with other Soul Images may also prefer keeping money separate, but this occurs most often for such practical reasons as needing to compartmentalize child support and alimony payments in a second marriage. Mercurial Lovers' strong value around keeping money separate is not tied to any particular practical concerns.

2. Mercurial Lovers often have a lifelong concern with gaining acceptance and respect from their parents. At issue is a feeling that acceptance is only possible if the Mercurial Lover person is "who the parent wants them to be"—a stance that is contradictory to the Mercurial Lover Soul Image.

3. We have found that couples in marital therapy who agree that their major issue is a poor sexual relationship are likely to both be Mercurial Lovers. Mercurial Lovers married to some of the other Soul Images may not find agreement from the partner regarding the centrality of sexual satisfaction.

4. "Upset" is a colloquial term. When we say we are upset, we mean that we are hurt, unhappy, and angry at the same time and about the same issue.

Chapter 6

1. Sometimes a consequence of such interdependence is the difficulty elderly Innocent Lovers have coping with life after the death of the partner. This can occur regardless of the partner's Soul Image, but will be especially true for couples in which both are

Innocent Lovers. In this case, their shared lifetime of healthy interdependence would have made more "independent" coping resources less necessary and therefore not well developed.

2. We have noticed that our individual psychotherapy clients who talk primarily about work are usually Mercurial or Steadfast Lovers, while those who talk primarily about their love relationship tend to be Romantic or Innocent Lovers.

Chapter 7

1. Steadfast Lovers consistently report having always been seen as responsible, mature, and older and wiser than their years. Even as children, they were sought out by their peers for advice and guidance; they were known for being trustworthy and level-headed.

Chapter 8

1. In Chapters 8 through 13, each of which presents couples whose Soul Images are different, the indication of complexes shown beside the text conforms to the chapter title; thus, in this Innocent Lover–Steadfast Lover chapter, the first named complex (e.g., Relatedness) is that of the Innocent Lover, and the contrasting complex (e.g., Separateness) is that of the Steadfast Lover.

2. When the complexes that are identified are not from an opposite pair, as is the case for Relatedness (whose opposite is Separateness) and Stability (whose opposite is Change [Instrumental]), the pair of complexes are separated by "and" rather than "vs." These complexes are labeled "complementary."

3. The George Burns and Gracie Allen comedy team represented a Steadfast Lover husband and an Innocent Lover wife in humorously exaggerated form; whereas Steadfast Lover wives and Innocent Lover husbands were depicted in the two couples on *The Honeymooners,* starring Jackie Gleason.

Chapter 12

1. Individuals who enjoy casual sexual encounters with no commitments to an intimate relationship are likely to be Mercurial Lovers rather than any of the other three Soul Images. This is consistent with the complexes that characterize them.

References

Abbey, E. *Desert Solitaire.* New York: Ballantine Books, 1968.

Austin, N. *Meaning and Being in Myth.* University Park, PA: The Pennsylvania State University Press, 1990.

Fulford, R. "Irving Singer on Love in the Twentieth Century." In Goicoechea, D., Ed., *The Nature and Pursuit of Love: The Philosophy of Irving Singer.* Amherst, NY: Prometheus Books, 1995.

Guggenbuhl-Craig, A. *Marriage Dead or Alive.* Zurich: Spring Publications, 1977.

Jacobi, J. *Complex, Archetype and Symbol.* Princeton, NJ: Princeton University Press, 1959/1971.

Jung, C. G. "Psychology and Alchemy." In *Collected Works,* vol. 12. Translated by R. F. C. Hull. Princeton, NJ: Princeton University Press, 1953.

Jung, C. G. "Symbols of Transformation." In *Collected Works,* vol. 5. Translated by R. F. C. Hull. Princeton, NJ: Princeton University Press, 1956.

Jung, C. G. "The Structure and Dynamics of the Psyche." In *Collected Works,* vol. 8. Translated by R. F. C. Hull. Princeton, NJ: Princeton University Press, 1960.

Jung, C. G. "Civilization in Transition." In *Collected Works,* vol. 10. Translated by R. F. C. Hull. Princeton, NJ: Princeton University Press, 1970.

Jung, C. G. "The Symbolic Life." In *Collected Works,* vol. 18. Translated by R. F. C. Hull. Princeton, NJ: Princeton University Press, 1976.

May, R. *Man's Search for Himself.* New York: Dell, 1973.

Meier, C. A. *Personality: The Individuation Process in Light of C. G. Jung's Typology.* Einsiedeln, Switzerland: Daimon, 1995.

Pinkola Estes, C. *Women Who Run with the Wolves.* New York: Ballantine Books, 1992.

Singer, I. *The Nature of Love,* vol. 3. Chicago: The University of Chicago Press, 1987.

Singer, I. *The Pursuit of Love.* Baltimore, MD: Johns Hopkins University Press, 1988.

Stevens, A. S. *Archetypes: A Natural History of the Self.* New York: Morrow, 1982.

Steinbeck, J. *Travels with Charley.* New York: Viking, 1962.

About the Authors

Alex T. Quenk, Ph.D., is a licensed clinical psychologist and diplomate Jungian analyst in independent practice. He received his master's degree from the University of Michigan in philosophy and his doctorate from the University of California at Berkeley in psychology. For the past thirty years his psychotherapeutic focus has been on individual and couples therapy. He has had a lifelong interest in the nature of individuality and the self, as well as an interest in the implicit philosophical assumptions of psychology. He is currently clinical associate professor in psychiatry at the University of New Mexico School of Medicine. He is also the author of *Psychological Types and Psychotherapy*.

Naomi L. Quenk, Ph.D., is a licensed clinical psychologist in independent practice. She received her master's degree from Brooklyn College and her doctorate from the University of California at Berkeley, both in psychology. For the past 20 years her psychotherapeutic focus has been on individual and couples therapy. Her enduring interest is in individual differences in normal personality functioning. She has written numerous research and theoretical articles exploring individual differences in personality, as well as several technical works relating to personality assessment. She is the author of *Beside Ourselves: Our Hidden Personality in Everyday Life* and *In The Grip: Our Hidden Personality*.

The Quenks live and work in Albuquerque, New Mexico. They have been married for thirty-three years and have three children. They have previously collaborated in writing several articles and chapters on personality and psychotherapy, and are coauthors of *Dream Thinking: The Logic, Magic, and Meaning of Your Dreams*.

Index

Psyche, 63, 318n
Psychic energy
  characteristics of, 35–36
  expression of, 135
  Innocent Lovers and, 113, 154, 234
  Jungian concept of, 35
  Mercurial Lovers and, 184, 258
  Romantic Lovers and, 93, 185, 235
  and Soul Images, 36–38
  Steadfast Lovers and, 155, 259
  strong and narrow, 36–37

Quarrels. See also Disagreements
  and acceptance, 303
  appraisals and, 58
  dynamics of, 64–66
  Innocent Lovers and, 128, 176, 225, 250
  Mercurial Lovers and, 86, 201, 225, 272
  Romantic Lovers and, 106, 201, 250, 295
  Steadfast Lovers and, 146, 176, 272, 295
  structure and causes of, 52, 148

Reciprocity, and intimacy, 28
Recreation
  Innocent Lovers and, 123, 169, 245
  Mercurial Lovers and, 264
  Romantic Lovers and, 245, 288
  Steadfast Lovers and, 141, 169, 264, 288
Relatedness
  Innocent Lovers and, 116, 156, 212, 233
  Romantic Lovers and, 14, 93, 186, 233, 279
  vs. separateness, 38, 156, 186, 212, 279
  vs. togetherness, 233
Relationships. See also Family relationships;
      Love relationships
  and archetypes, 3
  developing, 114
  enhancing, 96–98
  images of, 25–26
  stressful, 51
  themes of, 38–41
Religious archetypes, 3–4
Renewal, lovemaking as, 212
Rilke, Rainer Maria, 255
Rituals and celebrations, 289–290
Romantic Lovers, 91–92
  and being in love, 188, 236
  characteristics of, 15, 47
  and complexes, 92, 186, 199, 233, 278
  and Innocent Lovers, 231–233
  love relationships, 12, 204, 252

Romantic lovers (continued)
  and Mercurial Lovers, 181–182
  and shared complexes, 233
  and staying in love, 279
  and Steadfast Lovers, 277–278

Saint Exupery, Antoine de, 18
Sand, George, 1
Satisfaction and compatibility, 305–307
Self–differentiation
  vs. development, 162–164
  vs. self-transformation, 256–266
  Steadfast Lovers and, 136, 153, 157
Self-knowledge, Mercurial Lovers and, 75
Self-transformation
  vs. accommodation, 189
  vs. development, 209, 214, 220
  vs. enhancement, 186, 189, 194
  Mercurial Lovers and, 81, 186, 209, 256
  vs. self-differentiation, 256–266
  and staying in love, 261
Separate vacations, 218
Separateness
  and accommodation, 193
  and being loved, 220
  Mercurial Lovers and, 78, 186, 212, 256
  vs. relatedness, 38, 156, 186, 212, 279
  Steadfast Lovers and, 137, 156, 256, 279
  vs. togetherness, 187, 195, 198
Severe stress, impact of, 314–315
Sex
  Innocent Lovers and, 121
  loss of interest in, 242
  Romantic Lovers and, 101
  Steadfast Lovers and, 142
  withholding, 122, 243
Sexual relationships
  Innocent Lovers and, 121, 167
  Mercurial Lovers and, 267
  Romantic Lovers and, 101, 279
  Steadfast Lovers and, 167, 267, 279
Sexuality. See also Lovemaking
  and complexes, 195
  and desires, 101
  expression of, 37
  and passion, 212
Shared complexes, 283
  Innocent Lovers and, 233, 238, 241
  Mercurial Lovers and, 256, 260, 263
  Romantic Lovers and, 233, 238, 243
  Steadfast Lovers and, 256, 260, 263